DRIVE
THE STORY OF MY LIFE

LARRY BIRD

DRIVE

THE STORY OF MY LIFE

BY
LARRY BIRD WITH BOB RYAN

Foreword by Magic Johnson

DOUBLEDAY
NEW YORK LONDON TORONTO SYDNEY AUCKLAND

PUBLISHED BY DOUBLEDAY
a division of Bantam Doubleday Dell Publishing Group, Inc.,
666 Fifth Avenue, New York, New York 10103

DOUBLEDAY and the portrayal of an anchor with a dolphin are
trademarks of Doubleday, a division of Bantam Doubleday Dell
Publishing Group, Inc.

Library of Congress Cataloging-in-Publication Data

Bird, Larry, 1956–
    Drive: the story of my life/by Larry Bird with Bob Ryan. —1st ed.
      p.   cm.
    1. Bird, Larry, 1956– . 2. Basketball players—United States—
Biography. 3. Boston Celtics (Basketball team) I. Ryan, Bob, 1946– .
II. Title.
GV884.B57A3 1989
796.323'092—dc20
[B]   89-37228
                                             CIP

ISBN 0-385-24921-7

Book design by M 'N O Production Services, Inc.

Printed in the United States of America

November 1989

First Edition

To my grandmother
Lizzie Kerns

Acknowledgments

For their kind and invaluable assistance, I would like to thank my editor at Doubleday, Paul Bresnick, and his assistant, Mark Garofalo. I'd also like to give a very special thanks to Jill Leone for her tireless efforts in helping to make this book everything I wanted it to be.

CONTENTS

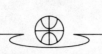

FOREWORD

The NBA had a great year on the floor and at the gate in 1988–89, but it was still missing a very important ingredient—Larry Bird.

When you don't have Larry Bird around, you don't have the Excitement . . . the Competitiveness . . . the Scare! Larry always has you on the edge of your seat, wondering what he'll do next.

Personally I missed him for another important reason. He's the one I've always measured myself against and it was definitely strange not being able to do that.

I admire Larry Bird for many reasons. Here are three:

1. He's got to be the most dedicated athlete imaginable. A lot of the guys I've played with and against are not really that dedicated. To them, it's just a job. With Larry, basketball is his *life*.

2. He has great heart and guts. They say he's not quick, but he makes up for any quickness he lacks with his guts, intelligence and determination.

3. He will make the big shot or big play. Of all the people I play against, the only one I truly *fear*—or worry about—is Larry Bird. Whenever we play Boston, it's always in the back of my mind that no matter what the game situation is Larry Bird can come back and beat us.

And it doesn't have to be with points either. The reason I love to watch Larry play is that he can dominate a game without even taking a shot. He is truly a guy who can make other players better. You'll see players who are so-so somewhere else hook up with him and improve their game greatly.

Ever since we played against each other in the 1979 NCAA finals in Salt Lake City, there has been a bond between us. It's like a marriage and we can't ever divorce each other—not that we want to. I had always liked the way Larry played the game, but it wasn't until I spent a day with him in French Lick doing a Converse commercial that I realized how much we really did have in common.

We talked about a lot of things that day, not just basketball. We discovered that we had a similar outlook on many things, including family.

When Larry first came along, it's no secret that many black players and fans refused to believe he was everything they said he was. The "playground people" doubted whether he was that good or whether he would *continue* to be that good. In time, he showed them. Now he's got the respect of both the basketball gurus *and* the playground gurus.

The league just wasn't the same without Larry Bird last year. The tickets that used to cost $100 when the Celtics came to town were back to $20 last year. The Celtics didn't have the same impact. The big thing when Boston comes in is not only the "Boo" but also the "Ooh."

I'm glad that "Ooh" is back with us.

—Magic Johnson
May 1989

PART I

WHERE
I COME FROM

1

I WAS STANDING THERE with the basketball in my hands and everyone was staring at me with a look of admiration in their eyes.

No, it wasn't after winning an NBA championship. It was on a summer afternoon in Hobart, Indiana, when I was thirteen years old. I can still remember how great I felt that day, the day I fell in love with basketball.

I was at my aunt's house up in Hobart, three hours north of my hometown, for a family get-together. When I was out walking around, some kids stopped me and asked me to join their basketball game. I had only played a little basketball in junior high because baseball had always been my favorite sport.

I took my first shot in the game and it went in. I took my second shot and that went in too. Even though I was playing against bigger kids that day, it seemed as if everything I lofted went in. The kids on my team started slapping me on the back and telling me what a great player I was . . . and I just loved it.

They asked me what team I played on and when I told them I didn't play on any team, they couldn't believe it. One of the boys said, "You must be the best player down there." Then a spokesman for the group asked, "Would you be able to come up next week and play with us again?"

That was it. I was hooked on basketball. I went back home

and started practicing every morning. I found that the more I did something, the better I got at it.

I went out for the high school basketball team and made the B team. Fortunately for me, Jim Jones was the coach. Coach Jones is the man I have to thank for drumming basketball fundamentals into my head. He taught me every basic maneuver there is and once he would show me something, it would just seem to click in my mind. It didn't matter what it was: a reverse pivot, boxing out, getting rebounds, whatever. Coach Jones taught me to utilize my left hand as well as my right. Once he told me that, I began to practice dribbling full-court with my left hand and I was amazed at how quickly my left hand adjusted.

I was progressing well and loving every minute of being on the team, even though I didn't get to play all that much as a freshman. During my sophomore year, I broke my ankle during a game and was out almost the whole season. I was really upset that I couldn't play, but I did try to keep practicing any way I could. I found that I could still shoot free throws while I was propped up on my crutches and I turned my attention to working on my passing, which I found was possible if I hobbled around on my cast.

As it turned out, I discovered from this adversity that I *loved* to pass! I thought passing was *it*—and I still do. I like to see the gleam in my teammate's eyes as he runs back down the court after scoring off one of my passes.

When I was finally able to come back from my injury, I was making passes no one had ever seen me make before and basketball was more fun than it had ever been before. Suddenly I had a whole new way to play. It was great because when you pass the ball that way it makes your teammates happy and it also makes it much easier for you to shoot. It just gave me a whole new dimension to my game. Besides, passing is more of an art than scoring. My feeling about passing is that it doesn't matter who's doing the scoring as long as it's *my* team. Everything was starting to come together.

I was put on the varsity team in my sophomore year and that year we went to the sectionals. This was a huge accomplishment for such a small high school team. After all, only about fourteen hundred people lived in the whole area, so everyone was extremely excited, including me. I didn't expect to make our tournament team because I hadn't been able to practice all season. But Coach Jones told me that if I worked hard, I just might be able to make the last spot on the tournament team.

Well, I worked harder than ever and on the day of the game there I was sitting on our bench, cheering our team on along with all the other people who were packed into the gym.

Suddenly I heard someone holler, "Bird!" I assumed it was a fan I knew from home, so I was busy scanning the stands when I heard someone call my name again. "Larry, *get in there!*" I realized the voice belonged to Coach Jones. I was getting into the game! My heart started pounding and I threw my warm-up jacket off and was at the scorer's table before I even knew it.

I was praying that I would play well, since the game was a real close one and this was my first game since I had broken my ankle.

The first time I get the ball, I launch it from about twenty feet out and it goes in. The crowd goes absolutely crazy while I'm passing everywhere, rebounding and sinking all my shots. Near the end of the game, we are down by only one point when I get a rebound and someone fouls me. I go to the free throw line and I try to pretend it's 6 A.M. in the gym back home and these are just two of the five hundred free throws that I shoot every morning. *Swish!* Both shots are good and we win the game by one point. Pandemonium!

The next day's headlines read: BIRD STEALS THE SHOW. That day my life was made. I couldn't believe that it was *my* name in all the stories and that something I loved to do— and could do well—could make so many people so happy. It was a new and exhilarating experience for me and I decided that day to dedicate myself to being the best basketball player I could possibly be.

From that point on, basketball was all I thought about, all I wanted to do. I couldn't wait for school to let out for the summer so I could play ball. I would play at 6 A.M. before school. I would duck into the gym in between classes to get a few shots up and play again after school into the early hours of the next morning, feeling that sleep was a rude intrusion on my practice time.

2

I GREW UP IN WEST BADEN SPRINGS and French Lick, Indiana, in Orange County in the southwest part of the state. The towns are only a mile or so apart. I have learned to enjoy life in Boston, but I always go home right after the last game of the season. I love the life back home; I always did. I still lead the simple life back there, spending time with my family and friends, fishing, golfing, working out, playing basketball.

Growing up wasn't always easy for me. My family didn't have much, so we appreciated anything we had. The way I grew up was very different from the way most people who I have met grew up.

First of all, sports was a big part of our lives—every day. There never was a day we didn't do *something,* whether it was baseball, basketball or football.

There were six of us Bird kids. Mike's the oldest at four years older than me; then there's Mark, three years older than me; then Linda, who is one year older than me; then Jeff, who's seven years younger than me; and then Eddie, who's ten years younger than me.

My father was Joe Bird and my mom's name is Georgia. Their parents had both lived in the area and Joe met Georgia Kerns when they were both working in a shoe factory over in Paoli, Indiana. My dad worked hard and he was very proud of the things he did.

One thing I found out when I went back to French Lick after I started playing with the Celtics is how proud the people are. They are proud of themselves and what they have, even if a lot of them don't have all that much. My family was certainly in the same boat.

But there are a lot of good people in that area and everyone works hard. They tell me that Orange County is the poorest county in the state, statistically speaking. I guess when you are living in a situation day-to-day, you just don't always realize the harsh reality of it. When I grew up, I didn't know how other people lived. I didn't know anything about Boston or New York or Philadelphia or anywhere else.

If someone from a big city tells me that my early life seems particularly difficult to them, I would have to tell them that I know we didn't have any money, but it didn't seem as if anyone *else* did either.

I just never realized how poor we were. Nobody in French Lick is wealthy. Everyone makes basically the same amount of money and everyone has basically the same values. It's the kind of small town where everyone stands up for his rights.

Sports are big, always have been. Especially basketball—giving rise to the term "Hoosier Hysteria" to describe Indiana's fascination and support of basketball. *Everyone* knows what's going on in sports and everyone who plays sports is extremely competitive.

The big employer in our area was the Kimball Piano and Organ Company—no question about that. There were also plants in the town of Jasper and the shoe factory where my mom and dad met in Paoli. The wages were not the same as they were in a big city, but people still put in a hard day's work and then they just enjoyed themselves. I think that is the way it should be: the American way. Sometimes today I look around at all the people who always seem to expect something more from their employers and I just can't understand it. I was brought up to work real hard every day and I do believe that's why I try to give 110 percent in every game I play—*my* workday.

The other major employer in town was what we referred to as "The Hotel," which is actually the French Lick Springs Hotel. It's a huge resort hotel located right across the street from the small downtown area of French Lick. It keeps changing hands and they keep renovating it and it's been a major resort hotel for many years.

A lot of townspeople work over there and it's something the town is proud of. What's funny is that when I grew up, I never did go over there. Sometimes kids from the high school would sell golf balls at the hotel's golf course, but as far as going into the hotel or just hanging around, we never did that.

When we weren't playing ball, we all hung out at a pool hall owned by a midget named Shorty Reader, a guy who went to school with my dad. Shorty was great. He'd always try to make sure every kid had a quarter in his pocket and a bottle of pop. He'd say, "Go to the store for me." Or "Sweep that floor for me." Shorty owned a Volkswagen and we used to drive over to Northwood, where we could pick up the Chicago Cubs games on the car radio. We would all cram into the car and listen for hours. I loved those times and I'm still a Cubs fan too.

My older brothers, Mike and Mark, were major influences in developing my motivation to excel—no doubt about that. Both Mike and Mark were great athletes and I always looked up to them. I still do. Of course, back then I was the tagalong little brother that they had to watch while my mom and dad worked. Since I was only about five or six at the time, I couldn't really be a regular member of the baseball team, so I had to pitch to both teams. We didn't have any fancy facilities and we'd just throw down some bases over at the Northwood golf course. When we played softball, we'd be lucky if we had six players. Right field was an out if the ball was hit in the air and a foul if it was hit on the ground.

Another one of our favorite places was a small softball field located right next to the house we were living in at the time. The field was all concrete and after you went about fifty yards, there was a wall. I could hit that wall every once in a while. My brothers got to where they could reach each level. Second tier was a double, third tier was a triple, over the rail was a home run.

Between the ages of five and ten, I used to take a rubber ball or a tennis ball and play up against the wall by myself for hours. I would be striking people out and have the ball come back, maybe try different angles and stuff. I would do that for hours and hours until somebody came to get me.

Anyway, we used to play ball every Sunday, for sure. We'd usually have two kids on a team and the pitcher would stand about forty feet away and throw just as hard as he could to the batter. If you ever caught ahold of one, you could knock it a country mile. The game moved right along. We still play it sometimes when I'm home.

The field wasn't a great place to play because it was right next to the house and we broke a lot of windows. We couldn't afford to replace the windows, so we blocked up the holes with cardboard.

My brothers were excellent athletes and they were incredibly competitive. Even though I was their little brother, they were constantly trying to beat me at any sport we were playing. If I was up at home plate, they would pitch harder to me than to anyone else. If I ever played poorly, they would be the first ones to give me a real hard time about it or even laugh at me. I never took too kindly to their razzing, so the three Bird brothers had some hellacious fights in those days. But the pressure they put on me only served to make me more determined to improve as fast as I could, so that I could beat them and get on *their* cases!

Speaking of sibling arguments, I used to get into it a bit with my sister Linda too. Under the circumstances, I don't think it could have been avoided. When I was little, I had to share a bedroom with Linda and you can imagine how that turned out. She was always telling me what to do and I was always talking back to her. Just in case you were wondering, we never argued over a messy room. I was a lot neater than she was, since I border on being an obsessively neat person. Anyway, sometimes the arguments got so bad that I had to go to my grandmother's all day. It makes me laugh today because I see what a great mother she is and realize that she was just trying to take care of me, but I was too young to appreciate it at the time.

Linda was also an exceptional athlete. It's ironic that of all the Bird kids she's the only one who ever made it to the Indiana State finals—for volleyball.

It's safe to say that while we weren't bad kids, we were definitely *active* kids. Personally I think my mother is a saint for riding herd on the six of us all those years while she worked two jobs and took care of the house too.

It seemed we were always roughhousing with each other, but as soon as someone outside the family gave one of us a problem, we became a united front, sticking up for one another. My father had taught us all to watch out for one another, no matter what the circumstances. As a matter of fact, he told us that if he ever heard we *didn't* stick up for one another, we shouldn't bother coming home. I think this type of upbringing prepared me for being a good teammate; not the fighting part, but the looking out for one another part. I'm always watching what's happening to my teammates out on the court. If they get trapped in a double-team, I'm right there for them and they know that I expect the same help from them. I feel this strengthens our team as a whole.

3

MONEY WAS ALWAYS AN ISSUE in our life. There were six kids and we just didn't have enough. Dad always worked, but he was lucky if he made $120 a week. Mom worked all the time as a waitress or a cook, sometimes working two jobs—but the best she'd wind up with would be $100. I can remember that whatever she made, she always needed an extra $20 or $30 for groceries. She'd go to the store on Saturday, but we'd generally start running out of things on Thursday. We really had to pinch those last two days. Mom never spent money on herself; anything she ever made she spent on us kids. Those were the days when you had accounts. I could go to the store, get something on Mom's list and put it on the account. But sometimes that got out of hand. Once we ran up a $600 or $700 bill, with no way to pay it. We were always in the hole for money. Mom worked something like eighty or ninety hours a week to make $100. It took $150 to feed the kids, so what can you do? Mom and Dad always worked so hard, but our family was too big for our means. All of us kids helped with our paper routes and odd jobs, but it still wasn't enough.

My mother always had a very positive influence on us. While she didn't push sports on us, she enjoyed them. She would take Mike, Mark, Linda and my friend Dave Qualkenbush to games. She'd go in snowstorms if they wanted to go. We bought a Corvair car in 1964 and Mom would pack up that little car with kids and off she'd go.

Mom always worked hard and she never complained. I just don't know where she got the strength. Mom never drank at all; she'd always been against it. And when Mom believes something is right, she'll stick to it. She's got a stubborn streak that I definitely inherited. I guess it's better to describe that trait as singlemindedness because it pushes both of us to stick to our position and stand up to anyone.

Mom worked at just about every restaurant in the area. It was great when she worked at the Villager in French Lick because it was right next to the basketball courts. We'd go over there after playing and she'd give us something cold to drink. We'd go back and play some more and then go back to the restaurant and she'd take care of us again.

She worked at another restaurant called Flick's and I can remember stopping over there after we had practiced or just played some ball and she'd ask if we wanted something to eat. She'd usually have some change from her tips and I'd say to her, "You always have tons of money." We'd be talking about $5 or $6, but that looked like a lot of money to me. She worked hard and then she took care of all the household bills, in addition to taking all the kids around. I guess every mother does that, but from my standpoint Mom's situation was a little tougher than most.

*   *   *

Though I went to high school in French Lick and people always associate me with French Lick, I grew up as much in West Baden as I did in French Lick. The towns are side by side with no natural boundary. Before they merged the high schools in the late fifties, the towns had quite a rivalry.

We moved quite a bit for different reasons. Sometimes it was because of the rent, sometimes because we could get a better furnace, and once simply because it was a house my mom really wanted to live in. In addition to that, we Bird boys took turns moving into my grandmother's house in French Lick.

The most memorable move for me was the one we made from West Baden to French Lick. I have to back up a bit. I had a job delivering papers and there was one house I was always afraid to deliver to because it looked as if ghosts were living there. There had been two porches, but one was torn down and the whole place looked dangerous and scary.

Every time we moved, we kids got really involved. Before we actually moved in, we'd have to help paint and wallpaper and so on. I was really excited about this move to French Lick and couldn't wait to get over there. Well, Mom took us over there and when we pulled up in the driveway my heart almost stopped beating. It was the scary house!

Living there was interesting. We had a stoker. You fed these chunks of coal in there and once in a while it got clogged up. A big piece of coal would get lodged in there somehow and smoke would come pouring out, just as if the house were on fire. Dad would have to get everybody out. We'd have to go outside and stand around in blankets while we were half-asleep, freezing, until Dad got the stove fixed. We spent half our winters there standing outside!

Once we made a very short move. We moved into that house that Mom really wanted. Linda and I moved almost all the furniture ourselves. We put the sofa, the beds and nearly everything else on our little red wagons and pulled them right down to the house. Mom said, "You kids are crazy. What are the neighbors going to think?" I said, "Mom, who cares?" I've never been one to worry too much about what other people think.

*   *   *

Dad worked at different jobs, but the one he enjoyed the most was at the Kimball factory, working on those pianos and organs. He was a sprayer and he was proud of his skill. Once he thought one of the pianos he had worked on was going to be on a television show. We all sat around the television set to watch that program, but we never did see that piano.

It seemed as if Dad was always switching jobs. His last job was working road construction in Louisville. He would leave on a Sunday night and come back on a Friday. I really don't know why he kept leaving Kimball—whether he would get fed up for some reason or just get mad or whatever—but he would always go back there. He'd say that if you worked on something big—like a piano or organ—you'd see it from the beginning and you would see it at the end of the project when you'd put on the finishing touches. He said then you'd have something to be proud of. Maybe that's why I'm never satisfied until I've put together a whole season of winning games—until the Celtics have won a championship—then I've seen the season through from beginning to end in a way that I can be proud of too.

Dad always encouraged us. When he was playing football with us, he would play quarterback and throw passes alternately to me, Mike and Mark. In his own way, he would challenge us too. He'd say to one of us, "You're better than he is. You have to show him."

I never heard my father brag about us, but other people tell me that when he was out with his friends he talked about us all the time, saying that he was very proud of all of us. Not that he would ever tell us that because my father never babied us. Everything he ever said was meant to make us strong and independent kids. He was closest to my youngest brother, Eddie, and he'd always say, "When Eddie grows up, he's going to be the best. I'm going to teach him."

Dad used to pitch horseshoes a bit, but his biggest recreation was hanging out with his friends. Dad was a great storyteller and joker and he was always popular with everyone. He loved to buy his friends a round of drinks in return for the drinks they bought for him. This could go on for hours at a time. As you can imagine, none of this sat too well with my mother. We kids never noticed the day-to-day effects, but we were aware that this ongoing situation was causing serious problems between Mom and Dad.

Things really started to go downhill between them when Dad took that construction job. We were living in a house that was really too much for him to afford and with Dad spending generously on his friends there was a terrific strain. Dad would be due home on a Friday, but if it had rained, there wouldn't have been work, so he would pass the day away with his buddies. He'd have cashed his check, but there wouldn't be a whole lot left by the time he got home. Eventually this was too much for Mom to take and they divorced. It's too bad because I know they loved each other a lot—even after the divorce. They just couldn't find a way to help themselves out of a difficult situation.

At this point, Dad seemed totally overwhelmed by the turn of events. He had to move in with his parents, but that still didn't help matters financially. He was having trouble making child support payments and I think he started to feel as if he was beating his head against a wall because things just weren't changing. For a while, little Eddie's visits to him on the weekends kept him going, but by Christmastime you could tell that Dad had lost the desire to go on. He was deeply depressed.

We all knew what he was going to do because he came right out and told us. Not that he wanted sympathy or anything. He simply said, "I am not going to be around much longer. No use me living this way. You kids would be better off if I was gone." It sounded pretty casual, but that's just the way he was brought up. It's just the way around French Lick; everyone is very straightforward and matter-of-fact about everything. There's no question Dad was strapped. After paying our bills, he only had about $20 left to show for a week's hard work—barely enough to buy lunch for the next week.

I think Mom just assumed that Dad was kidding around because he was always joking around about everything and she figured, "Why should this be anything different?" But when he told me, I could tell from looking in his eyes that he was going to do it. He said, "Things will be better off for you, your mom, Eddie and Jeff if I go ahead and take my life." I don't think he spent a lot of time thinking about it; I believe he made his decision quickly.

He was a couple of weeks behind on his payments to Mom and the police were sent out to my grandfather's house to get him. The policemen were friends—everybody in the town knows each other—and when they came he said, "Can I have until this afternoon to get some bills straightened out?" And they said, "Fine." But he knew that was the end of it. He had said he would never spend a day in jail; he was too proud for that.

Mom's brother owned a gas station. He went over there and said, "Hey, guys, I'll see you later. It's been great." They didn't know what was going on because he was always kidding around. He went to the bar, ordered half a pint—that's what they tell me—and then went back to my grandfather's house to drink it.

He called Mom up and told her what he was going to do. I don't know exactly how that conversation went. Anyway, the police came back. He got off the phone, took a shotgun and killed himself. Grandma and Grandpa were in the house at the time, but they didn't know what happened at first. When you live in the country, you hear hunters and you hear different sounds all the time. But the police came in and asked for Joe and there he was.

I was over at Granny Kerns's house. My sister Linda came by and she was crying. I wasn't surprised, but I was still shocked that it really happened. I was upset, but I understood. I felt as if I could cry, but I remembered what Dad told me and I remembered how tough he was. He was stubborn, but he was proud and I know in his mind he thought he was doing something to help the family financially. It wasn't insurance money, but Social Security. My mom received some money from his being in the service and it did help us out. But I would have given anything to just go on living the way we were than to have to lose my father.

I remember so many good times with my dad. He was a great father to all of us kids, always trying to push us all to be better. I missed him as soon as he was gone and I still miss him.

Dad's death was a big thing around town and people talked about it every day for the longest time. It wasn't something that happened every day, although now you seem to read about more and more people doing the same thing for many of the same reasons. It's sad when people just give up, especially these days when there's probably help somewhere for them if they just know where to ask for it, no matter what the problem is.

But, like I said, my father really thought he was helping us by doing this. I mentioned the word "tough" in reference to my father and I mean it. I think there is a lot of him in me in terms of my wanting to get out there and play, even when I'm injured. One time Dad came home from his construction job with a badly injured ankle. It took three men to pull his boot off. When they did, it looked as if somebody had taken a sledgehammer and had smashed his ankle. He said, "This thing's really killing me," but after that he never complained. He actually laughed about it, saying, "Can you believe this? Your old man can't handle it anymore."

The next day he put the boot on, tied it up as tight as he could and went off to work. I can't ever remember him missing work or even going to a doctor. Dad was really a tough man.

My mother wasn't the same for a long, long time, but she eventually came out of it. I hope she realizes that it wasn't her fault. It was just something that happened. The circumstances weren't good and Dad felt that this was the best way to handle the problems. People have their own minds and they do what they want to do. Dad lived his own life and I guess he felt as if it was time to die.

This all happened when I was nineteen years old and in between colleges. People have speculated as to what would have happened if Dad had lived long enough to see my basketball success at Indiana State. I do know this much: If he had been alive then, he and Mom would have been living in Terre Haute. It would have taken a little while, but things would have gotten a lot better. I'm sure of that.

If my dad was alive today, he'd be proud of me, but I don't think he'd be running off everywhere to see me play basketball games. Know why? Because I think he'd be running off to see Eddie play *his* basketball games at Indiana State, where Eddie is coming along great. I am so proud of Eddie and Jeff. They are both attending college and doing very well. I know Dad would be real proud of them too.

4

THERE ISN'T MUCH DOUBT that one of the most influential people in my life was my grandmother Lizzie Kerns. She was one of the nicest people I've ever met.

My brother Mike started the family custom of moving in with Granny Kerns during our high school years. I lived with her all through my senior year. She lives very close to the school, so I'd come over and eat lunch with her. On game days, I'd come over and take a nap from about four o'clock to seven-thirty, since game time was eight o'clock. I'd just go there, lie on the floor and go to sleep. Granny would come in at seven-thirty and say, "You'd better get up. You'll be playing in half an hour."

We used to shoot free throws every morning at six o'clock. One day I just wanted to sleep in. Granny woke me up and said, "Larry, those other boys are down there. You should be down there with them." I got up and went to free throw practice. She always had a nice way of handling things.

Mark and I would be at Granny's for supper and later on, just before it was time to go to bed, Mark would say, "Mmm, some popcorn would taste good right now. Larry, what would you think about some popcorn?" Granny wouldn't say a thing. But the next thing you knew, she'd have that pan out and you'd hear that popping sound in the kitchen.

We started moving in with her because we just didn't have enough room. It was always a problem. After Mike started it, Mark did it for a while and then me. Later on, Eddie used to eat lunch there every day.

To Granny, all her grandkids were equal. Oh, she read everything about me she could get her hands on and she knew I'd signed contracts for big money, but she never discussed it. She was proud of all her grandkids. None of us got special treatment. Granny loved all of us and that's the way it should be.

I loved to tease her. One day I said, "Granny, I'm going to buy you a new car." She never drove in her life and never had any intention of doing so. She said, "Well, I don't know." I said, "It would be nice. If you want, I'll get somebody to drive you." She said, "No, I don't need that." I was just kidding her, of course.

When I was a senior and living with her, I was involved in a project with some classmates in which we built a house. We got done early and I came home before school was out. She said, "What are you doing home?" I said, "There was a fire down at the school." She said, "Oh no." She went right down to my aunt's house and told her. The next thing you know, it was all over town.

I'd have given her anything, but what she really wanted was security. Granny just wanted to know she had enough to get by. She always told me one thing. She always said, "I'm not afraid to die. God is going to take care of me. When I get old and can't do it anymore, I'm not going to be afraid to die." That showed me a lot. Unfortunately, Granny passed away while I was writing this, so she was never able to see that I dedicated my book to her. But I do believe she always knew how much she meant to me.

5

IF ANYBODY IN OUR FAMILY appeared to be heading for a career in basketball, it was my brother Mark. It certainly wasn't me. I had little interest in basketball before I was thirteen or so. My mother would drive my brothers to the games. They'd go to the sectionals and stay all day. I wouldn't go, just didn't care to. I'd stay home and watch TV.

And I wasn't watching basketball either. I just remember one game. Evansville was playing Purdue, I think, and they were up by one point. A Purdue player shot a desperation heave from the baseline. The guy from Evansville jumped up above the rim, brought it down and was called for goaltending. That's the only game I ever remember watching when I was a kid in which I got excited. I remember watching it with my dad.

The first time I ever went to see a high school game was when my brother Mark played his last game. That was in 1969 and I was in ninth grade. By that time, I liked to play. I wound up on what we called the B team as a freshman, so I got to go to games and see Mark play. I remember the first time I ever got really emotional at one of those games. It was a real close game and Mark wound up being fouled. He had to make some big free throws. I was so scared we were going to get beat, but we won. There were tears streaming down my face and I remember thinking, "What's wrong with me? This is what I've been missing my whole life by not going to these games?" I was just so proud that Mark was my brother. One of my fondest memories is that after that big game, Mark was a hero and when we were all riding back to school on the bus, Mark sat right next to me. *Everyone* wanted Mark to sit next to them, but he came right over next to me. He made me feel so good when he did that.

I always thought Mark was an excellent player. He was about six-three or six-four and he could really shoot the eyes out of it. All day long, he would shoot, shoot, shoot. He'd have me rebounding for him while he shot. He could go out and hit six or seven in a row and he had a lot of range.

Mark went on scholarship to Oakland City College, which is near Jasper, Indiana. When Mark went to college, he said to the family, "Now, don't worry about it. When I get out, I'll be a big businessman and make millions of dollars and take good care of you." Mark was always watching out for us, sharing anything he had with us, sometimes slipping us younger kids a dollar or two whenever he could.

Up until this point in time, basketball was always around

and I played it once in a while but I was by no means obsessed with it. Baseball was my first love and I liked football a lot too. I did get a basketball for Christmas once and when I unwrapped it I thought it was the greatest thing I had ever seen in my life. It was better than a football, a bicycle or anything.

Remember those pot-bellied stoves? I got that basketball out and played in the snow. It lost air and I couldn't dribble it. I brought it in and put it next to the stove to get it heated and then I brought it back out. It would last two or three hours that way.

One night I left the ball by the stove by accident. I got up in the morning and discovered a basketball with bumps all over it. I kept that ball for two years because I couldn't afford a new one and when I would dribble the ball it would go this way or that.

But in those days I liked baseball a lot more than basketball. In Little League I pitched and played shortstop and then I played in a Babe Ruth League. Then when I was a freshman and Mark was a senior, I was supposed to start at third base. We had been practicing all spring, but then it rained for three days and we went inside with a pitching machine. I was the only freshman on the team that time.

Everybody got ten or fifteen swings, while I chased all the balls. It came my turn to bat. I get up there and the coach says, "Take three swings and pick up the balls and come in."

That did it. I never played again. I really felt that the coach had mistreated me and had done me wrong. I really wanted to play because Mark was on the team and I was the only freshman and I was supposed to start at third base. The coach had worked with me and had shown me a lot of good things, but it really killed me when he did that.

I guess I overreact when I think I've been slighted or when someone I care about has been slighted. I've always been that way. If I meet somebody and I don't like him right away, if maybe he says something I don't like before I start to know him and like him, I still hold that first thing he said against him. It is definitely not a good trait, but that's just the way my makeup is.

My football career had some of that element in it too. I went out for the team in the ninth grade. A good friend of mine was trying out with me. It was really hot and my friend and I were working hard, dragging the heavy equipment around the field for the various exercises. All of a sudden, my friend leaves me to finish carrying all that equipment because he's been excused early from practice for a dentist's appointment. Back then, I didn't even know what a dentist was, so, to me, it seemed unfair that the coach let my friend out of practice early but not me. So I just left too because in my young mind I was angry at not being treated the same.

After about a week, I wanted to come back. The coach said, "Fine, you can come back." He told all my friends to work me over in practice. They were working me over and working me over, but I loved it. I was just happy to be back. I'd have to sit out a game, but I was back on the team.

One day during practice I was on defense and this real big guy was running the ball. I mean, he was a *lot* bigger than me. I said to myself, "I am going to take this guy out!" He came across the line and I hit him as hard as I could. I turned over and he fell over and broke my collarbone right in half. I was out for the season. I remember being flat on my back thinking, "You really deserved that. You quit football and here you are, picking on the biggest guy out there. You thought you'd get in that one shot before practice was over." That was the end of my football career.

Later on, I wanted to resume playing baseball. I wanted to play baseball as a junior and senior, but I never did. By that time I had fallen in love with basketball and when spring came I just couldn't get myself to play baseball. I *had* to play basketball.

I had gotten that taste of what basketball could do for me that day up in Hobart. I had gotten excited at my brother's game. And by my sophomore year I was hooked on basketball. I could still take it or leave it during my freshman year, but by my sophomore year I hardly wanted to do anything else. I wasn't sure how good I was, but I just knew I couldn't get enough of it. It controlled my life from that point on.

I broke my ankle early in my sophomore year when a kid stepped on it going for a rebound. He was either running or jumping in there a bit late and he came down on my left ankle. I remember going over to the sideline and trying to walk it off. We went back into the locker room at halftime and Coach Jim Jones goes, "Aw, it's just a sprained ankle."

They taped it up real tight and I went back into the game. I went up and down about four times before I had to come out. Now they didn't want to untape it because of the swelling factor but I begged the assistant, Gary Holland, to cut the tape off. He did it and it hurt worse than before. We had it X-rayed and it was cracked in two or three places, plus there were torn ligaments. They had to wait a week to put on a cast because it was so swollen.

That's one cast that never made it to the finish line. I was doing everything with that thing on. We played football in the snow. I was punting with the thing on. About two weeks before it was supposed to come off, it fell off. The thing was beaten to death.

I wasn't a real good patient in those days. About the time I broke my collarbone, they were holding the Punt, Pass and Kick contest in our area and I was upset because I couldn't participate. So I became the guy who measures the distances. My doctor was up there in the stands and the next thing he knows I'm out there *throwing* the ball back to the competitors. That's not exactly what he had in mind. He went and told my mom.

When I returned to the team after breaking my ankle, I wound up being a hero with those two free throws at the end of the game.

I was about six-two then. By my junior year, I was up to almost six-four. I was playing all the time. In the summer, my friend Michael Cox and I would just play and play and play. When we'd sit down, we'd still be dribbling the basketball. We never wasted any time.

Remember that this is a small town and when you've got a coach, you've got a coach. Jim Jones was always around. He would be around, showing us something, and then Jonesie would say, "I'm leaving now, but I'll be back." He might come and go two or three times. You'd get it in your mind: "What if Coach comes back and we're not here?" You might think: "Let's go swimming . . . Aw, we can't."

Jonesie would say, "I'll be back in a minute." Then he would go play golf. He might show up four or five hours later, but he *always* came back. It was always on our minds: "We can't leave. Jonesie might come back and want to show us something new." In the summer, if Jonesie said he was coming back, he was coming back. You just didn't know *when*. And, boy, if you weren't there, you couldn't live it down. You'd think: "I let him down."

And yet you didn't really feel there was *pressure* on you. It was actually comforting. Coach Jones knew Coxie and I were playing. Maybe those other kids weren't playing, but we were playing.

During the school year, we'd meet him at six o'clock in the morning to shoot free throws. We'd see him all day at school. We'd practice. After practice, we'd stay on the court and mess around, shooting some more. He was with us fourteen hours a day. He even gave us haircuts. He did it all. If you were in a bigger town, it wouldn't be like that. But that was my life.

Mike and Mark were working in a steel mill up in Gary. My friend Dave Qualkenbush and I drove up there a few weekends to see them. One day Mark said, "A bunch of high school kids always play at that playground over there."

We went over there to play. Mark hadn't seen me play ball for a while and I had grown a little bit. We started playing and you talk about *domination*. We whipped every kid in Gary, Indiana. We whipped them all.

Mark came over and said, "Man, have you improved." He asked me if I had been playing much ball. I said, "Every day, all day."

We had a pretty good team in my junior year. We played a Christmas tournament game over at Jasper, one of our biggest rivals. I was only averaging about ten points a game, but I was doing everything else. I just wasn't shooting that much.

At halftime we were down by six or so and Coach Jones says to me, "If you don't start shooting the ball, you are going to sit next to me and you are not going to play anymore. You are hurting the team by not shooting when you are open." I went on and scored about twelve or fourteen points in the second half. From that point on, my game changed. I had to start scoring more, so I did.

6

WHEN I FIRST STARTED playing basketball, it was just another sport to play. As far as coaches were concerned, I did everything they told me to do, but basically I tried to get out of doing most of it. I just didn't care enough. I was on that B team as a freshman, but about the only time I'd get into games would be at the end.

After that great experience making those free throws and playing that good game at the end of my sophomore year, however, my attitude changed. I started paying attention to the things Jim Jones had to say.

I had known the man all my life. I thought of Jim Jones as someone who was always making remarks: "You've got to do this. You've got to do that." I could generally have cared less about the things he said to me then.

But once I started getting seriously interested in basketball, I *listened* when Jonesie told me something. A lot of kids still let it all go in one ear and out the other, but I've been blessed with a good memory and I was able to remember every piece of instruction.

I discovered that Coach Jones always gave sound advice: When Jonesie said to try something, it *worked*. He told me to work on my left hand and right away I could see an improvement in my game. He taught me that there was a lot more to the game of basketball than just shooting. A lot of kids just like to shoot and if they aren't hitting they get frustrated and don't play as well in other phases of the game. Shooting stopped being such a big thing with me.

Once I mastered the fundamentals, everything else

started coming along. I really wasn't that interested in scoring as such until Coach Jones gave me that lecture in the Jasper game. I figured, "If scoring is the only way to stay in the game and keep the man happy, then I'll just have to score some points."

Jonesie's practices included a lot of running and a lot of fundamental station drills. We didn't scrimmage all that much. He was more attuned to halfcourt workouts. At the end of practice, we would have to run those "suicide drills"—and they were killers for me. I'd run hard, but everybody knows I'm slow. But I was safe with Jonesie because he emphasized the fundamentals and I had those down.

Jonesie harped on those fundamentals. He hated it when we failed to box out on the boards. Years later the Celtics lost two regular season games one year because we didn't box out when the other team was shooting a free throw. We lost an extremely important game in the 1987 finals because we didn't rebound a missed free throw. I guarantee you that if you played for Springs Valley High School and Jim Jones and you didn't box out on the boards, you would soon be over on the bench.

Just being good at something changed my entire self-image. I had this skill and, what's more, it all came so easy to me once I started working at it. I didn't mind the hard work. I felt that every time I applied myself, I learned something new about the game.

My memory has always helped me to quickly pick up on things that I'm interested in. I think I've surprised people sometimes when they become aware of my recall capacity. Once, when I was doing a network interview, the producer ran a videotape of a previous year's NBA championship game so I could comment on the game. When they stopped the tape randomly, they were trying to figure out at what point of the game it was, so I told them right away. "It's the fourth quarter with five minutes and forty seconds left." The producer asked me how I could possibly have known that exact time and I told him I could tell from the fight song that was playing. He asked, "What fight song?" I explained, "I remember in that game the fight song was played three times. The last time they played the song the crowd was

going absolutely crazy. Houston had come back from being
seventeen points down and I remember looking up at the
clock at that point and there were five minutes and forty
seconds to go." I went on to describe the rest of the plays for
the producer before they appeared on the tape. I guess it's
things like that that earned me the nickname of "Kodak"
from Coach Bill Fitch.

I think this capability is true of me in more things than
just basketball. If I liked a subject in class, I would pay attention and do really well on the exam. But if I disliked a subject, it seemed as if that class took all day. With basketball,
everything went like clockwork. Things just seemed to click
for me.

I can visualize possible situations on the court before they
happen. That's how I come up with steals in the closing moments of games. Some golfers say that visualizing everything about a shot before they take it puts them in the right
frame of mind. That's how I feel about playing defense.

I know I can do certain things if it's a close game. Why
waste everything in the first or second quarter, when in a
close game you can save it for the end and defeat the opposing team? I think that over the years one of my best assets
has been the ability to make the right move at the right
time.

It's just like the use of your off-hand. You may go right all
night and save that move with your left hand for the very
end when you need it most. I've done that many times.

Of course, I am fortunate by being somewhat lefthanded to
start with. When I am eating, I automatically pick up the
fork with my left hand. It feels funny in my right hand. I
write lefthanded, but if a teacher sent me up to the black-
board, I'd go to my right hand.

The other thing that changed my entire game was my
growth in height. I was almost six-four as a junior, six-six or
so as a senior and I grew to six-nine. It's an entirely different
game when you're six-nine. I feel I had all the proper traits
at six-four, but I couldn't utilize them as well as I can at six-
nine. There is no question that my height has made a big
difference. Most people don't realize it, but I secretly wish I
was seven feet tall!

The first year they merged the high schools in West Baden and French Lick into Springs Valley High School in 1958, the basketball team went all the way to the Indiana State finals. After that we didn't have much of a basketball reputation. No matter how good we were, people didn't think all that much of us. The basic thing we had to do was to beat the larger towns around us, places such as Jasper, Paoli and Orleans. Beating those teams from Indianapolis and Muncie would have been the Indiana equivalent of beating the Celtics or the Lakers in the pros.

People in Indiana really *cared* about high school basketball. We were a lot like the team in the movie *Hoosiers*. Whoever wrote that story really had Indiana high school basketball pegged—it was right on the money. We have those town meetings, the way they do in the movie. People sit around the barbershop and talk about last night's game. The day after the game, someone will always come up to the players or the coach and say, "You should have done this or that."

After that first year, Springs Valley never went very far in the tournament. Our big goal every year was to win the sectionals. In Indiana the tournament is broken down into the sectionals, the regionals, the semi-states and the state finals. For us to win the sectionals would be great. To win the regionals would have been super. Anything else was way beyond our comprehension.

Coach Jones knew we were pretty good my junior and senior years and he tried to tell us we were good enough to play with the big boys, but we just didn't realize it.

We had an upheaval before our senior year even started. Coach Jones stunned us all by announcing that he was quitting as coach. Michael Cox and myself were at the bowling alley one day and Coach Jones walked in. "I'm getting out," he said. I'll tell you, that was a big shock. We loved the man. He had taught us all we knew. We almost broke down and cried.

Jonesie simply felt he had done enough coaching. He would stay at the school, but he'd be leaving the bench. "I'll be around," he said, "but I don't know if I'll come to any of the games. It might be hard on me in the first year." He was the biggest coaching influence I've ever had, but I always kid him that he's the *dumbest* coach I've ever had too. Didn't he walk away just as I was getting good? I wasn't through growing and when Coach Jones came back in the fall and saw how big I was and what kind of player I had become, he came to every game.

Coach Jones was only able to stay out of coaching for one year. He went to Princeton, Indiana, for a while and now he's been the head coach at Terre Haute North for the last several years.

The new coach was Jonesie's assistant, Gary Holland. He was a young fellow, just in his early or mid-twenties, and his personality was completely different than Coach Jones's. Jonesie ran a pretty tight ship. Under Coach Holland we had more offensive freedom. Holland knew what kind of talent he had and he basically turned us loose.

I have heard this story from other people. When we got back to school that September, Coach Holland walked into the office of the athletic director, Larry Pritchett, and said, "Looks like we've got an All-Stater here this year." Pritchett said, "You mean Larry?" And Holland said, "Yeah, he's six-seven now."

True enough. I *was* six-seven and I had been playing *every* day, *all* day. I had more confidence than ever in my game and I was ready for my senior year.

Springs Valley won our first game and then we lost two in a row. We went to play Orleans and they had a six-seven kid who was pretty good. I had only scored something like twenty-five and twenty-eight in those two losses, but I got forty-three on him. From that point on, everything just seemed to come easily for me. It seemed as if I could do whatever I wanted to do in a basketball game. After scoring forty-three, I felt, "If I want to score forty-three tonight, I can do it. Tomorrow night too and the night after that. Hey, if I want to get fifty, I can get fifty." I still liked to pass the ball and I brought it up the court a lot. The coach gave me the green light to do anything I wanted.

The players all got along great with Coach Holland. He had talked with me in the summer, explaining what he had in mind, and we never had a problem.

After those two losses, the season went more smoothly. We finished out the regular season and went into the tournament on a roll. We got through the sectionals and headed into the regionals. If we won the regionals we'd be in the semi-states.

Beezer Carnes was an old friend of mine and he was on the team. Whenever the rest of us would get up early and be in that gym at six o'clock to shoot free throws, Beezer would habitually sleep right through. During that entire season, I'll bet Beezer wasn't there but two or three times—and when he did show up, he was sleepwalking.

Beezer was always late for everything. The school bell would ring at a quarter to nine and Beezer would get there at five of nine. I'm sure you know the type.

I can remember Coach Holland saying, "Beezer, one of these days you are going to cost us a big game by missing some free throws." But we all knew Beezer. We knew how he was and we just took him for granted.

Sure enough, we get into the finals of the regionals against Bedford. We're up by six points with under two minutes to go in the game and they need the ball, so they start fouling Beezer, who actually wasn't that bad at the line, averaging about 70 percent.

So Beezer goes to the free throw line for a one-and-one. Miss. They come down and score.

We get it in bounds and Beezer gets the ball because he is our point guard. They foul him again and, sure enough, he misses again. They come down and score.

We are now only up by two and at this point we're trying like mad to keep the ball away from Beezer. We pass it around, however, and as soon as Beezer gets it they foul him again. He goes to the line, misses the front end of *another* one-and-one. Bedford keeps going and ends up winning the game.

Our chance to go to the semi-states was gone. We go into the locker room and Beezer isn't saying anything, but he's about ready to cry. Coach Holland got us all into a corner and said, "Remember that little conversation we had?"

And Beezer says, "Oh yeah, Coach. If I had to do it all over again, I would be there every day."

But that was Beezer. I remember another incident, which must have taken place the year before. We were playing well and Loogotee High comes into our gym for what they were saying was the biggest regular season game we'd had in ten of fifteen years. We must have had four or five thousand people crammed into our gym.

It gets to be a real close game and one or the other of us is up by one. We've got the ball and the coach calls for a time-out. The first thing he says when we get into the huddle is: "We have no more time-outs." Then he goes: "Try to get the ball to Larry . . . work it around." We take the ball out of bounds and throw it in to Beezer. He takes two or three dribbles and then can't find anybody for a second, so what does he do? He calls time out.

So it's a technical foul shot for them and then a jump ball. That was the rule in those days. They've got good foul shooters and now we've got to foul. They make the free throws. We lose the game.

Good old Beezer . . .

7

THE FIRST WHIFF OF RECRUITING I ever got was during my junior year when some scouts came to look over my teammate Steve Land. But after seeing us play, they started showing a little interest in me too.

Steve wound up going to Indiana, where he was the last man cut. He was the thirteenth man on a twelve-man team, I guess you'd say. He's a doctor now.

Things heated up during my senior year. The word was getting out about me. A writer in Jasper had written some articles and sent them out all around the state.

I wasn't very sophisticated in all this recruiting stuff.

We're talking about somebody who didn't exactly have a world view. I knew about Indiana University, of course. Bobby Knight had been there about two or three years by that time and people in the state were excited about I.U. But I wasn't a fan of college basketball. I knew next to nothing about it.

I just didn't have any interest in the outside world. Aside from visiting my relatives up in Hobart, I never really went very far out of town. That ride to Hobart took three and a half hours and to me seemed like forever.

When I was very young, we never had a car and not having a car was a big factor. Even when I got my license, we didn't have a car. But I was used to the situation. Mom always walked to work. Dad always got a ride to work.

I generally passed up the few chances I had to go anywhere. One of the men in town took my brothers to Chicago to see some baseball games a couple of times and I was invited to go along, but I just wouldn't go. Louisville was only about sixty miles away, but I probably didn't go there but twice in my life.

You can't believe what I didn't know. When I was in the sixth grade, another neighbor we used to do some work for took us to Louisville for a basketball game. I had no idea what was going on. We go in and the place is packed. We're up in the very top row and Mark says, "Boy, this is great."

I said to him, "Who's playing anyway?" He told me. I guess I didn't get it straight because I thought he told me it was a college game.

When we got home, Mark told me it had been a pro game. We were watching the Kentucky Colonels of the ABA. I said, "Why didn't you tell me? I would have watched it closer." I couldn't believe how big some of those pro guys were. But I really had no idea what was going on. Unbelievable, isn't it?

I didn't read all that much and I didn't watch that much TV. And nobody I knew traveled much. Since we didn't have a car or much money, we never took vacations. We thought going to Paoli was a big deal and that was about ten miles away. I jog that far now, but my mother still thinks that's a long trip.

So I was about as small town a kid as you could get and

when the scouts started coming in hard, I reacted the way you might expect. I'd say to each of them, "Hey, I don't want to visit your school." Finally I decided I would just pick one school and stay with it—if only to keep those recruiters off my back.

I did visit Kentucky. Joe B. Hall had come to see me play once and I didn't have a very good game. I got about twenty-five points and fifteen rebounds, but he said I was too slow and probably couldn't get off my shot against bigger guys. But for some reason, the Bird family went down there anyway on an official visit.

The things that Coach Hall had said bothered me. Here was a big-time coach who said I couldn't play for him. That helped motivate me to go to I.U. because I knew we would be playing Kentucky.

I went to I.U. and to Indiana State and I was planning a trip to Florida—because I had never been there and I was curious about *that*—but I never did get down there.

Purdue recruited me hard—*real hard*. The problem with Purdue was they had Wayne Walls and Walter Jordan, both forwards, coming in and there was no sense in going up there for a visit.

The man who recruited me the hardest was Denny Crum at Louisville. He was doing everything he could to get me to come down there and look at the school. Finally he said, "I'll tell you what. If I could beat you in a game of Horse, would you come for a visit?" I said, "Sure." I had no problem with that.

Coach Crum thought he was still a pretty decent player, but it was my court and I wasn't *too* worried. I started taking him real deep, out in three-point territory. I put him away in about eight shots.

He went over to Coach Holland and said, "Can this kid shoot this good from the outside?" And Holland says, "Well, you just saw him. You want to shoot some more?" Crum said, "No, I've seen enough." Coach Crum was just dying to get me to come down there, but I never did go.

Bobby Knight came to a lot of games. Mom wanted me to go to Indiana University. Coach Jones had gone to I.U. My dad liked I.U., but he also liked Indiana State. The truth is, he liked every school that came up. No matter which college you'd mention, he'd say, "Good place, Larry, good place." I think he just wanted to make sure that I did go to college somewhere, so he supported them all. In the end, it came down to I.U. It seemed as if *everybody* wanted me to go to I.U. and they really made the decision for me. In a way, I just went along with what they felt was best for me. My mom was happy, my dad was happy and Coach Jones was happy.

The big event after my senior year was the Kentucky–Indiana All-Star games. They play two of them each year and it's a big deal in that area. There was some controversy about my being selected at all because our area was not considered strong that year. But they generally had *somebody* from southern Indiana on the team and I was the one chosen to go. I was happy to be picked, but if I hadn't been chosen I really wouldn't have cared very much. I mean, it wasn't that much of a big deal to me.

I went up there for the All-Star practices. Kirby Olberman was the coach. He's got a starting five consisting of the "co-Mr. Basketballs" in Indiana—Steve Collier and Roy Taylor—and three other guys. I was put on the second unit.

When it was all said and done, my unit got the best of them in practice every day. That's the way I saw it anyway. Now we get to Louisville for the first game and we're up by eight points or so in the second half when he puts our unit in and we blow them away. We just take them apart.

We go to Indianapolis for the second game and the same thing happens. Our team was trailing in the first half, but when our unit went in, we went crazy and took complete control of the game once again. He starts the first unit in the second half and then the second unit is put in—everybody but me. So I'm just sitting there, wondering what is going on.

With about two minutes to go in the game, Coach Olberman comes over to me and says, "Hey, I forgot all about you. Why don't you go in now and get something?" I said. "Too late. I've already been embarrassed."

The coach got pretty angry at that and I don't blame him. But I thought what he did was wrong too. I put in my time, just like everyone else. Everybody else got to play. It would have been one thing if he had told me I wasn't good enough. But to come and say he had forgotten about me was another thing entirely. How can a coach forget about somebody after he's been practicing with him for two or three weeks?

I know I reacted wrong, but I was young. However, if I had to do it all over again, I would probably do the same thing because I know how embarrassed I felt that night. My values have changed. My outlook has changed. But I can remember how I felt that night, just sitting there—totally forgotten.

8

S INCE I DIDN'T REALLY KNOW much about college basketball or Indiana University or even Bobby Knight, for that matter, I started reading up on the school before I went up there.

I got excited about playing for Bobby Knight. I love that man. I admire him so much for what he has accomplished. I was really looking forward to playing for him.

He had asked me to get up there during the summer and get settled, which I did. I was reluctant to leave home right away, but he had asked me to come up, so I did it. I didn't have any problems at first.

Things went well in the beginning. Jim Wisman and I were shooting around on a court one day when Scotty May came over and introduced himself. Then Bobby Wilkerson came over. Jim and I played those two guys, two-on-two, and when it was over I said, "Oh no. There's no way I'll ever make *this* team." Scotty was making every shot. Those guys looked unbelievable to me. But we continued to play over there two or three nights a week. Kent Benson and somebody else would choose up the team. Scotty never did.

Kent Benson can be a nice guy, but, point-blank, he

treated me terribly. He treated us freshman as if we were idiots. That's why to this day I never treat rookies badly. I always try to take them under my wing.

Benson came down one day while I was shooting and just took my ball and went to the other end to shoot. He'd say, "You freshmen don't deserve a ball." Of course, Wisman and I would be the first two out there and Benson would come along and pull this stuff just about every day.

When they chose sides, we'd never play. Wisman and Wayne Radford and myself were the ones who always sat out. When someone did take a break, Radford would be the one they'd pick to go in. I never got to play. Benson had no idea what I could do. Finally Scotty May spoke up a little and I got to play, but Benson continued to treat me like a jerk, like I was nothing.

You'd see Bobby Wilkerson and some of the others around campus and they'd say hello and make you feel good. I couldn't believe the way Benson was acting. But I'm not saying that he was the reason I finally left. It wasn't just him—it was the school itself.

But ever since then, I've wanted the Celtics to beat Benson's team whenever we play. I got a big kick in 1985 when Kevin McHale set the Celtics' scoring record of fifty-six points in a game where Kent Benson was guarding him. Benson got so frustrated in the third period that he picked up two quick T's and then got ejected!

My problems really began when classes started. I wasn't much of a scholar to begin with, although I had gotten a good enough grade-point average to get into college. But I certainly wasn't ready for a school the size of Indiana University.

The school was way too big for me. There were too many students. One classroom could have held half of West Baden—or so it seemed to me. Thirty-three thousand students was not my idea of a school—it was more like a whole country to me. It was too far to go to your classes. I'd be thinking, "Which building do I go to next?" I walked around for two days, trying to figure out where I was going.

I knew I was really going to have to hit the books hard. In my senior year of high school, I started paying better attention in class. I felt it would not be a problem for me at I.U. if I listened, took notes and kept my head in it. But I'd go to a class and there would be three hundred people. I was intimidated by the size and it got so I just couldn't handle it. I felt awkward asking questions in front of all those people and I could see that it was going to be hard for me to take advantage of the educational opportunities there.

Things weren't much better socially. I had no money—and I mean *no* money. I arrived there with $75. Where was I supposed to get money? I had virtually no clothes. Knight had me room with Jim Wisman, who was a very worldly seventeen-year-old kid—just the opposite of me.

Jim may not have been wealthy, but he was solid middle-class. I came in with my few clothes and he just filled up the rest of the closet. He had a full wardrobe, while all I had was five or six pair of jeans, a couple of slacks, a few shirts, some T-shirts and my tennis shoes. I didn't have a sport coat or even a pair of dress shoes.

Wisman said I could wear anything of his that I wanted at any time and I ended up wearing all his clothes. He also gave me money when I needed it. But I couldn't go on that way for long. I said to myself, "How can I keep wearing Jim Wisman's clothes and accepting Jim Wisman's money?"

It didn't take too long for me to decide that I was in the wrong place. I figured I'd go back home, work for a year and try it someplace else. I.U. just didn't feel right to me.

Bobby Knight has said subsequently that he has learned a lot in the last fourteen years about how to treat kids. Recently he said that his thinking back then was since he had never catered to a Scott May or a Kent Benson or a Quinn Buckner, why should he have catered to a Larry Bird? Of course, the bottom line is that he had a great team—seven guys from the 1974–75 Indiana team would go on to spend time in the NBA—and he sure didn't need me.

But I do think Coach Knight knew he had a kid who could play. I say that because of what he's said since then and because of one little incident.

We were all down in the gym playing one day and this was

one time when I actually got into the game. Knight had been out of town and now he was back in Bloomington. Anyway, we're out there playing and I am moving without the ball— I'm moving, I'm cutting, I'm rebounding and I'm doing everything.

I make a nice backdoor cut and get open and Jim Crews— he's now the coach at Evansville—misses me. Suddenly you hear a voice. *His* voice. Nobody knew Coach Knight was back in town, but he sure was and he sure didn't like what he just saw.

He stopped that game. He came down and started yelling at the top of his lungs. I can just tell you it wasn't *me* he was screaming at.

We'll never know what would have happened if I had played on that I.U. team that year, but it would have been interesting if I had been around. That team lost just one game, but it was to Kentucky in the Mideast Regional and it knocked them out of the NCAA Tournament. They went on to win the whole thing the following season. I.U. is a great school with a great sports program and I'm sure that if I only could have hung in there, things would have worked out fine.

I really believe in my mind that if I had kept my head in my schoolwork and did everything Coach Knight had said and if someone had gotten hurt, I would have moved right into the starting five. It turned out that Scott May did break his wrist or something and although he did play in that Kentucky loss he wasn't himself. And I.U. only lost by two.

I never even made it to the official beginning of practice on October 15. When the time came, I just packed up, which didn't take me long. I didn't even tell Coach Knight. I just left.

I walked out to Highway 37 and hitchhiked. I figured I could catch a ride from someone heading back in my direction. A man picked me up in a truck and left me off in Mitchell and eventually I got home.

TYPICAL OF MY NATURE, I hadn't told anyone at home how unhappy I was, so they were surprised when I showed up. Their reaction wasn't good at all.

Everybody was disappointed. My family was upset and the townspeople were shocked. It was considered a great honor to play for Indiana University. At first, people kept hoping I had just made a rash decision and they could talk me into going back. I believe I came home on a Friday. On Sunday, somebody in the house said, "I'll take you back up there if you want to go." I said no. Once I make my mind up, I make it up.

That was the first extremely important decision I had ever made for myself and I was sticking to it. I knew everybody would be angry with me when I made it and that there would be a lot of pressure on me when I got back, but I didn't care.

Mom was so mad at me that she barely talked to me for a month. I went back to living at Granny's and Mom would walk into that house and not say a word to me. Mark was playing at Oakland City College at the time and I rode down with a friend to see a game. When we got there, Mom and Dad were already there. Dad started talking to me, but Mom wouldn't say a word.

She was convinced I was ruining my whole life by rejecting Indiana University. "You disappoint me," she'd say when she finally spoke. Mom would tell people, "He's never going back to college." She just didn't understand what the problem was.

Mom really took it hard. "What's he going to turn out to be? A bum?" I figured. "Well, if I do, I do." That was my response. A lot of people around town took it hard. But I didn't *like* it at I.U. It's like when people complain about their jobs. If you don't like it, why do it?

Sometimes you just don't feel that you have a choice. The only reason I quit I.U. was because I didn't feel comfortable there. I just couldn't motivate myself to get the job done. I wanted to work a year and I didn't want to go directly to another school.

I wanted to make some money and then decide about my future. I totally believed I was doing the right thing. I didn't have even a vague notion of becoming a professional basketball player at this point, so I didn't feel that I was jeopardizing any career opportunities. I didn't have any thoughts about turning pro until late in my college career. I just knew it was going to help me—both mentally and financially—to sit out that year.

When I got home, my dad supported my decision to leave. He said, "Look, son, if this is what you want to do, then that is what you should do. Don't look back. Just look ahead." Dad may have told someone else he was angry, but he never said that to me.

Despite leaving I.U. I still needed to play basketball. First I looked at Lincoln Trails College in Illinois. I liked it a little bit, but the school had no dormitories and I didn't want to go there for that reason. I came back home and people were after me to go to Northwood Institute, which was right there in West Baden. The next thing you know, I was enrolled there.

I don't think I lasted two weeks. I practiced with them for a couple of days before realizing there wasn't enough competition and I didn't belong there either.

I went to work at my uncle's gas station on and off for about a month and then I got a job in French Lick in what they call the Street Department.

I remember walking in the first day and one of the men said, "You don't need to be doing this. You should go back to school." Hey, I *loved* that job. I liked my crew and I liked everything we did.

We picked up trash once a week, which is where the press picked up that "garbage truck" stuff later on. We were out mowing grass in the summer and in the winter we took care of snow removal. We fixed roads. I was working outside and I loved every minute of it.

I was making about $140 and $150 a week and I was happy. I was able to save some money. I bought my first car, a 1964 Chevy. It was a piece of junk, but that was all right.

And, of course, I was playing ball.

I played some AAU ball for a team called Hancock Construction. We traveled around a bit and got some good competition. It was a great group of guys.

I was living with Granny then and I must have come home one time with a trophy from some tournament because after a while she would ask me each and every time I'd come home, "Larry, where's your trophy?"

Being down in French Lick didn't put me completely out of sight. College scouts were keeping track of me. When somebody comes to one of those games from out of town and he's a pretty sharp dresser, you know he's there for a reason. We'd go play a game and when we walked off the court there was usually somebody waiting there to see me.

But I already had an idea what I wanted to do. For a while in the very beginning, I was worried. I was thinking, "Maybe I *can't* get into another college now."

The most persistent recruiter was Bill Hodges of Indiana State and he assured me it was all going to be all right in the long run—even if I had to go to a junior college first. Hodges was down in French Lick every day and one day Mom got so mad at him always being around that she slammed the door in his face. My friend Tony Clark went with me to Terre Haute for a visit, however, and I liked the place. Remember, I had been interested in attending Indiana State all along anyway.

One day I had taken Granny to the Laundromat, when in walked Hodges. I told him about a kid named Kevin Carnes (Beezer's brother), who had played with Mark, and how I thought Indiana State could use him. Kevin had really improved his game since he got out of high school.

Hodges said, "Come on up and we'll put you guys through a scrimmage with our players and see how he looks." I said, "That's fair enough. I'll come up."

I grab Kevin and Mark and we take off for Terre Haute.

We're in jeans, T-shirts and tennis shoes—our usual attire. We get there and Hodges says, "Come on back to the locker room and we'll give you some shorts." We never played in shorts back home. We always played in blue jeans. We said, "We're fine. We'll play with what we've got." Hodges was horrified. "This is crazy," he said.

Hodges should have known what to expect from me. He should have remembered the first time he ever saw me play. There was a game scheduled between an Indiana high school All-Star team and an independent team. I was supposed to play on the independent team and he wanted to come down to talk to me before the game. This was after I left I.U.

He came down to French Lick and found me putting up some hay. It took us all day to do it and it was a hot day— must have been ninety degrees. When I finished, I was heading right over to play a game.

Hodges is a farmer himself. He knows how tough loading that hay is, especially on such a hot day. He thought I would be too tired to play. I scored forty-three points and had twenty-five rebounds before fouling out and we beat that All-Star team. After that Hodges was hounding me to go to Indiana State all the time.

So now we're out on that court at Indiana State. He gives us a guy named Jimmy Smith and some itty-bitty guy, John-something, to go along with Mark, Kevin and myself. We start the game and Kevin takes that ball, goes right around everybody and starts dishing it off to me. Mark was hitting from the outside. We played three games and we beat them every time. We drilled them. No contest. Hodges couldn't believe it. The I.S.U. players couldn't believe it either. They're saying, "Who *are* those guys?" We put on quite a show. Meanwhile, I wore my tennis shoes out.

Since I was a transfer from I.U., I had to sit out that first year. Bob King was the coach and and I wasn't sure what he really thought of me because I had really been Hodges's baby, not his.

I was put on a second unit during the practice and it was the same story as in those Indiana–Kentucky All-Star games. We pounded the first team every day. Coach King got to the point where he didn't know what he could do to protect the first team, so he made me sit down. I said, "That's it." I took my stuff to the locker room and I was ready to quit again. Coach King came into the locker room after me.

I said to Coach King, "Hey, if you're not going to let me practice, what am I going to do? These practices are my *games*. All I want to do is play basketball." He tried to explain to me why he was sitting me down. I had thought it was because I was messing up or something, but he said, "Look, Larry, I can't get anything done with these other guys. They're scared to death of you. You make them look like idiots. Now how are they going to go out and play a game?" When Coach King told me that, I realized it was a different matter.

It was rough not being able to play in the games, but I played basketball constantly that year. I played more than ever before. In between classes I would go down to the gym and shoot. When they went away on road trips, I played in that gym. The following summer I haunted the Terre Haute Boys' Club. I was always practicing there, always shooting baskets. I was a real "gym rat." I'd go home and eat, then come back to the gym and play some more. I mean, I practically lived in that gym.

BASKETBALL WAS MY DEFINITE FIRST LOVE, but that doesn't mean it was all I *ever* thought about.

In my junior year, I started dating a couple of girls, but nothing very serious. My whole life still revolved around basketball. I liked girls, but I was really in love with basketball and nothing else was close.

I had friends who had girlfriends and when they'd break

up they'd be messed up for a week. "Who needs that?" I thought. Half our team was angry with girls all the time. I could never understand that. They'd chase them around the school and then something would happen and they'd wind up getting angry. You could tell. So I really never wanted to get caught up in it. The way I looked at it, why even have girls around if you're always going to be upset with them?

Nevertheless, I did start going out with Janet Condra, a girl I had known since first grade. She came from a nice middle-class background. Her parents were nice people and they treated me great. We had nice times together, but we always seemed to be arguing about something stupid and we'd break up and then get back together again. This went on all the time. In the area where I grew up, everybody got married young and Janet definitely wanted to get married.

I wasn't ready to get married. Janet was a real nice girl, but I knew already that we were just too different from each other to make it a really happy, meaningful relationship. But like I said, everybody around us was getting married and the pressure that Janet seemed to be putting on me was, I'm sure now, the result of the pressure *she* was feeling from her family and friends. I know we were both too young to get married, but we went ahead with it anyway.

The wedding took place in early November, shortly after I entered Indiana State. We moved up there and I knew right away that it wasn't going to work. I tried to make it work, but there was just no way. We ended up getting a divorce. One day after the divorce went through, Janet came over and said that she wanted to get back together. We did try again—one more time—but it only lasted a few weeks. As it turned out, it was during those last few weeks together that Janet got pregnant. That really put a lot of pressure on me to stay with her, but no matter how I tried to figure it out in my mind, I just couldn't live with Janet anymore. There was no question I had made a mistake. I really felt badly about it, especially since, where I come from, divorce is considered to be about the worst thing that could happen.

That was a very rough time in my life, what with my father's death, changing colleges and the entire marriage/

divorce/baby situation. I remember thinking, "What's going on with my life?"

We had a little daughter, Corrie, who lives with Janet outside of Terre Haute. I can't honestly say I've had that much to do with her life because of my differences with Janet. I think about Corrie all the time, but what can I really do now? I can't go back and relive the first five or six years of her life. Corrie is a fine and beautiful young lady. Her mother has done a great job bringing her up in the best way possible. Corrie is also very athletic. She's good at everything she does and I'm really proud of her. To tell you the truth, I've never really known how to handle the situation, but I love her and anytime Corrie needs anything, I will be there for her.

Right around the time of my divorce from Janet, I met the woman who has meant the most in my life: Dinah Mattingly. I didn't know this when I first met Dinah because we were just friends for a long time. But whenever I spent time with Dinah, whether it was with our mutual friends or just the two of us, I would notice more and more how special she really was. We always had a blast together and laughed a lot.

During this terribly difficult time of my life, I feel it was Dinah who held me together, who brought my spirits back up or just listened when I was unhappy. She also bothered to take a real interest in my basketball activities (something Janet never did). As a matter of fact, Dinah would rebound for me for hours in the gym, when I'm sure she would have rather been doing something else.

I began to fall in love with Dinah. I realized she was the one. She was perfect for me. She was beautiful, athletic, understanding, funny, my friend. She had everything I could have ever wanted in a woman. We've been together since and I've never, ever looked back.

I T DIDN'T TAKE LONG to discover there was a world of difference in general public interest between the basketball programs at Indiana University and Indiana State.

Every game at Assembly Hall in Bloomington was sold-out. At Indiana State we weren't in the same situation. In the beginning of my first year of eligibility, I.S.U. was giving away $10,000 worth of gifts as an inducement for people to come to see the games at Hulman Center, our oncampus facility. The first night we draw four thousand people and I'm thinking: "They're giving away $10,000 and there's only four thousand people here? We've got problems."

Here we had this beautiful facility and people didn't seem to be interested in supporting us. I wasn't sure it was going to work. I said to myself, "I don't know if this is where I want to be." I knew I was going to stay at Indiana State, but at the same time I wasn't pleased with the turnout.

Then we really started playing well. All we did was win, win, win. Folks starting turning out. Around Christmastime we had a game—against Drake, I believe—when the students were away. We had a sellout anyway and we beat them (in overtime, if I'm not mistaken).

You could tell people were really getting into it and it was a completely different feeling from that point on. When the students came back from Christmas break, there weren't enough tickets to go around.

We wound up going twenty-five and three. We really played some great basketball games that year. We went on the road and just tore people up. In the last fifteen games or so, I think I averaged about forty points a game and I had the feeling I could do just about anything I wanted to on the court against just about anybody.

The turning point for me came in a loss against Purdue. I had about twenty-eight points and fifteen rebounds, but I felt a step slow against that level of competition. After that game I said, "I could have played a lot better. Why am I backing off, when I should be going straight ahead?"

Coach King helped me a lot. I enjoyed playing for him. He especially taught me about defense, which was his specialty: how to defend certain areas, how to cut off angles and all the basics you need to play good defense. If you wanted to work on offense, you had to do it on your own.

Coach King was a great coach as far as I was concerned and he was always fired up. We had a curtain hung in the gym to separate the courts and he would step through that curtain looking as if he wanted to fight somebody. The moment he stepped through, practice started. We worked and we worked *hard*. He always knew exactly what he wanted to work on. He studied the films and he was always well prepared.

We should have been at our peak in my junior year. We started off winning fourteen straight, but with all the publicity that was coming my way some of the other players didn't seem to be handling the imbalance of attention very well. After my sophomore year, I made third-team All-American and I was pretty excited about it. Somebody called me to give me the news and I was so proud that I called my uncle. Here I had gone from a high school player who had dropped out of college to a guy who made third-team All-American in his first year. That meant a lot to me.

Other people weren't so happy, I guess. After that great start, problems set in and we lost five in a row. I knew what the problems were, but I wasn't sure how to fix them. We had players thinking about being drafted by the pros, which usually happens to people in their senior years. It seemed as if everybody lost track of what we were trying to accomplish as a *team*.

Believe me, we had more talent than we had the year before. We were definitely good enough that year to go to the

NCAA Final Four. We had nowhere near as much talent the following year when we won thirty-three straight and went to the national championship game.

I was eligible for the NBA draft that year. Under the rules of the time, I was a so-called "junior eligible" because it had been four years since my original college class had entered school. I didn't have to "declare" for the draft. I didn't have to go anywhere either if I didn't want to. It was a nice situation to be in.

I had no intention of coming out. The pros didn't mean that much to me. I know it's impossible to imagine this happening now, with all the attention focused on the NBA and all those nationally televised games and the star recognition factor of NBA standouts such as Kareem Abdul-Jabbar, Magic Johnson and Michael Jordan, but at that time I don't think I had spent two minutes in my life thinking about playing in the pros.

I just liked my college life and had no desire to leave school. The money was no big factor. The only time I ever remember being aware of the kind of money that might be available was when I read something in the paper about David Thompson signing a new contract for $800,000.

I thought, "Wow, $800,000!" I was pretty impressed with that, but it was something I couldn't relate to my own situation.

You've got to understand that all I ever heard as long as I'd been playing was about everything I wasn't or everything I couldn't do. It was always: *He's from a small town. He can't run. He can't jump. He can't play against bigger guys. He's a step slow. He can't play defense.*

You hear all that, so you put the pros out of your mind. I figured, "When the time comes, I'll deal with it." That's always been my philosophy.

I wasn't paying attention to the 1978 draft. The only clue I had was from the Pacers. They had the number one pick and had an interest in me. I told them I was staying in school. They traded that pick to Portland and they got Johnny Davis and the third pick. They took Rick Robey with the third pick and Portland took Mychal Thompson at number one. I learned all this later.

I was out playing golf in Santa Claus, Indiana, when a man came up to me on one of the fairways and told me the Celtics had taken me sixth in the draft. I said, "What's that mean?" He said, "I don't know. Watch the evening news."

What it meant from the Celtics' standpoint was that they had both the sixth and eighth picks in the first round and were in a position to gamble on me. Even if I didn't sign right away, the rule said they would have a full calendar year from the day of the draft to sign me. If you're interested in trivia, the man they took at number eight was Freeman Williams, a guard from Portland State who would really fill it up. He never played a game for the Celtics, since he was involved in a big trade with Buffalo, who were moving to San Diego and who now are the Clippers.

The Celtics just didn't mean anything to me. I didn't know about the banners or the parquet floors or even Red Auerbach. I didn't know anything about all that Celtics' tradition.

I *had* heard of Bill Russell. In fact, my cousin and I used to play one-on-one over at his house in Shoals, Indiana. He had a little goal you could dunk on. We'd take turns. One day I'd be Bill Russell and he'd be Wilt Chamberlain and the next day we'd switch. But I had never actually seen Bill Russell play. Bill Russell was just a name to me.

They were *all* just names to me. I never saw Oscar Robertson play. I did happen to see the John Havlicek retirement ceremonies on TV when I was down in Kentucky playing on a postseason All-Star team. I had gone to that Colonels game in Louisville (the one I thought was a college game until I got home) and one Pacers game. And sometimes I'd see highlights of Dr. J. on TV. So much for my NBA knowledge—and interest.

By now, of course, I had decided to stay in school, but I wasn't telling my plans to anybody except Dinah. I told everyone I would make my decision at a later date. I only did that because I was stubborn and bullheaded and said to myself, "It's nobody's business what I'm going to do." I went to Florida with Dinah for a couple of weeks and then came back and told Coach King I was staying.

And why not? I was proud of the way I was handling myself. I was doing well in school. I had Dinah. I just loved my life at Indiana State.

Then something happened that threatened to change everything. Bob King suffered a serious heart attack and was not going to be able to coach the team. For the first time, I thought about leaving school. It was the Jim Jones situation all over again, except that I wasn't sure who the coach was going to be.

Believe me, I definitely would have left if Bill Hodges hadn't gotten the job. I really wanted to stay and I was very determined to become the first one in my whole family to graduate from college, but the only way I was staying was if Hodges got the job.

The first day Hodges was hired he came up to us and said, "Fellas, thanks a lot. I know you had a lot of input regarding my selection as your coach. Now let's get out there and start tearing somebody up."

When practice started that year, I honestly didn't know what to expect. We had a new coach and a lot of new people. Our most important addition was Carl Nicks, who had begun at I.S.U. and then had gone to a junior college. He was a six-two guard and we all felt he would definitely improve the team. The problem was getting him to come back to Terre Haute.

Carl had just torn his junior college league up. He was being recruited very heavily by a lot of big schools and he had a very strong interest in Tennessee.

When he was visiting us and trying to make up his mind, I sat down to have a talk with him. I said, "When you were here as a freshman, I tried to help you out. Now I need your help. We need you badly."

He said, "I don't know. I really want to go to Tennessee."

I said, "Look, Carl, it's my last year. I think we can have a great team, but we need you to finish it off. *You* will make the difference on this team." Carl came with us and he saved us on many a night.

We had some talent, but what we really had was a bunch of players who worked hard and did what they were told to do. We *all* played a role. We had guys like Brad Miley, a great defensive forward who couldn't shoot a lick, and Alex Gilbert, who couldn't shoot free throws and couldn't dribble but once or twice, but who could rebound and block shots and just act tough. We had Bob Heaton, whose specialty turned out to be game-winning shots.

We were a true team. We stood up for each other and we used to hang out together.

Before every home game, guys would say, "Larry, what's happening after the game?" I'd name a place and they'd say, "Okay, see you there later." That's the way we were.

There were twelve guys on that team and I'll bet that after every game, at least seven of them went somewhere with me and Dinah.

By this time, we "owned" the school and the town. In the beginning—back in my sophomore year—the people weren't believers. When we started winning, they realized the best team in Indiana was right there in Terre Haute. We blew I.U. right out of the water.

The more we won, the bigger we got. They started having pep rallies, Once after beating Purdue up there, we got back to find ten thousand people in that gym waiting for us. I didn't want anything to do with that. In my mind, we hadn't accomplished *anything* yet.

The way I saw it, what would really be impressive would be to see ten thousand people greeting us if we *lost* to Purdue. That would mean a lot more to me than having them there when you win. Well, those people in Terre Haute showed me something after we lost the NCAA title game to Michigan State. When we got back, there were I don't know how many thousands of people lining the streets all the way from the airport to the city. They'll probably never realize how grateful I am to all of them for that show of support.

That's the day I realized how much those people deserved that title. That's why I dedicated the 1984 Celtics championship to the people of Terre Haute. I'm still not sure if the people of Boston understood the meaning of that gesture, but that was the reason.

The tip-off that we might have something special going that year was the Purdue game. We had beaten them by thirty-two the year before after being up on them by forty and I knew they would be really psyched up for that game.

We got to their place and I overheard some of their pregame team meeting. They played a tape of the blowout game from the year before at I.S.U., with our fans going crazy. I told our team to be on the lookout because they really wanted to get back at us. Well, we just whipped them.

That's when I knew we had something. But I thought we had something the year before and then everything went bad. I knew I had another job in keeping everybody's head in what we were trying to do. I had another challenge. I knew we had to stay close as a team and that we had to keep things in perspective. Purdue was good, but there were much better teams out there.

There was one more loose end. I had to do something about the press because, in my opinion, they had a chance to mess up everything for us.

First of all, it would have been difficult to find anyone less prepared to be interviewed than I was when I got to Indiana State.

There were just a handful of press around at first, so it wasn't so bad. Then all of a sudden I'm this big college player and everybody wants to know what I'm all about. I wasn't ready to handle it. I didn't want to tell anybody anything.

The thing that really irked me occurred in one of the college hangouts I went to. I was sitting there talking to some friends when I noticed a fellow sitting near us—and he was writing things down! It just killed me. I didn't say anything to him, but I was hot. After that I was always looking over my shoulder.

If we were sitting there talking and a stranger came in and you could just sort of tell what he was up to, we were out of there. I realized that the better I got as a player, the more this was going to happen and that I'd really have to watch out. I asked my friends to help me out. We'd be in a place and I'd look at any stranger and say, "Who's that?" One of my friends would try to find out for me.

I was never relaxed getting up there and talking about the

game either. My attitude, which made sense to me at the time, was: "You were at the game. You saw what happened. Write it yourself."

The local writers didn't cause any problems. Somebody actually did an article about me working for the Street Department in French Lick and I liked it very much.

But once that story on me appeared in *Sports Illustrated,* the interest grew. By that time, I was settled in with my friends and I had my routine. That's when I started to look over my shoulder.

All I wanted during my senior year was to be left alone to enjoy my last year in college, especially since I had made the decision to return and not go into the NBA. I didn't want to be messing around with interviews. Ed McKee was our sports information director and he would say I should do this interview or that interview, but I didn't want to do any.

There was another major problem with the press interest in me and it came to a head early that season. We had just won a home game and now there were about fifteen or twenty press people in the room. I come out of the shower and they're all waiting for me. I scanned the room and the other players had their heads down. None of the press was talking to any of them. I had to be concerned about their feelings. The press only wanted to talk to me, when the other guys had played just as hard. As far as I was concerned, *they* were the glue.

I thought our team had a chance to do something that year and all I could think about was the way the team had fallen apart the year before. That's when I decided to cut the press off totally.

It turned out to be extremely difficult for Ed McKee, as well as for the coaches, but it was great for my teammates. They loved every minute of it. Of course, the first thing that happened was that when the writers started talking to the other players, they would ask about me. So we had to put a stop to that too. The players were told to answer question about the game or about themselves, but no questions about me.

I wasn't naïve enough to think I was going to keep my life a secret forever. I never got to the point of not talking to the press. I was just coming out of a tough period of my life and I wasn't ready to be probed.

The point was that I felt I should be able tell my story when I was more comfortable talking about it, which is what I'm doing now. You don't want to tell your story to somebody and then the next fellow down the road picks up on it and writes something else.

Believe me, I wasn't foolish enough to think people weren't going to find out that my dad had committed suicide or that I had been married and divorced and had a child. I just made up my mind that when the time came, I would tell my own story.

1 2

WE HAD GONE TO THE NIT in both my sophomore and junior years, but we hadn't gotten very far. When I was a sophomore, we had to go down to play the University of Houston at their place. I remember we were sitting around thinking we might be picked for the NCAA Tournament when Coach King came in and said, "Pack your bags, boys. We're going to Houston."

I thought, "Houston? Why do we have to go all the way down *there*?" We went down to Houston and got beat. I had forty-four or so, but I missed an off-balance shot that might have won the game for us.

The next year, after our season had fallen apart, we went back to the NIT. We beat Illinois State at home in a close game, but our season ended when we lost to Rutgers when James Bailey hit a last-second shot.

By my senior year, I had really developed as a player. I knew after my first year what I was going to need to do to improve. I had a pretty good year as a sophomore, but I knew

I needed more range on my shot, I needed to be able to take the ball low and make moves with both hands and I needed to control the ball a little better on the fast break.

Rebounding was never a problem. In high school, I had gotten about twenty a game and it never dawned on me exactly how good a total that was. All I knew was that I was getting more than anyone else on my team. When I got to college, it was just as easy.

Even when I got to the NBA and people told me, "You won't get any rebounds up there," I found it wasn't so hard. After playing with Dave Cowens and seeing how he would block out all the really *big* guys, all I saw was that I was rebounding against smaller people. No problem.

The big thing in between my junior and senior years was participation on an All-Star team with such players as Magic Johnson, Sidney Moncrief, James Bailey and a bunch of guys from Kentucky, such as Kyle Macy, Jack Givens, James Lee and Jay Shidler.

Joe B. Hall was coaching that team and I'll never forget the game we played in Kentucky when he started all his players from his NCAA championship team while Magic, Sidney and I just sat on the bench, looking at each other and laughing about the situation. Finally he put us in for about five minutes and we just went crazy, passing the ball around.

That senior year went like clockwork. We knew we were pretty good after beating Purdue at Purdue and from then on it was just a matter of keeping everybody's head in the game. We started to climb in the rankings.

It's nice to say you're number one, two, three or four, but what does it really mean? We didn't know *exactly* how good we were, but we never thought we were going to get beat. We didn't care who we played. The guys just followed my lead. If I said, "We're gonna beat these guys," they believed me and we'd just go out and win the game. Sure, we needed luck once in a while. Bob Heaton had to throw in a miracle shot from about sixty or seventy feet down at New Mexico State just to get us into overtime and we pulled that one out.

The most ridiculous game was against Bradley. Dick Versace, who's now coaching the Pacers, was their coach and he decided that he was going to stop Larry Bird.

The first time down the court, I could tell something crazy was going on. There were *three* players on me! I said to myself, "Why don't I move a little farther out and three of their players went with me. So we were basically playing four-on-two.

Two of our players wound up scoring thirty points and another had twenty-eight. Brad Miley had never scored twenty-eight points in his life—ever—and all of a sudden he gets twenty-eight. I wasn't going to rush anything. I scored once on an offensive rebound and once when I stole the ball and went down for a dunk. Dick Versace held me to four points. So what? I was two for two and I had about fifteen rebounds and a bunch of assists. We blew them out and I was happy with my game under the circumstances and my teammates had a blast.

It took a little while for Coach Hodges to get used to being the boss. His first day was total chaos. He told half the team to be there at two o'clock and the other half to be there at three. Of course, I was there an hour early anyway or else I would have missed his first practice. I thought, "What are we going to *do*?" But after that everything ran smoothly.

Things went great right up till the final game of the conference tournament against New Mexico State. I broke my left thumb when I reached down for a ball and one of their players brought it up quickly and hit the tip of my thumb.

I didn't really know what was going on at first. After the game, the press people were bugging me: "What's wrong with your thumb?" All I knew was that it hurt and I needed to see a doctor. It turned out it was broken in two places. That wasn't the best way for me to go into the NCAA Tournament.

We got by Virginia Tech and Oklahoma without any problems. Then we ran into Arkansas in the regional finals. That was a battle from beginning to end.

We thought we had the better team. They were bigger, but

we had better rebounders. They had Sidney Moncrief and he was a really great hard-nosed player.

Moncrief was on me in the second half and he was doing a good job, even though he is about five inches shorter. I had three or four fouls and I was afraid of making offensive moves that would give him a chance to take a charge.

They were up by one point late in the game. With about thirty seconds to go, one of their guys trips over Carl Nicks's leg and is called for traveling, giving us the ball back with a chance to win the game.

They were on me tight and I finally gave the ball to Steve Reed, a guard who was a good shooter, at the top of the key. He dropped it down to Heaton, who threw up a crazy left-handed shot. The ball went in the basket and we were in the Final Four.

Our semifinal opponent was DePaul. Mark Aguirre was a freshman then and he was scoring about twenty-five points a game. They had knocked off U.C.L.A. to get there and we knew it was going to be a rough game.

It really was a great game. I was hot. I was nine for nine or ten for ten or something like that in the first half. I was moving well that day. I had good footwork. A lot of times when I'm not scoring much it's because I don't have good balance. I had it that day.

Every time we thought we could take control of the game, they would come right back. Gary Garland was hitting everything for them.

It was another very tight game. I was actually scared to take the last shot because I had been so hot—I wound up shooting sixteen for nineteen—I was afraid I was due for a miss. Bobby Heaton won it for us with an offensive rebound.

So now it was Michigan State and Magic Johnson against Indiana State and Larry Bird for the national championship.

The press attention was enormous. The idea of the two of us playing for the NCAA title had captured everyone's imagination. I was pretty excited because I was looking forward to playing against Magic myself.

We had played together on that All-Star team coached by Joe B. Hall and one thing we had agreed on right away was that we both should have been playing. In practice, we had played together on a second unit that was beating the first team. I loved playing on the court with Magic.

Coach Hall got mad at us one day. We were playing our game when he said, "How can we work on this stuff if you guys are throwing these crazy passes and taking these stupid shots?" We said, "Coach, those shots are going *in*." I couldn't understand it. He was getting angry with *us* because we were embarrassing his first team.

Before our senior year, I watched Michigan State play against the Russians on TV. The Russians had beaten Kentucky, Indiana and Notre Dame. We only beat them by four or five. I'm always curious about anything connected with the Soviet Union and I was interested to see if Michigan State had improved. Well, Magic's team beat them.

Magic was just killing them with his rebounding and his coast-to-coast stuff. I said, "Right there, boys, you are looking at the team that's going to win the NCAA championship this year. Boy, they're good."

The buildup for the game was crazy. The semifinals were on Saturday afternoon and the championship game was on Monday night, so there were two full days for the press and the fans to get ready.

You couldn't concentrate because there were just too many people milling around. You'd go to practice and everybody would be at practice. You'd go to the hotel and they'd be at the hotel. Security was nonexistent. We went there hoping to have a good time and to win. It was impossible to have a good time. We would have been much better off it we had gotten away from the center of everything. We went about it the wrong way.

We thought it was just another game and that we would win. Everything had gone our way all year. We won every close game. We really didn't fear Michigan State. We were actually *too* cocky.

We didn't go in with a good game plan. First, we were going to put Carl Nicks, who was about six-two, on Magic, who was six-nine. At the last minute, we changed to Miley. It didn't make much difference because we didn't have *anybody* who could handle him. Magic was just too good on the break.

We thought we had proved that we could beat every kind of defense, but we had never seen anything like that zone of theirs. I couldn't do anything at all against it. I couldn't get the ball and make moves anywhere on the floor. They did a really good job on me.

In addition to all this, we weren't making our free throws. I went five for eight. We could have been right there at the end if we had made some foul shots, but we didn't do that either.

They just had too much firepower for us. We played a bad game, but they were better. I think if we played them ten times, we might have beaten them twice.

People always want to know if I was having problems with my thumb that day. I can honestly say I wasn't. I can't use that excuse. It was a little tender and sore, but when you're playing in a championship game the pain just goes away—unless you jam it or something.

When the game was over, I couldn't believe it. Not that we had lost—I could see who had the better team—but because it was all over. It took me a while to realize that was the last game I would ever play with this team. I said, "I can't believe it. All I've gone through the last five years . . . this has been the greatest time of my life and now it's over."

We were very proud of ourselves. We had done everything we wanted to do, but we came up short.

That senior year was everything I had ever dreamed of when I decided to come back for that final season. We just had a blast.

That team taught me a great deal about the game of basketball. We didn't have all that much raw talent, but we proved what you could accomplish when you have guys who really believe in each other, who work together and who know what it takes to win.

We had two guys—Alex Gilbert and Brad Miley—shooting 50 percent from the line. We had guys who couldn't dribble. If you told Alex Gilbert to take the ball and dribble as fast as he could with it, he'd never make it to midcourt.

Brad Miley couldn't shoot at all—either from the field or from the line. But he was a good defensive player and a good rebounder and he would always scrape up his ten or twelve points.

Somehow he would go six for six or five for five all the time that year. Steve Reed was a young kid who really didn't know what was going on, but he shot well, handled the ball well and just didn't make turnovers. And Carl Nicks just played as hard as he could. Sometimes he'd get hyper, but when the time came to settle down, he would always do it.

We were a man-to-man defensive team, geared to helping each other out. You never worried about anything because there was always somebody there to pick up your man if he got by. And we had guys willing to take that college charge, which is really a big thing in that game.

We honestly knew we weren't that good, skillwise. We just said, "Yeah, but we'll just wait till somebody beats us." The bottom line is that we knew what our strengths were and we stuck with them.

I don't think there's ever been another college team like us. There have been underdogs, like that North Carolina State team that won it all, but they had a lot more talent than we did. They had five draftable players. Carl Nicks was drafted number one and he kicked around in the pros for a little while, but except for me, that was it for the rest of our team.

I really believe the same thing could be done in the NBA if people truly dedicated themselves to winning. You take a team attitude like we had that senior year and put it on most NBA teams in the eighties and they would be great for years and years.

The entire college experience was great for me. In that short period of time, I learned more about myself and more about people than in the rest of my life put together. Everything was a learning experience for me. I got married and divorced. I had a child. I had to sit out a redshirt year as a transfer. I played against great competition. I helped change a mediocre basketball school into a powerhouse in three years. And it all happened so fast.

EVER HEAR ABOUT my college baseball career?
It wasn't a long one, but enough things happened
to make it seem that way. I had always loved playing
baseball. Although I never played on the Springs Valley baseball team, I had a lot of serious softball experience.

One summer I played on a big-time softball team with my
buddies. We're talking four, five, six games a week. We trav-
eled all over. Indiana. Ohio. Illinois. Kentucky. It was a blast.
I really got caught up in it. We won the state championship.
We played a game against a team that starred Joe Montana.
Obviously, Joe's always been great at *everything* he tries.

I played outfield and first and I batted third or fourth in
the lineup. My brother Mark batted second and Mike batted
third or fourth, whichever one I wasn't. If Mike was in his
home run groove, he'd bat fourth. But I hit a lot of home runs
myself. Our best hitter was a kid named Howie Johnson—
not the guy on the Mets—who hit about .700. You couldn't
get that kid out and it seemed as if he turned every single he
hit into a double.

It got to be serious business. The guys would bring their
wives and kids and some of them would complain because it
was either too hot during the day or too cold at night. You see
some of those guys now and they'll say, "Those were the best
days we ever had." We always had replacements ready—for
whatever reason. Sometimes another fellow just wouldn't
wise up. He'd be going for home runs and striking out when
he should have been advancing the runners, so we'd just go
out and get somebody else who could do the job.

Mike had a real home run trot. Every field we played on
had a fence and he liked to watch his shots go out. We played

a lot of games on a beautiful field they had in Jasper. The fence wasn't real far—maybe three hundred feet—but it was very high.

I loved to show off my arm. That's probably why it gives me trouble now. I'd be in left and when a single came my way I'd just rocket that ball into second base. And I loved to throw the ball to the plate.

Mike played some at third, at first and behind the plate. He'd always accuse me of setting him up to get creamed back there. He said I'd bounce them in to time it so he'd get run over.

We once played a team that went on to finish third in the nation. We lost two games to them in Jasper and they went onto Las Vegas for a big tournament and finished third. We're talking about a team that had a player who had hit two hundred or three hundred home runs. Now that's *cranking* it.

I loved baseball as much as I loved softball and I went to all of the I.S.U. baseball games. I got to be pretty good friends with some of the baseball players.

The coach, Bob Warren, was a good guy. After my last basketball season was over, he said to me, "When are you going to come out and hit some?" I said, "I wouldn't have any problem hitting a baseball." He'd just keep asking me and asking me and I kept saying I knew I could hit the ball. One day he finally says, "You want to come out and play in a doubleheader we've got coming up? If you do, you've got to come out and help us work on the field before the game."

We had a nice field and the players actually helped maintain it. We had to pull weeds and stuff. I said, "That's no problem."

The day comes and it's freezing cold. I'm out there pulling those weeds and my hands are freezing. I'm thinking, "If I have to take batting practice, it's going to kill my hands." Then I say to myself, "Why am I doing *this*?"

We start warming up and here come all these people. They're lucky if they can draw five hundred on an ordinary day and now they've got four thousand or so.

I didn't get to play until the sixth or seventh inning of the first game. Coach Warren sends me up to bat and I've never seen anybody pitch so fast. I try to watch the pitcher to see where he's releasing the ball, so I'll at least have a chance. I fouled one back, but he struck me out. Everybody went: *"Booooo!"* in a good-natured way.

Now I'm out in the field and it seems as if every ball is coming my way. I just wanted to make sure I caught the thing because I was used to catching that softball. Someone hit a little popup between me and the catcher. I was waiting for the pitcher to call one of us off, but he didn't. I was running as fast as I could when the catcher dived into me and hit me in the head with his shin guard.

All the time I'd been playing basketball I had never been knocked out. One baseball game and I get it. I was really hurt. They helped me up and I almost fell down again. I told Coach Warren to take me out of the game—*please!*

I went back to the dugout and all of a sudden my head cleared and everything just brightened up.

Coach Warren put me back in there during the third inning of the second game. This pitcher was throwing nothing but curves. He threw one and I just stepped back and said, "Wow!" Then he threw me another one and I hit it right in the gap.

I went to first base and stopped. I took off my helmet and threw it down. I was out of there. End of career: one for two, .500 average, two RBIs. I figured I couldn't do much better than that.

1 4

HERE'S ONE I BET NOBODY KNOWS. I had a chance to become the first player ever to play in an NCAA championship game and an NBA game a week later. Remember that during my entire senior year the Celtics had the NBA rights to me. They weren't having a very good season and there was a lot more going on back in Boston than I ever imagined.

When I was originally drafted by the Celtics, I couldn't have cared less about them. I had never been a fan of theirs and I had never followed them in any way.

Red Auerbach came to see us play a game in Cincinnati. He brought Dave Cowens, who had become his player/coach, along with him. Red really wanted to sign me and he made an interesting offer.

He said, "When you are out of the tournament, what would you think about finishing up the season with us?" We sat there and talked and he said he would pay me as if I had been there all season.

But he sort of upset me because he said, "You should be done in a week or two and then you can be playing in Boston." I said, "I plan on winning this whole thing." He was talking as if we were going to lose and it sort of aggravated me that Red was thinking we were going to get beat.

It actually did sound good to me, but I wanted to be at I.S.U. for graduation. It didn't work out that way, but I thought it was a pretty neat idea at the time.

At least I got my degree. I was so excited I remember running home and showing off my diploma to everyone, especially to Mom and Granny. Mom had always told me that she wanted me to the first person from either side of our family to get a college degree and I had done it!

I soon had another serious problem to deal with. Before I even had a chance to negotiate with the Celtics, I managed to do a pretty good job on my right index finger.

Through a series of complications, I found myself playing a softball game that spring *against* my brothers Mark and Mike. They thought I was supposed to be on their team and I had no idea I'd be playing against them until I showed up at the field. They were both furious about it, but it was just one of those crazy scheduling things that come up once in a while.

I'm out there in the outfield—in left center, actually— when Mike comes up to the plate. I start hollering at him. "Hey, hit it here! I'm ready for you." You know all that kind of stuff.

He hits the ball right on the seams and it's knuckling out toward me. I'm not one of those snatch-catchers, you know. I try to do it right. It was sinking and I go down on one knee and the ball hits my finger and bends it backward.

When Mike came running out to look at it, he started gagging. Dinah took me to see a doctor in Terre Haute. He took X rays and then decided he had to call a specialist in Indianapolis. I was told I had a shattered knuckle and they'd have to put pins in it. He said, "You're going to have to work hard with that finger to get it all the way back."

By that time, Bob Woolf was officially representing me and he was there at the game. He was probably having close to heart failure when he saw that finger pointing completely backward!

When I got to Boston, the first thing the Celtics' team physician, Dr. Thomas Silva, wanted to see was the finger. I held out the *other* index finger. Red took me out to see me shoot and I buried a bunch of jumpers. I said, "No problem. I've been working out all the time." That's when they started working on a contract.

Over the years there has been a tremendous calcium buildup, so that the finger is off at an angle and much larger than it should be. But I started making adjustments right away. One good thing about my body is that it's always allowed me to make the necessary adjustments. You hurt a finger and you try to make an adjustment with the other ones, making them do more work.

The first order of business before discussing a contract with the Boston Celtics was that of selecting an agent. I was very fortunate to have the interest and assistance of some of the best friends I have ever had, all of whom were and are very successful businessmen in the Terre Haute area. They were dubbed "The Committee" by the press before too long and the group consisted of Lu Meis, president of Meis Department Stores; John Royce, the president of Merchants Bank and Trust of Terre Haute; Paul Denehie, a vice-president of advertising and sales promotion for Meis Department Stores; and Ed Jukes, another bank vice-president. In addition, Coach Bob King had important input.

These men were nice enough to take the pressure off me of interviewing as many as sixty-five agents "narrowed down" from the hundreds that had sent mail or called me. They worked from a list of criteria that we had all worked on together.

The Committee finally recommended that I meet with two men, Mr. Reuven Katz of Cincinnati and Mr. Bob Woolf of Boston. Both men had excellent credentials, Mr. Katz doing a great job for people such as Johnny Bench and Mr. Woolf with people such as Carl Yastrzemski and Calvin Murphy, as well as with many past Celtics. Both had been in the business of representing athletes for many years and had great reputations for integrity.

In making their final "cuts," the key question The Committee asked of each candidate was: "If *you* don't get the job, whom would you recommend?" Almost all of them replied, "Bob Woolf." I was really impressed by that and when I met with him for three or four hours we talked about all kinds of different things. He was really sincere and even though he had all those years of experience, he was really down to earth and I felt I could trust him with anything I wanted to tell him. I decided that I wanted Mr. Woolf to represent me and it's a decision I've always been happy with. Over the years, Dinah and I have enjoyed our relationship with Mr. Woolf, his wife Anne and his children, Stacey, Gary and Tiffany.

My first contract negotiation was really kind of wild. I certainly wasn't prepared for it. Even though I had had such a great college career, as with all college seniors, you are still an unproven entity at the professional level. Red Auerbach is famous as one of the toughest negotiators in sports. He has rarely wavered from his negotiating process of trying to make his first offer his last offer as well. Red offered Mr. Woolf a $500,000 a year salary for me. I'm sure the labels *Too slow, Can't run* and *Can't jump* were mentioned more than once during the negotiations. Mr. Woolf told me he wanted to make me the highest-paid rookie in sports and I just left everything in his hands. I couldn't relate to all that money anyway, so I just told him to do the best he could in getting me a fair contract and to keep me updated on the progress while I continued to work out at home in French Lick.

Since the Celtics never budged from their first offer all summer, Mr. Woolf had to resort to any and all tactics he could think of to get them moving. He and Red exchanged heated words in private and waged a public battle through strategically timed press interviews that they each hoped would apply more pressure to the other side. Several times talks were officially broken off during the summer. This battle of wills was eventually referred to by the press as "The Hundred Days' War."

Mr. Woolf told me that he got lost one night on his way to a speaking engagement in a town thirty miles away from Boston and he had to ask directions from another motorist on the road. The driver yelled to him, "I'm only giving you directions if you promise to sign Larry Bird!" Eventually it appeared as if the Celtics and Mr. Woolf were at a stalemate in the negotiations. It got so bad that Mr. Woolf's kids had to come home from school because they were getting such a hard time from their classmates.

I did get a taste of "The Hundred Days' War" on one of my first visits to Boston. I thought people that I met on the streets would be polite and say, "Hope you can play for us." Instead, they were saying, "You've *got* to come here, we'll *never* make it without you!" I mean, these people really sounded *desperate*. I had recently learned of the Celtics' previous season record of 29–53, but I had seriously underestimated the public's perception of me as the "savior" of the Boston Celtics franchise. For the first time, I realized what a tremendous following the Celtics had and I knew that if I did come to play for Boston I'd really be thrown into the fire. I knew I would be stepping into something *big*. When I returned home, I told Dinah, "I didn't know what I was getting into until I went out there. You won't believe what it's like."

By the end of the summer, the situation was still gridlocked and finally the owner of the Celtics, Harry Mangurian, stepped into the negotiations and we were all able to come to an agreement before training camp that did give me the best contract ever paid to a rookie at that time. I was just happy to officially be a Boston Celtic and be able to get to *work*!

PART II

THE CAREER

1 5

WHEN I WASN'T WORKING OUT that summer, I started reading up on the Celtics and about Red so I could have a better idea of what the Celtics were all about. I also wanted to find out about the city of Boston. I was starting to get very excited. Most of all, I wanted to know what I could do to help make the Celtics a better basketball team.

The Celtics had their annual rookie camp during the first week in August in Marshfield, Massachusetts, at a place called Camp Milbrook. Red ran the camp in conjunction with his camp for children. He got a big kick out of riding around in a golf cart, overseeing the operation.

When I heard that Dave Cowens, Rick Robey, Tiny Archibald and some of the other veterans were going to be there at the rookie camp. I knew something was up. Somebody said to me, "They must be excited about the season." I knew better. I said, "They're just coming early to bust my chops."

Camp Milbrook wasn't exactly a glamorous place and Red wasn't exactly a gracious host. Dinah came with me, along with a friend of mine and his wife. I walk into the office and Red sees Dinah and he says, "What's *she* doing here?" I said, "She's with me."

I walk outside and look at the baskets and I see one that I swear was nine-feet-six. I look at the other one and it looks like it's ten-one or ten-two. I said, "Here I am. The Boston Celtics are supposed to have won all these championships and the baskets aren't even the right height? What am I doing here?"

Bill Fitch was the new coach and right away I realized that he intended to show me who was boss. When we started the scrimmages, he was doing everything he could to test me. Coach Fitch wanted to aggravate me and he just couldn't do it. He'd make me guard this player, then another one. He'd put me here, then he'd put me there. He tried to run me until I was ready to drop.

The real challenge was going to come at the regular training camp. I knew some of the veterans would be testing the rookie and I was right. Cedric Maxwell walked in and said to one of the guys—Curtis Rowe, I believe—"Hey, man, come here. Look, that's our *savior* over there." I wasn't too sure that *we* were going to get along. But I wasn't afraid of any of them. I was prepared to stand my ground with them all—if I had to.

Everyone was curious about Coach Fitch, but we didn't have to wait long to see what his approach was going to be. That very first day Curtis Rowe was jogging at half-speed and Fitch said to him, "Just take that jog up there by the door on the left, take a shower and get out of here. You've been cut." I'm thinking, "I can't believe this." And when Maxwell heard that, he just clammed up.

Maxwell really wanted a piece of me. He had all these veteran-type tricks and we would go at it every day. His playing style was different. He was unlike any player I had ever come across.

We had great battles in practice. Max had all these great moves, but I think he found out I was a little stronger than he had anticipated. And he really prepared me for NBA-style play—even if that may not have been his *original* intention.

Before practice, M. L. Carr would say, "Hey, rookie, let's go." Then we'd play one-on-one. Dave Cowens always wanted to play and I had a hard time with him at first. Eventually I stopped him. I stopped M.L. And I stopped Maxwell. I stopped all that "Let's get the rookie" mentality. I had to—just to get them all off my back!

Training camp was rough, but it was still basketball. I

think I made the transition from college to pro ball pretty easily.

Our first exhibition game was in Madison Square Garden against the 76ers. All I wanted to do at that stage was fit in and see if I could make some things happen. I wasn't trying to dominate. We had veterans such as Cowens, Maxwell, Carr, Chris Ford and Tiny Archibald to do that. I wanted to take things slowly.

Having my first game against the 76ers was special because that meant I'd be playing against Julius Erving. I had met him once at a banquet and I just couldn't believe I was meeting him. I just couldn't wait to *play* against him to see how good he really was. In time, I would find out. Man, would I *ever* find out.

As a rookie, it's very important to earn respect, first from your teammates and then from the rest of the league. They test you more and more as the season goes on to see what you're made of.

I didn't notice much along those lines in the beginning because I was simply concentrating on trying to play well. As the season progresses, you find that your opponents are pushing you a little harder and then a little harder and then you realize you're being tested. But once you get their respect, you can start giving it back to them.

I honestly believe the physical nature of this league is completely overblown. That's all you hear—that you've got to be strong and you've got to be physical—but there's much more to the NBA than that. Sometimes you take some unnecessary shots, but you learn to put up with that stuff.

I discovered I had come to an interesting team. On the one hand, we had people such as Max and M.L., who did a lot of talking. On the other hand, we had people such as Tiny and Don Chaney, who didn't say a whole lot. I found that I was attracted to both types.

I saw where Coach Fitch was coming from the first time we met. I hadn't seen many people like him, but I had him pegged. He wanted to make sure he was in *total control*. He wanted me to listen to *everything* he said, so I just went along with the program, which I thought I should do, because, after

all, he was the coach. I tried to do everything he asked me to
do and I think that once he found out that I was "tough" and
always played hard, I don't think he had any problem with
me. He started backing off a bit.

I played with that right index finger taped to the middle
finger all through training camp and the exhibition season,
as well as during the first game of the regular season. But I
really wasn't that pleased with the feeling. I couldn't get a
good grip on the ball.

I stopped taping the finger from top to bottom before the
second game of the season. I just taped the top joint in order
to give it more flexibility and I went out and scored twenty-
eight against Cleveland. Not too many games later, I threw
the tape away entirely during halftime of a home game
against Kansas City. I had been afraid of getting the finger
jammed or hit, but I decided I had to stop babying myself.
I've never taped that finger since.

After that game in Cleveland, I didn't think I was going to
have any serious problems. My big concern was to be consistent, so the guys on the team would know they could count
on me every night. That was really my only concern. I wasn't
concerned about totals of points or rebounds.

I was now doing what I'd wanted to do for many years. I was
playing and thinking about basketball twenty-four hours a
day. The first three months or so of that season I thought
were neat. I was just traveling and playing basketball and I
didn't have to worry about anything else.

I was starting to hold my own in the team byplay. When
Maxwell and M.L. would start in saying stuff trying to get us
going, I'd join in. Then when somebody on the opposing team
would start smarting off back to them, I'd get *hot*. We were
sticking together and *everybody* was involved.

I thought we were building something very special. Max
and M.L. were always saying something and the rest of us
had to back them up. Here I am in my learning stages and
they're doing all this stuff to fire me up.

As it kept going and going, I realized that this was exactly
the life I wanted.

I even played in the All-Star Game, but since it was my

first year in the league, I really didn't feel I deserved to be selected. I can remember standing there during the introductions, listening to all the names being called out, and I felt, "What am *I* doing here?"

I was happy just to play a little bit and I was pleased when Billy Cunningham kept me out there in the overtime. I wasn't really trying to do a lot. I just wanted to fit in and see just how good the other players were when they played together. I had a nice balance of points, assists and rebounds and I considered it to be a very successful day. I even hit the first three-pointer in the history of the All-Star Game and we won in the OT.

In general, I'm not really an All-Star Game person. The first one was great, but it's really not my kind of game. I won the All-Star MVP in 1982 just by hitting a few shots late, but for my money Robert Parish should have gotten the award.

The All-Star break seemed to refresh me. One reason was that the Celtics always head right out to the West Coast following the All-Star Game and that trip has always agreed with me. During my first Coast trip, I was feeling exceptionally good. I remember thinking, "This is awful scary." Everything was falling into place. I felt that if I kept improving—and I had no reason to think I wouldn't—I could become a great player and that's definitely what I was shooting for.

My biggest defensive worry was trying to keep players like Dr. J. from just doing whatever they wanted to do on the court. I was afraid they were going to go around me every time or that I would get caught back on the fast break in an isolated situation.

My teammates very quickly started to help each other out, however, and that saved me. I needed help. If you put me out there and asked me to guard a Dr. J. one-on-one, he'd have beaten me every time. Once we all learned about each other and started covering up for each other, it was a lot easier.

I loved my teammates. I had never met a character like Cedric Maxwell. He was such a great player, but he used to get in moods where we'd play a weak team and he'd say, "Go ahead, boys. You'll have to pull me along tonight." He just wouldn't get up to his highest level of play for the lesser teams.

I'd say, "C'mon, Max, let's just go play a good half, get way ahead and then you can sit down."

"No, not me. Put somebody else in," he'd reply.

That was just Maxwell's way, so on those nights we'd just have to play around him. But when the big games came or even games against half-decent teams, Max would play extremely well. Then it would be; "Give me the ball. I'm going to carry *you guys* tonight."

Max was always talking trash. He'd say all this stuff to get somebody to react, so *he* would get fired up. We used to do anything we could to get someone on the other team to say something that would get Max riled up.

Sometimes he'd come into the locker room after doing an interview and say, "Hey, we've got to get serious tonight. I just said something they're not going to like." So then we'd have to go play even harder. He'd do it all the time.

"Hey, boys, I opened my mouth again. I shouldn't have said it, but I did."

That was Max. To me, he was a good team man. When you *had* to get something accomplished, he was a great, great teammate. He was the key man for us in game seven of the 1984 Laker series. That's the night he said, "Jump on my back, boys." And we did.

M. L. Carr was another one who kept us fired up. We always had to back *him* up too. He was just as bad as Max because he would even pick on the *fans*. He was good-natured, but if he felt you weren't doing the job on the court, he'd let you know about it. Coaches might sometime beat around the bush, but M.L. would say, "Hey, why don't you tell the coach to take you out of the game? You're lousy tonight."

M.L. would add, "You're not playing hard. You sick or something? If you don't want to play, I'll go in there." It was great. You *need* a guy like that around. I told the front office that if they ever let him retire, they'd never be able to replace him. That prediction turned out to be accurate. Everyone on the team respected M. L. Carr.

Chris Ford. I had never heard of him. I didn't even know

he existed until I paid that visit to Boston in the spring of 1979. I went into the locker room and I heard a voice over there in the corner saying, "Hey, Larry Bird! Come over here and talk to me, Larry Bird!" It was Chris Ford. I thought, "Who *is* this guy?"

What an interesting player. Here's a fellow who was even slower than *I* was and he was a *guard*. He looked as if he was always just holding on, as if he was ready to die, but had one more gasp while he tried to hold onto that cliff. And just when you'd think he'd had it, Chris would pop a three-pointer on you. What a competitor.

Dave Cowens. Dave treated me right. He tried to take care of me. He'd pick me up to go to practices and games. Sometimes we'd go out and eat together afterward. I regret we didn't hang around as much as we could have. My relationship with Dave was good, but it could have been much better.

Tiny Archibald was—well—a moody guy. You never knew whether he'd come into practice hollering, screaming and giggling or whether he'd come in and not say a word. If Tiny was in a joking mood, we'd have a great time. If Tiny came in and didn't say a word, nobody else said a word either.

Tiny's moods didn't bother me. We had M.L. and Max to do all the talking. I like those quiet guys too. You can't have twelve guys yakking all the time—not if you want to get along.

I knew right away I was going to like playing with Tiny. I was fascinated with the way he moved, the way he got his shots off and the way he passed. It was a very easy adjustment for me to play with him.

My closest friend on the team was Rick Robey. We had met playing in those All-Star games two years earlier and we definitely hit it off. I found out right away that if you wanted somebody to go out to eat with or go to the movies with you, Rick Robey was your man. He was always ready to go anywhere and do anything.

The bad thing about Rick was that he didn't know when to go home. We'd go out and do different things and after a while I'd say, "Rick, I'm tired. Let's go home." Rick would answer, "Well, I feel great!" It took me a whole year to figure out that the reason I was tired and he wasn't was that I was playing forty minutes a game and he was playing five!

Even now Rick says that the best thing that happened to my career was *him* getting traded to Phoenix—and in many ways I've got to agree with him.

We were roommates during road games and Rick took care of answering the phone. I hate the phone anyway, so that was ideal for me. So in that sense Rick watched over me, but he was still slowly killing me by keeping me out so late.

Cowens got hurt in late January of 1980 and Robey started at center for the next month. He had some fantastic games. There was no question he could play.

It was no accident that my first MVP season came the year *after* we traded Rick to Phoenix for Dennis Johnson. Rick knew it. When I got the MVP, he called up and said, "I leave and you go crazy." It was true.

The Celtics had only won twenty-nine games the year before my rookie season, but the two groups had nothing in common. M.L. was new. He had come over from Detroit as a free agent. I was new. Gerald Henderson was new. Tiny had been hurt the year before and hadn't been himself. Cowens didn't have to worry about playing and coaching the team at the same time anymore and he was in fantastic shape. And Fitch was the new coach.

Bill Fitch was good for me. He stayed right on me and helped me improve in many areas. He could take out a film and show me immediately what I was doing right—and what I was doing wrong. He knew when to pull me from games at exactly the right time. He would never let me get too cocky.

I think he thought the entire situation out because he knew exactly what he was doing with me. Just as soon as I was ready to make the big splash, he would pull me back a little. In my second year, when I missed my first nine shots in a game in Oakland, he just sat me down and said, "Look, you're just going to have days like this."

Fitch had been in the marines and there was a lot of the drill sergeant in him. Some of his practices were killers. Once we flew all day to the West Coast and then got off the plane and practiced for two and a half hours. Normally your road practices aren't as strenuous as your home practices, but we once practiced for over three hours in San Antonio. Coach Fitch was trying to make the team as good as he possibly could.

There couldn't have been a better coach for me. If I had a coach who didn't push guys and sort of let you go your own way, I would have been confused. I've been blessed with a lot of good coaches. I knew when I had a good one and when I had one that wasn't so good. Bill Fitch was a good coach.

Our record reflected that. When the regular season was over, we had won sixty-one games. That thirty-two-game gain over the previous year is still the biggest single-season turnaround in NBA history.

1 6

R IGHT FROM THE START, people were wondering how I would manage to handle the press. After deciding not to talk with them during my senior year at Indiana State, I had a pretty bad image in the eyes of a lot of people.

In my head, it wasn't going to be a problem. I knew that once I got into the NBA, I would just about *have* to give interviews I didn't do it to look good. I did it because it was a part of my job.

I really had no reason not to do interviews. Once you get to the pro level, everyone must be man enough to take care of himself. In the pros, everyone knew that if I played well, I was going to get the press attention automatically.

After I got there and the rest of the players saw I could play, I don't think there were any hard feelings. They saw me having to stick around in every new city to do all those interviews and after a while I think they actually felt sorry for me.

The whole experience really wasn't so bad and I wasn't thinking about it as much as people thought. I just did it. First, I set some rules—the most important one being that no one could come to my home for an interview because I am an intensely private person and I like to think of my home as a refuge from the spotlight of being a celebrity. I preferred to do interviews after practice or games—not before. I believe things have worked out and that people have generally been very fair to me.

The one thing I've learned is that interviews really don't take up that much of your time after a game and that's even true in postgame playoff situations. I always dress in the trainer's room, so that when I make my appearance after a game I am fully clothed and ready to go on my way as soon as the interviews are over. When I enter the locker room, I always glance at the clock. Say it's twenty after ten. When the group interview is over, it's generally only twenty-five of eleven or maybe twenty of. Sometimes you look out at all the people and you say, "I'm going to be out there for *hours*." Instead, it's only fifteen or twenty minutes.

I've seldom had any problems with people writing critical articles about me. But sometimes somebody will send a critical article to Mom or Dinah and they'll get upset, then I'll be upset because *they're* upset. I don't usually read those stories anyway. Everyone has his own opinion and I respect that a lot more now than when I was in college.

I tried to stay out of sight that first year. I had no idea what to expect when I first went to Boston and I wasn't interested in doing much, other than playing basketball and learning to fit in with my teammates. When we went out to eat on occasion, Dinah and I just picked our spots. I didn't venture out too far.

It took me two or three years to discover how great a city Boston really is. We both fell in love with Boston.

Selecting a house led to a funny story. I came out to Boston without Dinah and Mr. Woolf was taking me around to look at different houses. When we came to a certain house, I took a look at it and said, "That's the one I want."

It turned out that it was right next door to Mr. Woolf's house. I liked the house because it's only a few minutes away from Hellenic College, where we practice, and because it was just a comfortable house—not too big and not too small—and it had a nice yard.

Before I left home, I told Dinah I was going to look at some houses and then she could come out and look at some and we'd choose. Before she came out there, however, I had already bought that one. Luckily Dinah liked the house a lot too.

I found that living in Boston was less bothersome in some ways than living in French Lick. There are so many pro athletes in Boston that people are used to seeing them around. Most people are very friendly.

That doesn't mean I can just run over to the Chestnut Hill Mall, a few minutes from my house. You've got to use your head. If you want to sign autographs all day, you go where the people are. The movies are no problem. I know some places where we can go to eat without much interruption. But sometimes someone will say, "Let's go to *this* restaurant," and I have to start thinking about how many people are likely to be there before I go.

It never fails. If you think there will be a lot of people someplace, you'll find there's no one there. But when you think, "Oh, there won't be anybody *there*," then there'll be about a hundred people, all wanting autographs.

Sometimes it's fun just to drive around. Once I was creeping along in traffic on Storrow Drive, a road that runs along the Charles River. A fellow and his girlfriend were in the car next to me and they were sitting very close together. We were going very slowly and when she saw me she started hitting him, pointing me out, and he smacked into the car in front of him, a fender-bender if I ever saw one. I started laughing because that poor guy was so embarrassed.

No one can ever be fully prepared to live a celebrity's life. It can get really ridiculous sometimes. It just so happens that

I like to do my own yardwork. But I can no longer mow my own front lawn.

If I go out there, it's like an open invitation to the public to stop in. I did it for three years and loved every minute of it—when I could actually do it. But one day I counted fifteen people in my yard waiting for me.

One year a buddy helped me paint a railing. He said, "I'll paint the front and you paint the back." I'm out there painting the back and I walk around the front for something. *Boom*—here they come. After a while he said, "Get back there. I'm too busy talking to everyone and I'm not getting any painting done."

People drive by constantly and honk the horn, no matter what time it is. We'll be inside watching TV and we'll hear that *beep-beep*. I'll say to Dinah, "There go the fans." But Saturday night can be bad. They'll be out all night and they've been known to come by at two in the morning, beating on the door.

But we've really come to love Boston and we're considering keeping a home there when I retire. The city turned out to be everything we didn't think it was going to be. I love the area. I love the sports opportunities. It's a tough city and I like that. I don't know why, but I just have that perception.

Before I came to Boston, I had never seen a hockey game in my life and now I'm watching Bruins games all the time. I was always a Cubs fan, but now I follow the Red Sox. If I could go to Fenway Park without a hassle, I'd get season tickets. I could sit up there in a box, I suppose, but I don't like to rush in and rush out.

That situation is frustrating because I'd love to stop into Fenway after practice and watch the game. It's a great place, but the two or three times I've gone there, all I've done is sign autographs for three hours each time. I never even got to my seat! I'd go to baseball games all the time if it weren't for those autograph requests. I don't feel right turning the fans down for autographs, so I just don't go to see the Red Sox anymore.

And I'd like to walk on that field just one time. Major league parks just give you a certain feeling. I'd like to grab a bat too. I can guarantee you I could hit one over the Green Monster.

I can't really relate to signing autographs. What does it all mean anyway? I looked up to my father and he wasn't a celebrity. He was just a workingman. I respect my brothers. It's like the time a man once said to me, "You're my son's biggest idol." I replied, "Why aren't *you* his idol? He said, "Because I don't play basketball." I said, "That doesn't mean anything." I think he sort of got my hint. I told him that my father was always my idol.

I learned to cope with all this as I went along. When I was in college, I got a lot of publicity, but I didn't take it to heart because I knew I had my whole life to live. I knew I was heading for a whole new set of experiences, but I had no idea what the scope of them would be. The day I left Terre Haute to go to Boston, I remember thinking to myself, "What am I *doing*? Where am I *going*?"

I had only been to Boston twice—once to watch the Celtics play and once to buy a house. I loaded up all my stuff and when the day came to leave I was actually scared of the unknown. I was thinking, "Is this what you really want?" I drove out there by myself and the whole time I'm thinking, "This is a whole new life. I'm going to live in a city I never dreamed I'd be living in."

But my biggest concern was how the Celtics—not the public—were going to react to me. I know people were figuring, "Here comes that 'Hick from French Lick,'" a phrase I had come up with at a press conference. The most important thing to me was showing the Celtics that I could play basketball. After I got going in training camp, I knew I was going to fit in.

I didn't know I was going to escalate into a three-time NBA MVP, but I knew I was going to be able to play in this league. I didn't worry about anything else.

As a rookie entering a team with a lot of key veterans, I knew my place. I just wanted to get along, but I was never exactly sure what anyone was thinking, especially Bill Fitch. During training camp, he came up to me one day and said, "Write down on this piece of paper how many games you think we are going to win this year." I put down forty-seven. I figured, "They won twenty-nine the year before. They'll go *crazy* if we win that many."

Fitch said, "That's awfully high. You must really think something is going to happen around here." When we finished the season, we had won sixty-one games. I'm still waiting for Coach Fitch to come back on that one.

Once I started playing, I realized that I was farther along than I thought. All the things they had been saying—*He can't get a shot off. He can't jump. He can't run*—turned out to be either not true or irrelevant. I was rebounding, I was filling the lanes on the break and I found that my body was a lot better than I thought it was, as far as staying up with the guys and taking the beating and banging. The pushing and holding and the physical stuff wasn't as big a deal as I thought it would be.

I started to hit my stride with a forty-five-point game in Phoenix right after the All-Star break. I said, "I can play in this league. I'm not backing down against any of them." I was willing to pay my dues, but I was holding my own against everybody and I felt that if I kept improving, it wouldn't take me long to be where I wanted to be.

The sixty-one games we won in 1979–80 was the best record in the league and we naturally thought we had a great chance to win the championship. But Philadelphia destroyed us.

We swept Houston in the first round. Chris Ford had a great series. He managed to play great team defense while still doing a good job on Calvin Murphy, always a dangerous scorer. Every coach I had ever had always told us how important it was to learn how to cut off angles and Chris was a master of that. And if Chris was ever beaten on a play, he still wouldn't quit. He'd always make that extra effort. He'd always try to help out and that makes such a big difference to team defense. Chris sure knew how to play team basketball.

Then Philly beat us at home in the first game and we never recovered. When we got down, three games to one, the press asked, "What are you guys going to do?" I figured, "No problem. We'll beat them at home, for sure, and then go back over there and take care of business." We had played so well the week before against Houston that I was sure we'd snap out of it. So Philly came into town and beat us again. End of season.

I said to myself, "I can't believe the season's over." It was basically the same feeling I had after the Michigan State game. So much had happened and it had all been good—except for Philly.

Someone told me, "You look tired." He was right. I *was* tired. I was really worn out. When that series was over, it was raining in Boston and I just stayed home and slept for three or four days. I really felt bad about getting beaten so early.

I was a rookie, which means, by definition, that I didn't really know what was going on. I had always felt I was a winner and I thought we had a chance to win the whole thing. I didn't like the feeling of losing and that served as a motivation for me the following season. I didn't feel right until we won the championship that second year. It honestly took me that long to get over it because I believed we had a better team than the one that played against Philly. The next year I was determined not to go home early. Of course, when we won it the following season, we weren't the same team at all.

Over all, things were coming together at the end of that first year. I had made an adequate adjustment to the NBA and to living in Boston. I still wasn't as comfortable as I wanted to be, but I knew I'd get there.

And perhaps the biggest thing I had learned that year was how important beating Philadelphia was to everyone in Boston. I got a little taste of it during the regular season, but it didn't have the real impact until we got into the playoffs.

YOU DIDN'T KNOW WHETHER TO LAUGH or feel sorry for the guy. Bill Fitch was busy being "Mr. Drill Sergeant" and the poor fellow had obviously never had to run like this.

By the time he'd get to midcourt, he'd be so far behind everyone that he'd have to turn around and go back the other way. He'd get halfway down there and everybody else would be coming the other way again. He was always stuck in between. He was going from free throw line to free throw line. Everybody on the team was saying, "Who *is* this guy? He can't even get up and down the court."

That's the way it was for Robert Parish during his first month as a Boston Celtic.

Then Kevin McHale got right off a plane from Italy—he and his agent had been threatening to take his act to Milan—and walked onto our practice court at Hellenic College. He had been holding out, but now he was signed.

We knew Fitch would really have it in for him. He had already told the press that as far as he was concerned, McHale could have stayed in Italy. I remember we were stretching and Fitch was already calling him "Spaghetti Man."

I'll never forget my first encounter with Kevin. I started up for my shot and all of a sudden a hand was there and I had to shoot high. I was thinking, "Just luck." I drove the next time I had the ball and he blocked it from the side. I said, "*This* guy is an unbelievable defensive player."

That was our introduction to Kevin McHale.

Parish and McHale had both become Celtics on the day of the draft. We had the number one pick that year, thanks to a trade with Detroit. We also had the thirteenth pick. Red and Coach Fitch traded those picks to Golden State for the third pick and Robert Parish, who had spent four years with the Warriors but who never had realized his full potential. With that third pick we took McHale. Suddenly we had one seven-footer and one six-eleven guy.

It turned out that Robert just needed time to get in shape and an opportunity to play. He got that sooner than anyone expected because early in the exhibition season Dave Cowens came up with a big surprise to all of us by announcing his retirement.

We were in Terre Haute, of all places. We had scheduled exhibitions in Indianapolis, Terre Haute and Evansville and were spending the week with Terre Haute as a base.

We were sitting on the bus, waiting to leave for a game with the Chicago Bulls in Evansville. After a while, it seemed as if we should have left already and people were saying, "Come on, let's go!" Then Dave walked on the bus and asked Coach Fitch to come outside so he could have a word with him.

We still didn't have a clue. Dave gets on the bus and says, "I've got to tell you something." Then he proceeds to make a speech. Dave says, "I want to wish you luck, but I think it's time for me to retire."

We were stunned. Then M. L. Carr stands up and says, "Hey, if you're not a part of this team anymore, get off our bus. We've got a game to play!" He was just kidding, maybe trying to help us absorb the shock a little better.

It was a pretty somber ride to Evansville. Initially there was some joking, but then reality settled in and there wasn't much said the rest of the way down there. Dave *had* been acting a bit funny in practice. It did seem as if he really wasn't into it. We had all worked hard the year before and we all knew we'd be working hard again and we felt Dave had probably been through so much that he just thought it was time for him to get out. I was sad because I was looking forward to playing with him that year.

Dave told people he just didn't think he could do it anymore because his ankles were bothering him, but I really didn't buy it then—and I still don't. I think it was all in his head. I think Dave had made up his mind to get out.

Dave's leaving really shook me up. You can read about something like that, but when you're actually living it, you just sit there and say, "Can you believe this?" You're in the town where you played in college and Dave Cowens retires.

Another older player who packed it in during that training camp was Pete Maravich. He had joined us in January of my rookie year and although he did have some good games for us I never really thought he felt comfortable with the team. You could tell he just didn't have enough spark. He was there for that one last hurrah, but you could tell he really wasn't into it either. He never even played an exhibition game.

But I never doubted that "Pistol Pete" loved the game and I had a lot of respect for him. His early death from a heart problem in 1987 was a complete shock. We'd see Pete once or twice a year and I really got to like him. He had changed his entire lifestyle and he had a legitimate love for people. It was just amazing that something like that happened to him.

By this time, I was getting used to these veterans calling it quits. When I was a rookie, Ernie DiGregorio just walked out of the locker room one day during training camp and never returned. That was too bad because I honestly think he could have been a great backup to Tiny.

Once Cowens left, Parish really started getting in shape. By Thanksgiving, he was a monster and it was apparent that the Celtics had a better team than we had the year before. Playing with these guys put me more at ease. I just didn't have to do as much. There was no great pressure to come up with big scoring numbers and I could just concentrate on playing consistent all-around basketball. The one major difference was that with Cowens gone they were looking more to me at the end of the game. Going to Dave the year before was fine with me—I was just a rookie.

The following year, however, our offensive game plan revolved more and more around me. If we were running, the ball went to Tiny. Otherwise it started going more and more through me.

We were winning and we were working hard, but so was Philadelphia. The rivalry had always been something special in the NBA, but now it was bigger than ever. Every day we'd check the standings to see how Philly had done the night before and I'm sure the 76ers were doing the same thing with us.

My personal rivalry with Julius Erving was growing. It's still the most exciting confrontation I've ever had at the forward spot. In my first couple of years, Dr. J. was at his peak and I was just starting to come on. It was a battle every time.

The most important thing I had to do while guarding Dr. J. was to get help. When he started going along that baseline, you knew what was on his mind. He wanted to dunk. Once he got a step on you, there was nothing you could do. Any daylight at all and Dr. J. would jam it through.

Some people said, "You should just give him the outside shot." Well, when the good doctor was on the left side, he had a very good bank shot and I was scared to death of that, so that wasn't necessarily the answer either. Julius Erving also was a much better defensive player than most people gave him credit for.

We never spoke on the court. It was said that I yelled things at him one night, but that was M.L. talking trash from the bench, not me. Believe me, I never said a word to Dr. J. on the court.

1 8

T HERE'S NO QUESTION THAT Parish and McHale made us a much better team.

Once Dave retired and Robert got in shape, he showed us he was going to be a great player. He was filling the lanes on our fast break, he was dunking, he was blocking shots and he had a good outlet pass.

Then when you brought Kevin off the bench, it was double doses of everything. Kevin was the total package. He *also* rebounded and blocked shots and ran the break—and he was a killer inside. We didn't really have a shot blocker the year before. The only team with fewer rejections than us was San Diego. When Robert and Kevin showed up, we went right to second place in blocks, trailing only San Antonio.

Their presence certainly made *me* a much better defensive player. I could now guard anybody I wanted to because I knew I could run my man to either one of those big men. Max was guarding all the quicker guys anyway and now I had the power forwards.

They all said that Max was a weak defensive player before Coach Fitch arrived. Bill got on him and Max turned himself into a very good defensive forward. He accepted challenges from the NBA's great offensive forwards for the next few years and he did a great job for us. But both of us benefited a lot from playing with Parish and McHale.

We breezed through the 1980–81 season. We only won one more game than the year before, but it was still a great achievement because we weren't sneaking up on anybody this time. It all came down to a Boston Garden showdown with Philly on the final day of the regular season. The winner would have the best record in the league and the home court advantage for the entire playoffs. It was no different than a playoff game. It wasn't the best-played game ever played, but it was a very emotional game and our crowd was really into it.

We won by four, but not before Andrew Toney put fear in our hearts. It seemed as if every time he touched the ball, it was a swish. Andrew had to retire early because of an injury, but he was a *great* player for the Sixers in the early eighties.

I remember one playoff game that year when we had Chris Ford guarding him, M.L. guarding him and then even *me* guarding him—and none of us could stop him. With the exception of Michael Jordan, I have never been more afraid of an opponent at the shooting guard position than Andrew Toney.

To me, there wasn't much difference between the two when it came to the sheer ability to score. Michael has always come off more picks (until they moved him to point guard late in the 1988–89 season), whereas Andrew would just throw his guy off and go. Just when the 76ers *really* needed a basket is exactly when Andrew would get it.

And that man could pass a basketball. There was one All-Star Game when Andrew was making some bullet passes. Players were cutting down the lane and he would thread the needle every time. Andrew Toney was a total player.

Our first playoff series in 1981 was against Chicago. We took them in four straight and the major thing I recall about that series was one basket I made early in the fourth period of game four.

Chicago Stadium may be the noisiest place of them all and the fans were *really* raucous by the end of the third period. It was a close game and during the huddle between the third and fourth periods, Coach Fitch said, "Will somebody please do *something* to quiet these people down?"

We went out there and passed the ball a couple of times. It came to me and I tossed up a three-pointer with about twelve or fifteen seconds left on the twenty-four-second clock. The thing went in and we got that crowd quieted down—just the way Coach Fitch wanted.

So now it was Boston and Philly in the Eastern Conference championships. They beat us by one at home in game one and there went the home court advantage we had worked eighty-two games to get. We won the second game, but they took care of us in games three and four at their place, so for the second year in a row they had us down, three games to one, with game five in the Boston Garden.

We were down by six with about a minute and a half left and they had the ball. But Tiny came up with a big three-point play on the break and we were lucky enough to pull that game out and send the series back to Philadelphia for game six.

That's the game Celtics fans remember mainly for one thing that happened. We were down by ten or so in the third period when, for some reason or another, Max went into the stands for a loose ball and wound up getting into a fight with *one of their fans!*

That really got us going because we've always been the type of team to rally around one of our guys if there's a problem, just the way me and my own brothers did. We just started clicking and we wound up winning that game by two points.

I'll never forget the sight of Tiny flipping up a hook from the corner a split second after the final buzzer sounded. The ball went right into the basket. It didn't count, but Tiny was so happy he made it.

McHale saved that game for us with the biggest block I had ever seen in my life. We should have had the game put away, but I lost the ball at the other end and now here was Toney, getting into the lane for a shot that would have tied up the game. Andrew thought he was in the clear, but Kevin came over and made a huge play, knocking the ball off the glass and then retrieving it.

I've played in a lot of playoff games, but there is no doubt in my mind that the most *emotional* one of them all was that seventh game. This was Philly and not even L.A. could get the Boston fans riled up the way the 76ers could in those days. My mother seldom comes out to Boston, but even *she* felt she had to come to the Garden for this game.

The 76ers weren't fazed. With five minutes to go, they were up by nine. That's when Jake O'Donnell and Darell Garreston—two good veteran officials—put the whistles away. When you're talking about refs just "letting them play," you should get out the videotape of that game. It was going to take a real hatchet job for someone to get called for a foul in those last five minutes.

I remember driving in and either Bobby Jones or Lionel Hollins tried to take the charge. Maybe it *was* a charge, but there was no call. I remember M.L. stealing a cross-court pass from Dr. J. and thinking we had it won, but we turned it over and gave it right back.

Most of all, I remember Darryl Dawkins getting the ball

down on the left side of the lane. The score was tied with a little over a minute to go. He went up and there were three of us on him. He missed the shot and I grabbed the rebound on the other side of the basket and took off.

It was a semi-break situation. I was coming down the left side of the court. I believe Hollins was back for them and I sort of made it look as though I was thinking about passing and then pulled up from about seventeen feet and banked one in off the glass.

I hate to bank shots. Why I decided to bank *that* one I'll never know. I just don't like to bank and I certainly didn't want to bank from that far out. Who can explain why you do what you do at moments like that?

We won that game by one point and all I can say is that if we had lost it we wouldn't have felt embarrassed. We had no complaints about the officiating because they were letting *everything* go. Players were knocking each other down all over the court. Dawkins was clearing out and we were hammering Dawkins. We were all beating each other to death.

If a guy grabs your arm when you're going to shoot, that's one thing and a foul should be called. But if you're just bumping each other going for a loose ball or you're trying to take a charge, that's fine. That was a rough, tough ballgame. Those last five minutes were all-out war. I've never been through anything so brutal.

The scene inside and outside the Boston Garden was unbelievable. You play in order to get people excited, but you then have to make your way to the locker room against the tide of fans pouring onto the court, which they *always* do in Boston. That can be difficult because after playing in a game that was as physical and as emotional as that one, you are *totally* drained.

The fans had not been able to celebrate a playoff victory over Philadelphia since 1969, so they really let it all out. They were still outside cheering on Causeway Street, right in front of the Boston Garden, two hours after the game. There is a walkway suspended between the Garden itself and the Annelex Building next door and we were standing in front of the windows, waving to the crowd.

*   *   *

We players couldn't celebrate too long or too wildly because
we still had another series to play. The fans undoubtedly
thought the championship was wrapped up by beating Philly
because L.A., the defending champion, was already out of it
and our opponent in the finals was going to be Houston, a
team that didn't even have a winning record during the regular season.

We couldn't afford to think that way. We knew Houston
had gotten that far for a reason—and that reason was Moses
Malone. Their coach, Del Harris, had decided to scrap all
thoughts of a running game and and concentrate on playing
good defense and walking the ball up the floor and powering
it in to Moses.

One thing I've learned about playing against Moses is that
it really makes you want to concentrate on your own rebounding. I was young then and still figuring out what was
going on and I know this is the first time I really started
thinking about the necessity of rebounding in the playoffs.
Even in 1988, when I shot 35 percent against Detroit, I was
the leading rebounder in the series. No matter what else is
happening, I always get into a rebounding mood in the playoffs.

It's really necessary to think about rebounding when
you're playing against Moses. He's the quickest jumper I've
ever seen and he's relentless. He's very dangerous when he
follows up his own shots and he has a way of spreading his
arms that treats you as if you aren't even there.

We split the first two games at home and we were lucky to
win the one we did. Houston was playing its best ball at the
beginning of that series. They had already beaten Los Angeles, they had set some kind of a playoff record for victories
on the road and they certainly weren't intimidated by us. I
mean, that Houston team was peaking at just the right time.

We went back to Houston tied at one game apiece and we
knew we *had* to win that third game. We get down there and
Max is talking junk again. He says to us, "Let's get out there,
win that game and pluck those turkeys." We went out and
held them to seventy-one points.

But they came back to tie the series up in game four and now the question was: *What's the matter with Bird?* That's because I had scored eight points in both games down there. All of a sudden, Robert Reid is this great defensive force.

Robert *is* a good defensive player, but he's no Michael Cooper. I couldn't understand what all the fuss was about. I couldn't hit a shot, but otherwise I thought I was playing good basketball. I was passing the ball well, playing great defense and I had twenty-one rebounds in each of the first two games. No forward has done anything like that since. You'd think by this time people would realize there's more to the game than scoring. Everybody in the press and in the stands seemed to be concerned, but I was happy with the way I was playing. I figured I'd start to hit—sooner or later.

Game five belonged to Max. It was the most fired up I'd ever seen him and it told me how badly he wanted that championship. He could smell it. He was getting great position underneath and we were all feeding him. He had twenty-eight points (plus fifteen rebounds) and we won by twenty-nine. Max was just awesome in that one.

We were one game away from accomplishing our goal and we were all locked in. But as soon as we got in town, the weirdest thing happened. Just before we were going to practice, we heard the Pope was shot. We're all sitting around and somebody comes into the locker room and says, "Somebody just shot the Pope!" CBS had a TV monitor set up at center court and we kept drifting over to see the coverage. I just couldn't believe it.

I had no intention of letting that series go back to Boston. I had friends from Indiana down in Houston to help me celebrate my first championship and some of them said it was all right with them if we didn't win the game because they wouldn't mind going back to Boston.

I said, "No way. We've got to do it *tonight*. Everyone is ready to go."

We were up by seventeen in the third quarter when Houston started making a comeback. Allan Leavell started hitting everything and the place was rocking. We finally pulled ourselves together and were still leading by three when I got the ball in the corner and said, "This has got to be *it*. It's all in my hands."

I threw up a three-pointer and when that ball went through the nets my heart started *pounding*. I mean, that sucker was really beating fast. I knew it was all over and I was just so happy. They called a time-out and I just ran into the huddle and started jumping all over Eric Fernsten. Coach Fitch was able to pull the starters late in the game and we just sat there saying, "Can you believe it?"

The locker room was chaos. We didn't even know how we were supposed to act. We were just running around in circles in there.

We went out and had our pictures taken and that's when I grabbed Red's cigar and stuck it in my mouth. To this day, I love that picture more than any other photo I have. When we got home, I told Dinah, "Believe it or not, we may have a dynasty here. Maybe we can win four or five championships in a row."

That was the first time I ever experienced the true feeling of winning. When you're first celebrating, you don't fully realize the scope of what you've done. You can only do that a bit later, when things settle down. The most amazing thing about winning a game like that is you're so full of energy you feel as if you could go out there and play two or three more games.

The next three or four days after winning a title are fantastic. In Boston, you have a parade and a gathering at City Hall Plaza and that's always something to look forward to. When that's over, you're ready to go home and hear what your friends have to say about it.

If I was happy, you can imagine how overjoyed the veterans were. Take a person like Chris Ford. He was getting near the end of his career and things hadn't always been pleasant when he was in Detroit.

He had worked had for that title. He wasn't sleeping. He was losing so much weight in those playoffs that I thought he might fade away. I remember telling Chris and his wife Kathy, "Really go out and have a good time. Live it up like it's the only one you're going to get because you never know."

The great feeling carries over all summer. Any day that

summer I got into a bad mood, I would just think about the experience of winning a championship, and it would snap me right out of it. That feeling lasted all the way up to the beginning of training camp. Then you realize you've got to go out there and try to do it again. You've got to keep things going.

1 9

A YEAR LATER, my new experience was learning how to act after *losing* a championship.

As I said, I thought we had a dynasty going. We won sixty-three games and I expected us to win the championship. We had that good a team. We were young. We had a good bench. We had people who really knew how to play.

Perhaps the only uncertainty was at the guard spot. Chris Ford was a year older, but we still had Tiny, Gerald Henderson and M.L. We had also added Danny Ainge.

Typical of me at the time, I hadn't paid much attention to the Danny Ainge story. I had never seen him play on TV or anything. I just knew he was a baseball player for the Toronto Blue Jays who had also been drafted by the Celtics, who had to go through a court trial to sign him.

When he came to Boston, everybody was telling me about how Danny had dropped thirty-seven or something on U.C.L.A. or how he had gone the length of the court to beat Notre Dame at the buzzer in the NCAAs. It was all news to me.

I first saw him the night of as Philadelphia game. He was sitting at the press table next to our physician, Dr. Silva, and just by looking at him you could tell he was an athlete. I went out to eat with him after the game and there was no doubt he was eager to play.

He impressed me right away. I recall saying to Dinah,

"Boy, this kid is going to be great." But his first practice was something I'm sure *he* won't forget. He went zero for nineteen to start. He missed the first one and Max went, "Zero for one." Then "Zero for two . . . Zero for three . . . Zero for four," and so on, right up to nineteen.

Coach Fitch was going crazy. He was all over Danny, telling him he was shooting his batting average. He was on him *hard*. Everybody loved it.

Right after Danny was activated in early December, Tiny got the flu and Coach Fitch threw Danny right in there. He didn't do badly for a player who never even had a training camp, but once Tiny got back Danny was basically a spare tire for the rest of the regular season.

We got off to a rough start in the playoffs against a pretty good Washington team. They had Jeff Ruland and Rick Mahorn, who had already been nicknamed "McFilthy and McNasty" by Johnny Most, our loyal radio announcer. They had Spencer Haywood, and they had a pretty good rookie in Frankie Johnson, who was one of those little guys you had to start guarding as soon as he crossed midcourt.

Spencer Haywood was talking some *serious* stuff and he was threatening us with voodoo. I'm not kidding. He'd be out there before games, sprinkling stuff around, telling us he was putting a curse on us.

That's all Max and M.L. had to see. Max said, "Voodoo, right. We're going to go out there and pull their plugs. Lights *out,* suckers!" Meanwhile, M.L. is going, "He may be putting that voodoo on us, but we've got some stuff to put on *them*. That's called jumpers from twenty and blocked shots."

Ruland was really giving us a whole lot of trouble, as much with his passing as his scoring. The guy was a great inside scorer and when you started paying too much attention to that, he'd pick you apart with his passes. Then when Frankie got hot, it was fuel to the fire. One night in that series, he hit one of the longest nondesperation threes I've ever seen.

They beat us in the second game at home, but we dug in defensively and took both the third and the fourth games in the Capital Centre. Game four went to overtime and it was quite a game. But it wasn't as good as game five, which went to double overtime. That was a real spurty game and we were very fortunate to win.

So now it was the Celtics and the 76ers for the third straight year and you can imagine how cocky we were feeling after we beat them by *forty* in the first game. We felt we had everything in order. We didn't think anybody could beat us.

Guess what? Philly came back and dumped us in the next game. The guy who really hurt us was Caldwell Jones, who didn't shoot the ball much as a rule. We left him alone, as we normally did, and he drilled five jumpers in the second half. He just demoralized us. All of a sudden our cockiness was gone. Philly had knocked us down a peg.

Things continued going badly in the third game because in the very first minute we lost Tiny for the series when he messed up his shoulder diving for a ball. We lost that game and the next one too and again for the third straight year we were down, three games to one, to the 76ers.

We regained a lot of our confidence when we beat them by about thirty in game five. Our crowd was great. They started chanting, *"See you Sunday! See you Sunday!"* because that's when game seven would be. The next game was just plain weird. They couldn't hit the broad side of a barn and we beat them by a ridiculous score—88–75.

We chartered right back home after that game and there was a mob to greet us at the airport. I was with Ford, Robey and McHale and I needed a ride home. They decided they had to go greet the fans and I knew that was going to be a big mistake. But they insisted on going over there and saying, "Hi, fans. Thank you very much."

We were in a van of some kind and I decided it would be more intelligent to stay inside. Those people saw us coming and they went crazy. Somebody stole Ford's bag out of the back. They broke mirrors. They smashed windows. It was near three o'clock in the morning and they had been waiting for hours, which only added to their overzealous reactions.

The seventh game was a disaster for us. Just about everyone in the world thought we would win. We were at home. We had momentum. The 76ers had been humiliated, losing by thirty in the fifth game and only scoring seventy-five points *at home* in the next game. Their own newspapers were calling them the "75ers."

And the Sixers turned it all around and blew us out.

We played terrible basketball. We didn't execute in the halfcourt and we didn't run. Dr. J. buried us. He was making jumper after jumper. He just took over the game.

It was hard to accept. You go home in the summer and you wake up and wait for everybody to say, "Why? You guys had all the talent and you had the bench. Why did you let Philly come in and get you?" You could talk about losing Tiny for the last four games, but that's not a good enough excuse. You just wind up with the complete opposite feeling of the one you had the year before.

Every morning you wake up and you say, "How could that have happened?" You can't wait for the summer to end, so the next season can get started. That summer of 1982, I worked more on conditioning than I ever had before and I tried to expand my game.

For two years, I had had Caldwell Jones and Bobby Jones taking turns guarding me and I wanted to figure out a way to combat them. I needed more range to get Caldwell, who was seven feet tall, out on the floor more so I could go around him and I worked on a lot of stuff underneath so I could do more there against Bobby, who was six-nine. I felt we'd be playing the Sixers again in the conference finals.

Every season is a learning experience in some way and that's the year I discovered what it was like to cope with a major injury. My regular season goal always was—and always will be—to play eighty-two consistently good basketball games a year. In my first two seasons, I had been able to suit up for every game, but I ran out of luck in late February of 1982.

We were playing Milwaukee at home and in the second quarter I was guarding Harvey Catchings, who was six-nine and more known for his rebounding and defense than his scoring. I remember going for a rebound and then seeing his elbow—too late. I turned my head and he caught me right in the face. I immediately knew something was wrong because my mouth didn't work very well.

We called a time-out and I went directly to the dressing room, along with Doc Silva. At first, I was dazed, but after a while I started feeling better. Then I tried walking around the room and I knew something still wasn't right.

I sat there longer than normal during the halftime break and although I knew something was wrong, it wasn't as bad as it had been before. I went back into the game during the third quarter.

After the game (we won), I was checked over again because I still didn't feel right. I looked in the mirror and saw there was an indentation maybe the size of a nickel on the side of my face. By this time, I couldn't move my mouth well at all and it was beginning to swell.

I refused the doctors' request to stay in the hospital overnight. I went for X rays the next morning and they learned I had shattered the "zygomatic arch" and I would need an operation to fix it. That's the first time I ever heard anyone use that term. The second time was when it turned up as a reference in the movie *Diner* a bit later that year.

The Celtics went away to Texas for a three-game trip and we won them all. We beat New York at home, went back out and beat Detroit and then when the team came home the fireworks really started.

I was looking and feeling better, but the doctor who had operated on me insisted that I shouldn't play until the stitches had been taken out and the face had healed properly. Meanwhile, Red started saying I should play, that the doctor didn't know anything about professional athletes, and how much better they healed than normal people. Bob Woolf got involved and at one point there was quite a row because he thought the team was pressuring me into playing when I should be healing. I decided that I was going to play— stitches or no stitches. I did and I never had any problems.

I have nothing against Harvey Catchings. He wrote me a letter of apology. When many people told me what kind of a guy he was, I believed them. I wasn't upset about it because things like that happen in a game. Harvey had never been known to throw vicious elbows and he had never been known to hurt people on purpose.

Since it had been a pretty serious injury and since I had

lost some of my conditioning, Coach Fitch did the only reasonable thing and brought me back slowly. I came off the bench and it was working out well for the team, which, by this time, was really playing well.

Coach Fitch liked me as the sixth man so much that he just kept using me that way, long past the time when I was ready to return to the starting lineup. The team was winning with this lineup—our winning streak eventually reached ten—and I think Coach Fitch was having too much fun with it to change anything.

I have nothing against being a sixth man. I'm one of those people who says it doesn't matter who starts the game as much as who finishes it. If being a sixth man was good enough for Frank Ramsey, John Havlicek, Paul Silas and Kevin McHale, just to name a few, it was good enough for me. I didn't mind watching for a while and knowing that, in my case, when Coach Fitch called my name I would be staying in there for the rest of the game. I wasn't going to need a rest. I really liked the experience.

But I knew I would be going back to the starting lineup by the playoffs and that remaining as the sixth man too long would hurt my timing as a starter. If I was going to be a sixth man all the time, I think it would have been a great role. But everybody knew that wasn't going to happen. I needed to get back as a starter and re-establish that particular routine.

2 0

A BASKETBALL TEAM consists of twelve men—not five or six. If the team is going to function properly, every member must have a role and that includes off the court, as well as on. The problem is that the public only pays attention to the ones who play the most minutes.

Eric Fernsten had been on the team for my first three years. He didn't play very much, but he was a very important member of the Celtics. He was six-ten and could play both center and forward. The most important things he did for our team were never seen by the public.

Eric was perfect for our team because he did everything and anything Coach Fitch asked. What he wanted to do was practice. His games were like mine while I was being red-shirted at Indiana State. He *lived* for practices. You may find this difficult to believe, but he really didn't care that much about playing in the games.

Eric would walk into practice and say, "Today is *my* day." Then he'd go out and give you a real battle. He made the players he practiced against better—and that includes me. If Coach Fitch told him he wanted him to tackle you—which happened about three quarters of the time—that's what he'd do. He would get me so frustrated, he'd make me want to play harder. He would do everything to you that you *hated* in an opponent.

Fernsten came up with a hernia in 1982 and he didn't have a very good training camp as a result. The team cut him and I think I can safely say we never replaced Eric Fernsten. We've had other hardworking bench players, guys such as Greg Kite who gave their all to the team, but we never again found a guy quite like Fernsten.

At the same time Fernie was having his troubles, Chris Ford was struggling too. When Chris hurt his knee in training camp, we all knew that it was basically the end for him.

We were all pulling for him and it was a sad day for our team when he got cut. I remember guys saying, "Fordie got cut. What are we going to do?" Chris meant a lot to the team.

Coach Fitch was changing a little himself. He went from being tough all the time to picking his spots. He knew what we had to do to get in shape. He knew how we needed to prepare for games. He began slacking off. We still worked hard, but it wasn't all-out, the way it had been. If we played well and things were going all right, he'd sort of let us go. There were no more three-hour practices, followed by one-hour film sessions.

*   *   *

The one key addition to the team was Quinn Buckner. We got him from Milwaukee when Dave Cowens unretired—which didn't really surprise me—and went to play for the Bucks. The Celtics were able to extract Buckner from Milwaukee as compensation. Quinn and I hit it off immediately.

Quinn was a big-time sweater. The first day of training camp he came in and started dropping water all over the floor. The floor stayed so wet that we couldn't practice. We all loved the guy right away. Quinn must have gone through twenty pairs of shoes just in training camp, as they'd all be soaked clean through.

He was a senior at Indiana when I was there, but we never met because he was away playing on some All-Star team. He always told me that if he had been there, I never would have left I.U. When he got there, he said, "Where's this Bird kid?" They told him I had already gone and he couldn't believe it because he had heard so many good things about me. He said they told him, "You won't believe this kid. He's skinny, but he's a ballplayer." I'm sorry I missed out on that relationship.

I made up for it when he came to the Celtics, however. He became one of the best friends I've ever had.

He was built like a football player and he had actually been a starting defensive back at I.U. for a couple of years before he quit that sport. I'd always say to him, "What did you play football for?"

He said, "I was crazy. Once I was knocked down hard on the field and as I was laying there I said, 'What am I *doing* out here on this football field?'" He quit football right after that.

Quinn didn't live very far from me and we wound up spending a lot of time together. We'd go out after practice and eat dinner at each other's house. I valued his friendship because Quinn Buckner is the kind of person who will *be* there when you want somebody.

We were still a good club, but we were not the completely dominant team we had been the two previous years. We just

kind of drifted along on our skill and our reputation and we
didn't exactly go into the playoffs with a lot of momentum.

The one big thing that happened to me came late in the
season in a game at home against Indiana. We had gone to
Market Square Arena the game before and the Pacers had
really put it to us. We still had enough pride left that something like that would serve as an incentive to get ready for
the return match.

I always like to play against Indiana in Boston, more so
than at their place. Our public relations director, Jeff Twiss,
always lets me know if the game is being televised back to
Indiana and if it is I *really* want to do well because everybody
I know will be watching.

This game starts and points are coming easy. I was hot
from the outside and I was also getting a lot of lay-ups because we were running very well that night.

We've got a message board in the Garden and as I kept
scoring everyone knew I was getting close to Sam Jones's
regular season Celtics' scoring record, which was fifty-one. I
wound up with fifty-three.

The playoffs were an immediate struggle. That was Philly's
monster year, so we weren't either the division or conference
champs. We had to play Atlanta in a best two-of-three "miniseries" and we needed three games to beat a team we should
have blown away. We wouldn't even have won the first one at
home if it weren't for some clutch jumpers from Quin.

One funny thing happened in that series. Danny and Tree
Rollins got into it and that's the famous incident where
Rollins bit Ainge on the hand.

Danny was coming down the lane and Tree gave him a
shot with his elbow. Danny just blew up. He called Tree a
sissy and some other stuff and Tree said, "I'll see you later."

When Tree finally did get him, Danny retaliated by charg-
ing him and bringing him down with a great tackle at the
ankles. Everybody just piled in there—yes, me too—and
when they pulled them apart Danny was laughing. He said,
"That big sissy just *bit* me." That's pretty funny, since Danny
is six-four and Tree is about seven-two. Here was Tree

throwing elbows at everybody and then winding up biting somebody. I'm sure Tree has a different version, for sure.

I wish I could forget the next series. We played Milwaukee and in the first game I dislocated the pinkie on my right hand. I remember that I thought we needed some spark and I was trying to pick up my own game a little bit when I went diving after a loose ball near midcourt.

I caught my finger on someone's arm—or shoulder—and the finger just bent back. I went to the bench and had it sort of popped back in there, but it was so sore that I could hardly move it.

I've dislocated it three times since and for the last several years I've been playing with it taped so I won't do it anymore. If I didn't tape it, it would keep sliding out at the least bit of contact. I've had it checked out and a doctor told me that the only way to treat it is to have a plastic knuckle inserted after I retire. All the ligaments in there are torn and there is nothing else anyone can do about it.

The Bucks beat us at home in that first game. It was very cold at practice the next day and I could feel myself getting sick. When I woke up the next day, I was dizzy. I had no idea what was happening. A doctor came over and I found out that I had a temperature. When I tried to walk, I could barely maintain my balance.

What I had was the flu. This went on for two days and it took me out of game two. That was the first playoff game I had ever missed and it really killed me. Danny was sensational. He had twenty-four at the half and we had a lead. But the Bucks came on, won the game and now we were down, two games to none, heading back to Milwaukee.

Game three was another big game for Milwaukee. Something was wrong. The whole team was down. We just didn't have our old energy. I can remember sitting there and looking around and you could just tell that we all looked like zombies or something.

The Milwaukee crowd was loving it. When we arrived at the arena for the fourth game, everybody was waving little brooms and chanting, *"Sweep! Sweep! Sweep!"* With the shape we were in, there was no way we were going to win game four after losing that third game. We were beaten by the time we got to the lay-up line.

Oh, we tried to talk it up. Guys were saying, "Let's not get embarrassed. Let's go out there and win." But we just didn't have it.

We would have had trouble with Milwaukee under any circumstances. They really wanted it bad. Marques Johnson played very well. Bob Lanier played well. This was Don Nelson's first chance to coach a playoff series against the Celtics and I read where he said that what he wanted most of all was to have Red Auerbach respect his team. Four straight wins will get anybody's attention. Anytime somebody beats you four straight, you have to say they're a better team, but we knew we *should* have been a better team. We knew that all year.

Sitting in the locker room after being swept by the Bucks was the worst feeling I've ever had playing basketball. I had known great moments, had won a championship and had had a lot of good games, but at that moment it seemed like the end of the world. I was sitting there, knowing we had enough talent to win but that we didn't. Right then and there, I knew *something* had to happen.

A lot of people accused the team of flat-out quitting on Bill Fitch, but I'm not sure that was the case. We were just down. After having the home court advantage and then losing two games in the Boston Garden, we all kind of looked at each other and said, "Well, *whose* fault is it? Your fault? My fault? The coaches' fault?" I don't think we quit on him. I think we just died as a team. All the spark, all the enjoyment, all the rah-rah we had those first three years—all of a sudden it was gone.

Maybe it all started when Eric Fernsten and Chris Ford were cut. But there is no doubt that something was a bit off all season and it all came crashing down on our heads in that Milwaukee series.

SAT IN THAT LOCKER ROOM after the fourth Milwaukee game and made a vow. I said that I was taking this loss very personally, that I was going home to work harder than I ever have in my life and that I was going to come back and have a great year.

When I say I'm going to go home and play ball, that basically means *by myself*. I never did like to scrimmage against people. When I was at Indiana State, some retired professionals came to play against us. After we got done whipping them, we said, "They're not that good."

We were forgetting that the reason they were playing against us was to *get* in shape. They weren't trying to beat anybody. They were just trying to get in condition. I said to one of my friends, "If I ever get in that league, I'll never do that."

Even when I was young, the way I liked to practice was by myself or with no more than one other guy. I always felt I could get more work done by myself than with three or four guys standing around.

The way I see it, if I put two hours in by myself, then someone who is working out with somebody else has to put *four* hours in in order to beat me. That's the way I've always gone about it.

That summer I went home and put in *more* hours—and got up *more* shots—than I ever had before. I couldn't get that Milwaukee mess out of my mind.

I was sitting home one day not long after the end of the playoffs when someone called me and said Bill Fitch would no longer be coaching the Celtics. I was both shocked and sad.

After that fourth Milwaukee game, I remember saying in a TV interview that wherever else people wanted to lay the blame for what happened, it did not belong on Bill Fitch's shoulders. I said we had never gone into a game unprepared and that I thought he was the best coach in the league. And I believed it. I really didn't know what had gone on upstairs to cause the Celtics and Coach Fitch to part company—apparently there was some sort of mutual decision that it was time for him to go—but I was apprehensive about what would happen with him gone. I just hoped that the coach who replaced him would feel strongly about the Celtics and would lead us in the right direction. I also thought I would have to work harder in order to impress whoever it was that would succeed Coach Fitch.

Coach Fitch never indicated to me that he might not be returning. He seemed just as upset as everyone else about what happened against Milwaukee. We had a little meeting and he said, "I hope you have a good summer."

To me, he was a great coach. I looked up to him so much. I didn't really know how I was going to react without him around. He had sort of guided me along all those years. I felt pretty sad about the whole thing, to tell you the truth. I felt I owned Bill Fitch a lot.

I was pleased when K. C. Jones got the job. I thought he deserved it after being the assistant for many years and I knew he was the kind of coach who would do a good job with us.

The next bombshell was *really* personal. Red traded Rick Robey to Phoenix for Dennis Johnson. I certainly wasn't upset that we had traded for Dennis Johnson. I loved his style and I knew he would help us. But I was sad that they had traded Rick away.

That was the very first time anyone I was really close to had been traded. I thought about all the fun we had. "At least," I figured, "he's going to Phoenix, which is one of my favorite places." He always loved that town too, so that made it easier. And if they wanted him badly enough to trade Dennis Johnson for him, I assumed that meant he'd get a lot of playing time. It turns out what the Celtics were doing was trading my best friend in the game for one of the best players I've ever seen.

While there are always shocks and disappointments in professional sports, there are surprises and fulfillments that you don't always expect either. When the then-owner, Harry Mangurian, sold the team to Don Gaston, Alan Cohen and Paul Dupee, the new owners wanted to negotiate a new contract for me, even though I still had one more year to go on my old one. Red and Mr. Woolf negotiated on and off all that summer and when I returned for training camp, I sat down with Mr. Woolf, Red and Jan Volk and we came to an agreement.

Let me tell you, that contract meant so much to me because the Celtics gave it to me right after we got swept by Milwaukee. That made me feel so good! Kevin got a new contract too. The new management didn't wait; they came in after we got swept and everybody was in a down mood. That made me so proud to be a Celtic and inspired me to go out and try to do even more for the team.

2 2

THE 1982–83 SEASON was not a good one for Tiny Archibald. Somehow Tiny got caught up in our general deterioration. His passes weren't quite as crisp and his mind just didn't seem to be into it anymore. I don't know whether you can say he was suffering from burnout or whether he was just upset with the way things were going, but I do know that Tiny wasn't the same player he had been during my first three seasons.

When we went to camp in '83, Tiny was no longer with the Celtics. He had been put on waivers that summer and had been picked up by the Bucks. This was another sad event because I had never played with a guard quite like Archibald.

You could always tell when Tiny was ready to play, ready to go. On defense, he was a guy you always had to cover up for because people loved to take advantage of his size, but on offense he never needed any help.

Tiny could get you any kind of shot you wanted. All you'd have to do was give him the ball and go fill a lane. I believe I got more nice fifteen-foot spot shots on the break than I've had any time before or since. I remember first playing with Tiny during my rookie camp in '79 and thinking, "This guy is going to make it real easy for me."

I learned that to play best with Tiny, you should start to position yourself when he crossed midcourt. The idea was to stay just a bit behind him and when he started to make his move and get around his man, that's when you should take off. After a while I could tell when Tiny had it in his eyes to go to the hoop, so then I would go to the boards.

Tiny going to the hoop was a great sight. He had absolutely no fear at all and he could use his right hand as well as his left. When Danny Ainge came to the team, I thought he was as tough as any guard I had seen, but Tiny was a special case, considering his age and all he had been through.

I wasn't a fan back in the early seventies and so at first I didn't realize that Tiny had once led the league in both scoring and assists. All I know is that Tiny sacrificed a lot for our team. He could have had more points and more assists, but he sort of held back, just doing the job Coach Fitch asked him to do. I honestly believe the only guard in the league doing as good a job for his team as Tiny was doing for ours was Magic Johnson. I know Tiny had a lot of problems in Boston the year before I came and that's why I think Bill Fitch deserves a lot of credit for sticking with Tiny and getting the best effort out of him.

One of the great confrontations I ever saw in training camp was that first year, when Ernie DiGregorio and Tiny were in camp together. From the day Ernie came in, you could tell that Tiny was thinking, "That *my* position. If Ernie is going to beat me out, he'll have to be awfully tough."

I don't know whether or not Ernie was going to make the team before he walked out, but I believe he would have been a good role player. Bring him in when Tiny needed a break—which wouldn't have been too often, I'll admit—and we would have been covered. Ernie wasn't exactly the same type of player, but he had the same type of explosive effect on a team. We all could have adjusted to his particular style easily. But one day Ernie went into the locker room and never came back.

Ernie has said in later years that it was the dumbest mistake he ever made. When he just walked out, I was thinking, "How can these guys do that? This is the NBA. This is what it's all about." I just sort of stood back and wondered why they quit.

Now I can understand what happened a little better. But I would have loved to have seen those two little guys go head-to-head every day. They were both competitors, but I never saw a competitor quite like Tiny. Anytime we'd have a little scuffle, Tiny would be right in there, no matter how big the guys were.

Tiny just loved to post up underneath the basket. He could go to his left or to his right and he could really draw fouls down there. Sometimes his small size even worked to his advantage.

When Tiny lost it, he lost it quickly. In this league, you're going to have your ups and downs. The problem is, when you are down, it seems as if you are *never* going to get over it. It's just like Cowens and Havlicek. Cowens could have helped us that year and if Havlicek could have held on one more year to be on our 1979–80 team, he could have played for several more years.

I'm certain of that because for a few years he used to suit up and scrimmage with us on his birthday, which is April 8. What a shame he retired when he did because he could have helped us. John couldn't have gone out and played forty minutes a night, but he would have been a great asset coming off the bench. He would have been somebody to look up to, the way Dr. J. was during his final couple of years with the 76ers.

John knows. He has said to me, "If I knew that you were

coming along and you were going to be as good as you are, I would have stayed." He meant it. We missed each other by just one year. And if Cowens had hung in there, we would have had an amazing team—even better than the one we had.

I've been fortunate enough to play with such great players as Cowens, Archibald, Kevin McHale, Robert Parish, Dennis Johnson and Bill Walton and I would have loved to have played on the same team with John Havlicek.

Tiny was gone, but Dennis Johnson was with us now and I knew right away we were going to love him. I had always liked his style when he played with Seattle and Phoenix. I thought he was a competitor and a great team player. He just didn't like to lose. You could see he was great in the big games. The idea of having Dennis on the Celtics had me pumped up right away.

During training camp, I discovered how well Dennis could take it to the basket. He could drive on *anybody* and if he didn't make the basket he would probably draw the foul. Over the years, I was to learn that the surefire way to know exactly what a game meant to D.J. was to see how often he took it to the basket. When D.J. takes it the basket, it means he *thinks* it's a big game and you can count on him playing especially well.

With D.J. in there, we were scoring a little better than we had been, even though he didn't push it up the floor as fast as Tiny did. It was just that our ball movement seemed to be excellent. I really thought our outlook was great as we started the 1983 exhibition season.

We knew it wasn't going to be an ordinary season when we got into a big row with the 76ers during one of the exhibition games. For years, the Celtics stayed away from the Boston Garden for exhibitions because they didn't draw very well. But now things had changed and we were playing the 76ers at home.

Philly was the defending champion, so it really wasn't an ordinary exhibition—especially in our own building. We respected Philly as competitors, but we didn't like them. It was a serious game.

It started with Max and Moses, who was now playing for Philly. They got into a scuffle near the basket and when Moses said something Max wound up throwing the ball at him. Moses came back and tackled Max and then pandemonium broke loose.

I almost forgot about Marc Iavaroni. Somebody was at the foul line. There was a lot of yapping going on. The ball went up and Iavaroni's arm got hooked with mine and I threw him off. He came back at me and we started fighting. That's when Billy Cunningham came out and before it was over his coat somehow got ripped. What a way to start the season—and this was only an exhibition game!

Philly hung with us for a while that year, but by January we were in charge of the race. Our front line was as good as anybody's, we had a nice guard rotation with D.J., Gerald Henderson, Danny and Buckner and we had more scoring off the bench from Scott Wedman. Aside from my elbow acting up every once in a while, I was having a good year. And everybody was relaxed playing for K. C. Jones.

There was no bigger Bill Fitch fan on the ball club than me, but I had to admit that under K.C. everyone on the team seemed to be a lot more at ease. K.C. represented a fresh breath of air. Coach Fitch got us where we were and at that time I didn't see the need for a change. After K.C. took over and I saw the changed attitude of the players, I knew it had been the right decision.

People just naturally wanted to play for K.C. He never embarrassed anyone publicly and he also dealt with people in a straightforward manner. There were none of the mind games that Coach Fitch loved to play with the younger players to get them to play harder.

The press is always asking about the relationship between K.C. and Bill Fitch. K.C. never said much about it to us. We all knew there was some friction between the two of them, mainly because of their different approaches to the game, but I think they got along a lot better during Coach Fitch's final year than they did before. Still, K.C. tended to hang out more with the players.

Life under K.C. was completely different than it had been

with Bill. Coach Fitch loved his practices. K.C. wasn't that fanatical about them. If he thought you looked tired in a game or when you arrived at practice, he would take it easy on you. "Are you tired? Why don't you take it easy today?" There were no favorites. He would do that for anybody.

We worked hard. K.C. would say, "All I'm asking you guys is that when you come to play, you play to win." We always felt that's exactly what we did. After a while, everybody looked fresher. Everyone felt a little better about himself and the team.

Technically, we basically stuck to the same plays we had run the year before. But there was some tinkering and over the years we gradually changed just about everything.

We wound up winning sixty-two games and that gave us the home court advantage for every playoff series. There weren't going to be any excuses if the Celtics didn't win the championship.

We opened up with Washington and there was nothing memorable about that series. Gene Shue was generally able to slow down the tempo against us, but the best they could do was win the third game in overtime at their place. That was the only game either team broke 100 in the series.

The fun started after that. We were playing New York and I knew it wasn't going to be easy—if only because of Bernard King. This was Bernard at his best. He was coming off a series in which he had *averaged* an amazing forty-four points a game against Detroit.

We won the first two games at home, but Kevin and Max couldn't leave well enough alone. We go down to New York for game three and Kevin starts yapping about "throwing dirt on their grave." Then Max is smarting off about how "Bernard isn't getting any forty on me."

The atmosphere in Madison Square Garden was great. I had seen the place a little alive before, but nothing like this. The fans were up the whole game.

The Knicks beat us in the third game and then Bernard went crazy on us in the next game. He got forty-three. Sorry, Max. The worst part was that we weren't doing any running at all. The Knicks had completely taken away our fast break.

We won the fifth game at home, so now it was back to New York. Bernard comes up big again, scoring twenty-nine in the first half and forty-four in the game. They had us by thirteen with about four minutes left, but we made a run and got back in the game. I even had a chance to tie it with a bank shot, but I missed. Max got the rebound, but he missed too and the series was tied at three games apiece.

We needed a police escort to get away from Madison Square Garden. The bus driver had to drive the wrong way on a one-way street to get us out of there, but he delivered us to the airport and we were able to fly back to Boston.

Very often I have strong positive feelings before big games, but I wasn't sure about that seventh game. I knew that if Bernard stayed hot, it would go down to the wire. The only thing making me feel good at all was that we were playing in the Boston Garden.

Some days everything just clicks and I could tell early in the first quarter I was going to play really well. I was in the kind of groove where I knew I could do anything I wanted to at any time and my main thought was simply to get myself in a position to receive the ball as often as possible.

I was fortunate enough to be in a great rhythm the entire game. There was a moment relatively late in the game—after we were up by fourteen or fifteen—when I received the ball farther out than I wanted to and I wound up banking it in, even though I wasn't trying to bank. After I made *that* shot, I knew they didn't have a chance.

In a situation like that, I try to take it one quarter at a time. If I have a good first quarter, that's over with. Then the second quarter. The third. And so on. After the first quarter, I knew things were going well, so then I wanted to draw the defense toward me so I could get the ball down low to Max and get him some easy baskets.

The best thing about having that series over was saying good-bye to Bernard King for the rest of the playoffs. During those playoffs, Bernard was automatic—the best scoring machine I have ever seen.

His release was amazing. You'd always seem to come within a fraction of getting a piece of his shot, but he wouldn't allow it. He always had you off-balance. And the

Knicks seemed to go to him every time. We *tried* to get the ball out of his hands, but we always seemed to be late.

What's really incredible about what Bernard did in those playoffs was that he was doing it with dislocated fingers on *both* hands! He seemed to be steering the ball up, shooting it off the bottom of his hands.and he'd still get forty.

You can imagine how the New York crowd loved him. One night in the Garden, K.C. put M.L. in. Almost immediately, Bernard got his legs tangled and tripped, hurting one of his fingers. This was on M.L.'s first trip up the floor. When Bernard went out, so did M.L. The crowd was delirious. They thought K.C. had sent M.L. into the game to hurt Bernard!

That was a fun series to play in and I came away with a lot of admiration for Hubie Brown. As a matter of fact, that's one coach I wish I could have played for during my career.

I realize there are many people reading this who think I'm crazy, but I just happen to like his attitude. It was always fun playing when he coached. You'd hear Hubie hollering at his guys, "Get *up* on him!" Or "You can stop him! You can stop him!" I would laugh. He'd holler that kind of stuff all the time to his players, but I liked and respected that man.

It strikes me that Hubie is a man who knows *exactly* what he wants done and how to do it. I like people who think that way. I think that the series his team played against us in '84 showed how great a coach he is. He's very demanding, yes, but all I know is how well they played us. If they had gotten by us, they would have had a good shot at the championship.

There was nothing out of the ordinary in our next series. We had a chance to avenge our sweep against Milwaukee the year before and we did. The only game they got was the fourth. The circumstances had turned around a great deal. All the problems we had the year before were history.

We were finally going to have *our* shot at Los Angeles. It's the series the press wanted, the fans wanted and we players wanted.

Early in the first game, we all wondered why. We had been sitting around in Boston since Wednesday, while they had to fly in on Saturday after beating Phoenix on Friday. We should have been ready. They should have been tired.

Instead, they had us down by eighteen in the first quarter before we started playing. We got back in the game, but not before Magic had picked us apart.

We needed to win the second game and we started off much better. We even had them by thirteen in the first half, but they weren't disturbed by that and with twenty seconds to go they were leading by two and Kevin was at the line.

I'll never forget it. He missed the first one and now he's worried, so now he's trying to *guide* the ball in. He didn't make that one either. What we didn't know until we saw the tape was that while he was lining up that second shot Kevin's knees were clacking back and forth. They were really *shaking*. Oh, we got on him *hard*. Max was leading it, calling him "Clacker" and "Slacker" and "Knee Shaker." Everybody said, "How would you like to have Kevin taking the last shot of the game?" It was so funny.

After the misses, L.A. called time. When they threw it in, we had some pressure on in the backcourt and Gerald Henderson stole a pass from James Worthy and laid it in to tie the score. I never saw him coming. To me, he just came from nowhere.

That was the play of the series. We got into overtime and beat them. Robert made more big plays and Scott Wedman drilled a jumper from right in front of the L.A. bench to beat them. It was beautiful ball movement, with the ball going around the horn from right to left to the player who was probably our best pure shooter. But Gerald is the one who gave us a chance to win. If we had lost that game, we were staring at another Milwaukee.

We went to L.A. and they just destroyed us in the third game. We were pathetic. It was a *very* discouraging performance.

I knew a lot of people in the press thought we were lucky to win the second game and didn't think we had a chance anyway. I wanted to prove them wrong, but after a performance like that one I was starting to think they were right.

When the reporters asked me about the game, I told them we played like a bunch of sissies. I said, "A bunch of children can play better than that—even if they had never played the game before." I said if the Celtics played like that again, the Lakers were going to blow us out of the series.

A couple of the players reminded me that I should make sure I was talking about "we" and not "you." Of course they were right. But M.L. came up to me and said, "I hope you get us fired up." Sure enough, next game we came back.

The fourth game was a great one for us. We were down by five with just under a minute left in regulation when Robert made a three-point play. Michael Cooper missed. Robert rebounded and I wound up making two free throws to get us into overtime. We had a chance to win it when Robert stole an in-bounds pass with four seconds left, but I missed the shot.

We caught some more breaks in the overtime. The score was tied late in the game when Magic missed two free throws. I came down and posted up in the lane. Fortunately for me, I had Magic—not Cooper—on me and I was able to make the shot with sixteen seconds left. I could maneuver better and get the shot right where I wanted it with Magic— better than I could have with Cooper, who would have been all over me.

Worthy was fouled right after that. When he went to the line, he missed the first one and Max was standing there, giving him the "choke" sign. I thought, "Oh no." Worthy sank the second one. Then M.L. steals the ball at midcourt and as he headed downcourt, I was afraid he was going to dribble it off his ankle or something. But M.L. drove in for a dunk to put the game away.

There was a lot of talk that year about the difference between the Eastern Conference and the Western Conference styles of basketball. The East was supposed to be a more physical, defensively oriented brand of ball, while the West was supposed to be a more wide-open finesse game. The Celtics and Lakers were said to represent the style of play of their respective conferences.

There's some truth to that, but I think all it meant to us was that we had to come out and be tougher than the Lakers—prove to them we *wanted it more*. For three and a half games, that wasn't the case. Suddenly we realized that if we were going to beat the Lakers we were going to have to play better defense, but, most of all, we had to prove to them that we wanted to win the championship more than they did.

We never did shoot well in that series. We wound up winning despite shooting something like 40 percent from the floor. Some people called it "1950s basketball."

We were a good rebounding team anyway. We just had to turn it up a notch. I also realized that if I was going to get the job done against Michael Cooper. I'd have to play a more physical inside game and take more advantage of my two advantages over him: size and strength.

What changed that series was our physical play and our offensive rebounding. We seemed to be getting all the loose balls and all the garbage points inside. We were all making that extra effort. The series was won in the trenches. I took Cooper inside so much I wound up making more free throws than field goals in six of the seven games and that ordinarily doesn't happen more than about six times during a whole eighty-two-game regular season.

Our other great asset was Dennis Johnson. D.J. is simply the best player I've ever played with on the Celtics. Kevin is great. Robert is great. I've played with other great players. But when I look at other teams, there is always a player on that team who seems to symbolize the whole team. When I think of our *own* team, the guy I think of is D.J.

When I look at him, I think, "The guy will do *anything* to win." And D.J. *knows* how to win. D.J. is a clutch player who can win the big game for you—no matter what it takes.

D.J. is a very intelligent basketball player. I picked up on that immediately. When he first came and we got into tight games, he would always look for me. He'd wait for me to make my move and then he'd get me the ball. Believe me when I say he made me a better player.

I could talk about him all day. Getting Dennis Johnson was a great move by the Celtics.

When we got back to Boston for game five, it was *hot*. It can get hot in June when you live in Boston, but this was *really* hot. The Garden is not air-conditioned, so we all knew the fifth game was going to be played in serious heat.

But we were home. To me, that was all that mattered. The

thinking and attitude when you play at home is completely
different. We were prepared. We knew we had to run. We
wanted to get out running, get them sweaty and get the
crowd into it early in the ballgame.

People came dressed in ways I had never seen at an NBA
game. T-shirts. Shorts. Women in halters. Men with no
shirts. Believe it or not, the game time temperature inside
the Garden was ninety-seven degrees. The Boston people
knew this was something unique. They weren't just a sports
crowd—they were a *party* crowd.

It was hot, but we didn't care because we were already so
fired up. We knew the Lakers *had* to be miserable. They were
used to playing in the air-conditioned comfort of the Forum.
This just wasn't their idea of basketball.

But it was *ours*. Just from warming up, we knew it was
going to be a great crowd. If the crowd is in the game when
you first come out of the tunnel, you know you're going to
play well. *Everybody* was into it. Max was pumped up. "It's
game five," he said, "a crucial game. We *have* to win this
game."

It was our game from the start. We were moving the ball,
we were running, we were ripping off the rebounds and we
were playing good defense. We had everything going. Max
was going crazy down low. Robert was spinning and hitting
his hooks. The court just seemed wide open for us and we
definitely took advantage of it. We won a game we needed to
win—a very good sign.

Then we had to go back to L.A. We got off pretty well and
we were leading by eleven with about five minutes left in the
third quarter, when suddenly the game turned completely
around. Byron Scott started sinking every shot he took and
we fell apart, losing the game.

But our collective state of mind as a team was still good.
We knew that there was one game for the championship and
that it was going to be in our place. We knew that the crowd
had really been a tremendous ally in game five and that
they'd be up for this game too. We weren't looking at the
game emotionally as much as we did professionally. We just
wanted to get our rest and try to play the way we did in game
five.

We all met at Hellenic College and took a bus to the Garden together. Quinn Buckner and his wife Rhonda picked me up to go to the Hellenic and for the first few minutes after I got into the car, there was total silence. I asked Rhonda if anything was wrong.

"Larry," she said, "Promise me one thing—that you *will* win this game tonight." I looked at her and said, "Rhonda, don't worry about it. I'll take care of it. I can tell you right now we are going to win tonight. Just relax at the game and have a good time." Rhonda said, "If *you* tell me that, I'll believe it."

We had a little extra incentive because M.L. had been hit in the eye following the sixth game and was going to need to wear goggles for the last game. Somebody hit me with a hot dog and a beer after that game and someone got M.L. in the eye with something more serious.

M.L. came walking in with his new goggles and said, "Let's go, boys, it's game time." Danny was walking around with a doctor's stethoscope—don't ask me why or how he got it—checking everybody's heartbeat. He went up to Max and said, "Nah, your heart's not even beating." Then he walked over to M.L. and said, "Wow, your heart's pumping like crazy!"

M.L. says, "Hey, I'm ready. Max probably isn't even ready to play, but I am."

That's when Max jumps up and says, "I *am* ready. Get on my back tonight, boys. This is my game. Just give me the ball."

Max wasn't kidding. We got the ball into him and Worthy, who was only in his second year, couldn't do anything to stop him. Max wound up with twenty-four, but it seemed like five times that. He was fourteen for seven from the line, which gives you an idea how Max frustrated Worthy and all the L.A. inside people that night. Max really took it to the Lakers.

We decided to test Max early. He's not like Kevin. You didn't have to give him the ball in perfect position. If Kevin gets the ball in certain spots, you know he'll score every time. All you had to do with Max was give him the ball anywhere in the low post. He had great hands, so you didn't have to be very precise with your pass. Once he got the ball, he could get any shot he wanted when he was in the groove. We had respect for Worthy even then, but when Max really wanted the ball we made sure he got it.

The other teammate who came up big was Danny, who came off the bench and hit some jumpers to get us going during a somewhat sluggish portion of the first half.

We were up by thirteen after three quarters, but they got it down to three with under a minute to play. I got a chance to ice it. I came off a pick down low and drifted to the foul line. Kareem switched off, but I got the shot up over him and I thought it was going in. When that ball hit the back rim and kicked out, my heart almost quit. That *could* have been the game.

Magic came right down the court on a fast break, but he never really had control of the ball and Robert blocked the shot. D.J., who was sensational in the final four games, made two free throws—he was twelve for twelve from the line— and we had the game and the championship won. From that point on, the Lakers just kept fouling. The crowd was surging around the court and the Garden was going absolutely crazy. All we were thinking about was getting out of there.

The winning feeling is indescribable. You look up at the clock and it is eleven-thirty or a quarter to twelve and you're saying, "I wish I could freeze this time for twenty-four hours." Because the next time you look up, it's one o'clock. When we won it in 1986, it was an afternoon game and there was more time to enjoy it with the guys you won it with. But late at night, you know you're just going to go home and you don't really want to do that. You want the thrill of victory to last as long as it possibly can. You want to savor it to the fullest.

The parade and the civic ceremonies later are nice, but it's not like the moment *right there*—the next four or five hours. What you do is wind up staying awake all night, since you're so excited that you can't really sleep.

The circumstances don't even allow you to celebrate properly. You know you've got to go out and talk to the press and you barely have enough time to sit and think about it. What

I try to do after winning a championship is go into the trainer's room right away and get my thoughts together. But everybody goes there now. Everybody's running around and it's just crazy in there.

That night I remember resting for a while on the trainer's table. Red came in right away. My heart was just about ready to pound straight out of my chest again. Red and I sat there and just talked together about it because, you know, you just don't get that feeling very often. Finally he said, "You've got to go out there."

So I went out to meet the press. It was a madhouse, but if that's what winning brings, it's all right with me. As a pro, winning the championship is the most enjoyable time you're going to have. You want to milk it because you know it's only going to last until the next season gets under way.

23

WHAT A REVERSAL! We went from losing to Milwaukee in four straight to winning the championship over the Lakers in seven in one year. It was just a great year—from the time we got to camp, to the end.

They gave me the series MVP. It was nice, but I didn't get carried away by it. Max won it in '81 and I thought he deserved it. I thought I had played well enough to win it this time, but I didn't really care right after the game. I remember walking in and being handed this envelope and finding out I had won a car. I walked over and started talking to Chris Ford. All I was interested in was talking to my teammates.

That was also the season in which I received my first regular season MVP. I knew I had a good year. Early in the season I had some good games, but not necessarily great ones. After the All-Star Game, I had some great ones.

When we won the title, I said, "This one is dedicated to Terre Haute." I meant it. The fans had been so great to me when I was at Indiana State and we had come so close to winning that NCAA title for them. Dedicating this NBA title to them was the best I could do to make up for the loss to Michigan State. In their eyes at least, I had finally beaten Magic.

I went to Terre Haute for a celebration. First they were talking about flying me into a park via helicopter for a rally, but they were afraid there would be too many people in too confined an area. We had an outing and I was given gifts from the college, the Boys' Club and other people. I made a speech. It was a great day for me.

This was a great championship for many reasons. K.C.'s first year. The memory of the Milwaukee sweep. The way we came back in the series, almost losing game two at home and being blown out in game three in L.A. Finally beating Magic's team. I was proud of myself and our team when I stood up in Terre Haute and told them, "We got beat in '79, but this is the one I wanted."

The 1984–85 season started off very surprisingly. We knew there might have to be some kind of a shift in our backcourt situation because Danny Ainge deserved more playing time, but there hadn't been any rumblings about a trade. That's why we were stunned when we learned during the exhibition season that Gerald Henderson had been traded to Seattle for a first round pick two years down the road.

We were in Houston at the time and we knew something was up when Gerald didn't go to the game. All I could think of at the time was how Gerald had saved the championship in the L.A. series by stealing that Worthy pass and making a tougher shot than people give him credit for.

Gerald had progressed into being a great player—for the Celtics. I believed then that he was a lot better for us than he would have been for anyone else and I think that's been proven. He just fit in with us. He could hit the shot when he had it. He could draw fouls. He could pass and he didn't make a lot of mistakes. He could also get right up on you defensively. I thought he was a valuable player for us and I was sad when I heard about that deal.

Gerald got quick revenge the first time he came back to the Garden as a Sonic. The crowd gave him quite an ovation and he went out there and kicked our butts. Seattle beat us. He had about fifteen assists and when the game was over he took that basketball and spiked the thing.

We all knew Ainge had to start playing more, but when you're a player you don't think the same way they do in management. We recognized Danny's value, but we felt badly about Gerald. Danny brought a lot to the team. He was a big guard with quickness who could shoot, who covered a lot of ground on defense and who could make things happen.

Danny had a tough time his first two or three years. He played a lot with one eye on the bench and I've always said you just can't play that way. With D.J., Gerald, Danny and Quinn, a coach had a lot of choices. Eventually management made a choice. Trading Gerald for a draft pick appeared to be a great move, because Seattle wound up being a lottery team in 1985–86 and the Celtics wound up with the second pick in the draft. Unfortunately, we were never able to cash in on that pick because the player was Len Bias.

D.J. was the only one of the Celtic guards who played completely relaxed.

Quinn Buckner was another one who played with one eye on the court and the other on the bench. He seemed to be reluctant to go out there and play his whole game.

Quinn had a funny release on his shot. When he went to the free throw line, we would kind of cover our faces because we knew if it was coming off, it was coming off *hard*.

Defense was Quinn's strength. He was smart and he had very quick and strong hands. A rebounder had to be careful when Quinn was around because he had a sneaky way of coming underneath you as you brought the ball down and knocking it away. He must have done that a million times. I was always conscious of him when he played for Milwaukee.

He was a very smart player. He helped me a great deal on defense, telling me how I should play a certain guy, and what I should do in this or that situation. I might be playing a man who was getting hot. He might turn right two or three times and Quinn would say, "Make him go left, but be sure Kevin or Robert are in the vicinity.

We got very friendly and I started bringing him back to French Lick. Everyone treated him great. We're talking about Indiana University country and everybody in my area knows who Quinn Buckner is.

Danny made the most of his opportunity when Gerald was traded. We clicked in the way we usually did. We won fifteen of our first sixteen and twenty-two of our first twenty-six. Our old friends Philly put the pressure on and we didn't get any real breathing room in the race until there were about fifteen games to go. We finished with sixty-three wins, five games better than the 76ers.

Kevin was just getting better and better. He had won the Sixth Man Award the two previous years and there was no longer any doubt he was one of the best ten players in the league. When Maxwell hurt his knee and had to go for an operation in February, Kevin became a starter and began putting bigger and bigger numbers on the board.

Detroit came in on a Sunday afternoon. Kevin always had success against Detroit because they didn't really have anybody who could guard him. But that game was something special. Kevin broke my regular season record of fifty-three points that game by scoring fifty-six. "Mr. Automatic" was just awesome.

A week later, we had a rare Sunday off. No game or practice. Mike Cole, who used to work for the Celtics, was running a road race for charity and he asked me to come fire the starting gun. Then I thought about actually running the five-mile race. I asked K.C. and he said, "If you want to run, go ahead."

I got down there and stretched pretty well. I knew I'd probably wind up being a little sore because it had been a long time since I had run for distance. I ran the race and I felt pretty good. After the race we had a little party.

We were leaving the next day to play Atlanta in New Orleans and when I got up I felt pretty sore. I was also feeling the aftereffects of Saturday night's game. We had played in New Jersey and I didn't get back home until two or three in the morning. The race had been at noon.

Well, we go down to New Orleans and the day of the game I tell people I'm stiffer than ever. I figured I'd really have to loosen up in order to play. I got out there early and ran a mile or so, trying to get loosened up. My legs and ankles were sore and I couldn't understand it. I said, "I only ran five miles. What is this?"

When the fans started coming in, I began getting psyched up for the game because it seemed as if *everybody* was wearing green. This was supposed to be a Hawks' home game, but that crowd had to be 75 percent Boston. That's got to get you fired up.

We start playing and I don't think there is anything unusual going on. Later on I was told I had thirty-two at the half, but I didn't realize I was scoring that much. I remember Dominique Wilkins was having a good game for Atlanta, but I still didn't think I was doing anything special.

I did get hot in the third quarter. Things were really flowing and I remember going to the free throw line and hearing the PA man say I had fifty or fifty-one. I said, "I *can't* have that many points." I thought I was hearing things.

Then I hit a shot and the PA announcer comes on and says that Larry Bird needs three points to break the Celtics' record. D.J. came up to me and said, "We're going to bust Kevin's record tonight." By the time, I was putting in shots from everywhere. People were all over me and I was shooting and making my shots anyway. I would have come out, but my teammates kept encouraging me to keep going.

Kevin was all for it. I remember getting the ball over by the Hawks' bench, getting fouled, shooting it and making it. It was a three-pointer and I thought I was going to have a crack at a four-point play. What I didn't know until later was that a bunch of guys at the end of the Atlanta bench actually fell right off the bench when I made that shot!

Bill Saar was the referee and he disallowed the basket. I made the two free throws, giving me fifty-eight. By this time, I was tired. I came down on a break, pulled up for a three and missed it. It was a complete brick. The ball bounced back to

Kevin. He passed it to me. I threw it to D.J. and ran to the line. He passed it back to me and I tossed it up. The buzzer went off while the ball was in the air. The shot went in and I had a sixty-point game.

How can you explain something like that? I hit a couple of shots in that game I've never hit—before or since. Weird off-balance runners; things like that.

When the game was over, D.J. and Quinn came running over, jumping on me, and I said, "Hey, get off me. I'm so tired, I just want to get out of here." We went into the locker room and everybody was running around. A guy came into the locker room and wanted me to sign the basketball and give it to charity. I said, "Sorry, but *I'm* keeping this one. I don't get sixty every night." So I signed my uniform for the guy instead.

There were all kinds of Celtics' fans outside after the game, but I couldn't do much for them because I was so tired. The race and playing a game like that had drained me. All I wanted to do was get back to the hotel and go to bed. I met some friends there, had some dinner and went to bed. So much for my one visit to New Orleans.

In the big scheme of things, I wouldn't consider it one of my great games. It was just a freaky fun thing. I scored big, but I didn't rebound well and I didn't pass that well. When I think of my great games, this is not one that comes to mind. For example, there was that game in Utah a month earlier in which I had a triple-double and nine steals in just thirty-three minutes. Now *that's* a great game.

We had lost our game in Los Angeles the day before and I ran into Pace Mannion of the Jazz right after our shootaround the next morning in the Salt Palace. "We always get you guys at the right time," he said. "You're coming from Los Angeles, you're on a rough trip and then you have to play us. It's going to be our night."

I said, "Hey, you don't even have anyone on your team who can guard me." I was just kidding around, right?

As it turned out, I was hot from the beginning, hitting three-pointers, passing well and rebounding well. Sometimes you're just in the right place at the right time and this

was one of those nights. I was fluid and everything felt perfect.

Once while I was taking the ball out of bounds in front of
Frank Layden, I turned and said to him, "Don't you have
anyone who can stop me?" He laughed because he knew our
whole team was playing really well, even though Robert,
Max and Quinn were all injured and not even in uniform, so
there wasn't much he could do about the situation. We were
off to a great start, up 34–10 in the first quarter.

In addition to a triple-double, I was making a lot of steals.
I was able to sneak up behind Mark Eaton on some entry
passes and I even picked off an in-bounds pass or two. By the
end of the third quarter, I had the triple-double, plus nine
steals.

When K.C. asked me if I wanted to go back in because of
the nine steals and a chance for that fourth double-figure
category, I told him no. It was great of him to think that way
for my sake, but my purpose every time we play is for the
Celtics to win the game. I've never felt the greater purpose of
my playing well is to break personal records, but it *is* to help
my team win games. I felt I had already done that, so why go
back in again? The other players were playing great ball and
we were all satisfied and happy with our performances and,
as far as I'm concerned, that's the way basketball is supposed
to be played.

2 4

SOMETIMES WHEN YOU LOOK BACK at certain events,
the reason things happened the way they did seems
pretty obvious. Yet when something is actually
happening and you're right in the middle of it, you can't
seem to get a handle on what's going on.

We were winning a lot of games in the second half of that 1984–85 season, but we just weren't the same team. For one thing, we didn't have the real Cedric Maxwell.

Max had injured his knee and had to have an operation. Even before his operation, he wasn't really happy. I noticed that he didn't seem to be into it 100 percent the way he had been in past years. Maybe it was the constant discomfort in his knee that had him out of sorts. There is nothing worse for a professional athlete than to be hampered or completely sidelined by an injury—it takes you out of your everyday routine and deprives you of the ability to accomplish your goals. While Max was going to therapy, Kevin was starting in his place. When the playoffs came around and Kevin was still in the starting lineup, Max was definitely upset. The Celtics did not feel Max was ready to fully contribute and were afraid to take a chance on him. Max never did like coming off the bench; he was definitely the type of person who needs to start.

Some guys are like that. Your friends say, "You *start* for the Celtics. Isn't that great!" But when you become a sixth man, even though you may be more valuable to your team than any starter, you still want to hear your name being called in the warm-up introductions.

Whatever his thinking, Max was definitely not the same old Max—and we weren't the same old Celtics.

Toward the end of that season, I began having problems with my right elbow. I had always been a reckless player, diving around for loose balls without thinking of the consequences. Time after time I would land on my elbow. I guess all that banging finally caught up with me.

The elbow would stiffen up on me, but at first I was able to work the stiffness out and play decently. As the season progressed, it bothered me more on the road than at home. Before the playoffs were over, it became a major problem.

I missed two games with the bad elbow at the end of March and the beginning of April. By the tail end of the season, after we had the league's best record wrapped up, I was trying to cut down my minutes by coming off the bench.

*   *   *

Our first playoff opponent was Cleveland, where George Karl had done a good job with a team a lot of people didn't think was that good. I was anticipating a tough series because—no matter *who* was in those uniforms—Cleveland always seemed to give us a rough time.

I knew Phil Hubbard would be on me and I respected him. He was a banger, who would push me and use his hands on me. The big thing on my mind was, once again, rebounding.

The Cavs were more difficult to play than ever that year. We won two very close games at home and then my elbow started to act up. At the shootaround on the day of the third game, my elbow was so sore I couldn't shoot at all. I attempted twenty free throws, but I couldn't do anything else.

I went back to the hotel room for a nap and when I woke up the elbow was stiff. I couldn't even bend it. When I called K.C., he told me to stay in the room and ice the elbow and watch the game on TV. He figured there would be a fourth game if we lost this one and maybe I'd be feeling better. As it turned out, we lost a close game.

The fun started when I got to practice the next day. The fans had really had a good time at the Richfield Coliseum the night before. They were yelling, *"We want Bird!"* I had taken some therapy in the morning and the elbow started to loosen up. When the press came to ask me what I thought of the Cleveland fans, I was ready.

I said, "They want Bird? Tomorrow night they are going to get him—both barrels. I'm coming out strong and the Celtics are gonna win." I didn't really say anything bad about Cleveland and the fans because the truth is, I've always enjoyed playing there. The fans there have always been into it and that's the way I like to see the fans get— *involved.*

The atmosphere the next night was great. I knew what we would be in for when I came out for my early warm-up. There were anti-Bird and anti-Celtics signs all over the place. People were coming down to courtside just to holler things at me while I warmed up. When we came out for the lay-up line, they booed every time I touched the ball. The emotions were running high—just the way I like it.

It turned out to be a physical game, with banging and pushing all night long. The game was close all the way through and we wouldn't have pulled it out without Ray Williams.

The Celtics had picked Ray up after the All-Star Game and I was excited when we got him because I knew he was a tough kid who could hit the outside shot and also make things happen inside with his ability to penetrate. One night at the Garden, I was going backdoor and, with his back to me completely, Ray got a bounce pass through to me for a lay-up. I still don't know how he did that, but I went right over to him and thanked him and told him it was the best pass I had ever received.

Ray and I always had excellent eye contact. Late in this Cleveland game, he made a thread-the-needle pass while I was cutting along the baseline. I caught the ball, was fouled on the shot and made two game-clinching free throws. We held on at the end and won what turned out to be a fun Cleveland series on a good note.

Next up was Detroit. That's the series where Vinnie Johnson and Terry Tyler scared us after we won the first two games at home. Tyler killed us in the third game and Vinnie was out of control in the fourth game, really living up to his "Microwave" nickname, as he dropped twenty-two points on us in the fourth quarter. We tried everybody—M.L., D.J., Ray—but we just couldn't stop him. People on our bench were just sitting there, going, "Oh no." We'd all seen Vinnie get hot before, but nothing like this.

A funny thing happened late in game four. We were down by three and passing the ball around when M.L. shot the ball while standing on the out-of-bounds line. I told him, "That was pretty clever thinking. We're down by three, so you go for four." After that we started calling him "Mr. Four-Point Man."

My elbow was bothering me somewhat in game four, but nothing major. I was thinking, "Let's just beat these guys. Then I can go home and get it worked on."

It wasn't too bad in the fifth game. I had Kelly Tripucka on me and my objective was to take him low as often as possible. We won that game to go up, three games to two.

We knew game six was important because Red was there. Usually, we don't see much of Red on the road until the finals, but here he was, walking around, smoking that cigar, but he wasn't saying much.

We played a solid game. We moved the ball and we played intelligent basketball and we beat them to win the series. After the game Dan Roundfield walked in and started shaking hands, saying, "I won't be around here anymore." Things had broken down between him and the team and he spent the second half of that game in street clothes. That was his last game as a Piston.

At that point, we really didn't have a lot to fear with Detroit. They had Isiah Thomas, who reminded me of Tiny Archibald, although he was a better outside shooter than Tiny. You could see he wanted to take control of that team. He was a little frustrated because he was playing hard every night and couldn't always get the others to follow his lead. They had Bill Laimbeer, but he hadn't gotten as good as he would get. They still needed players to help out those two. They didn't yet have the size or the ability to handle the better teams. As everyone knows, Detroit is a much more balanced team now and has made great strides in winning the 1989 season championship.

There wasn't much to the Philly series in the Eastern Conference finals. The 76ers were no longer really our equals. We took them in five. The last game was close, but I was able to steal the ball from Andrew Toney to save it.

It was Boston and Los Angeles once again for the championship. The one visit was a new format in the championship series. Instead of the old two-two-one formula, where if you had the home court advantage you'd have the first, second, fifth and seventh games at home, they had come up with a two-three-two format, with your home games being games one, two, six and seven. This would put you in the opponents' city for the better part of a week—much too long—and would take away the home court for what I always think is a key game in any series—game five.

Wish I could blame what eventually happened on the elbow, but I can't because we were home enough for me to have it worked on. Give the credit to the Lakers.

We started off very well, blowing them out at home in the first game. We were moving, running and playing great defense. We went to the bench and Scotty Wedman was phenomenal. He kept hitting and hitting and wound up shooting eleven for eleven from the field.

We were lucky because we caught the Lakers just right. We were relaxing in Boston, while they were going six games with Denver. I know they figured they were looking at a five-game series with Denver when they went up, three games to one. All they had to do was win at home. Instead, they lost and had to go back to Denver. When they came out to play us, they hadn't prepared the way they wanted to and they looked fatigued.

We were happy about the way we played, but we had been through it with Philly in '82 and knew game two would be starting all over. If you recall, we beat them by forty in the first game at home and lost the second game, not to mention the series.

History was about to repeat itself. The Lakers jumped all over us in the second game. Magic took over immediately. They were pounding us at the half and then Kareem really kicked in. He had been terrible in the first game and you knew he had too much pride not to bounce back. The great ones always do. He wound up with thirty points, seventeen rebounds and eight assists.

We went to L.A. and they drilled us again. It was a rerun of the third game in '84. I was worried because our minds didn't seem to be in it. There wasn't any dissension on the team, but at the same time our old fire was missing. At one point that week, we decided to have a team meeting. Some of the guys wanted to have it at the hotel, while some wanted to have it at the Forum. We wound up with half the team showing up at the Forum and the other half at the hotel. For some reason, we just weren't in synch as a team.

We had one game left in us. The fourth game was up for grabs and it came down to the score tied and us with the ball. Someone threw it to me, but there were two guys running at me, so I passed it to D.J. He made the shot at the buzzer to win the game and tie the series.

We celebrated that one, but we still didn't have our old fire. L.A. proved that by handling us easily in the fifth game. Going back to Boston, we needed to win both games at home if we were going to retain our championship.

I wasn't shooting all that great in the series and people assumed it was my elbow. To tell you the truth, it had a lot more to do with Michael Cooper than with my elbow.

Michael Cooper had been in the league as long as I had and I had always thought he was a good defensive player, but by this time I was really paying attention to him. Going up against him was different than playing against anyone else. That was true of the Lakers as a whole. No other team was as subtle defensively as they were and no individual on the Lakers was better defensively than Michael Cooper.

First of all, Michael Cooper obviously studies the films a lot. Most players will just go out there and see whether you're going to be hot or cold and then see what they can do against you. Michael comes into the game with a plan.

If you like to catch the ball from thirteen feet, Michael will make you get it from fifteen feet. He relies on keeping himself between you and the basket—the first thing you're taught, isn't it?—and he slides with you. He's always watching out for you from the corner of his eye.

Michael *never* leaves you. He doesn't worry about anyone else. A lot of players intend to concentrate on you, but they get caught up in the game one way or the other and let you get away. Michael never does. He never loses his concentration.

He knows he is a defensive player and that his offense is secondary, just icing on the cake. His pride is defense. Michael boxes out a little better than everyone else and he contests the entry pass better. When you put the ball on the floor and get him faked out, you're not home-free because Michael will come up behind you. He never quits on the play. If he can't make the play himself, he brings someone in to help. In fact, everything he does is a step ahead of anyone else in the league who guards me.

Michael is generally quick, but where he is especially good is when he goes to his left. Most people can slide to the right all right, but for some reason they don't go that well from right to left. Michael slides equally well either way. And he may be thin, but he's a lot stronger than he looks. You can try to push him around, but he will battle you. He will contest every inch you try to take from him.

He feels that because I have the ball so much, if he can slow me down, he can hamper our entire offense. Michael knows why he's out there. He's the best because he seriously cuts down on the number of my shots.

Against some teams, when I'm hot I'm going to get off twenty or twenty-five shots. There's no way I'm getting that many shots against Michael Cooper. You start thinking, "I'd better make every shot I take because I'm not going to get that many of them." I once had an eleven for thirteen game against him. I also think I had back-to-back games against him in which I only had eleven shots in each game.

I heard he told people that one year when he went on vacation to Europe he took videotapes of Celtics games. After playing against him, I can believe it.

He wasn't much of an offensive threat when he started out, but he changed that too. One time, early in my career, I decided that I was working so hard on offense that I would relax on defense and let Michael shoot. He burned me. Everyone knows he made himself into a great three-point shooter. I just love his game. He knows he isn't going to play more than twenty-five or thirty minutes, so when he comes in he gives it everything he's got. The Lakers can use his offense, but if it's not there he *really* concentrates on his defense.

We hardly ever talk on the court. However, once I made a shot over him and I said something to him. Michael came right back with a basket on me and said, "You can't play *defense* either." I never said another word to him. As far as opponents go, I have always admired Magic the most. But when it comes to guys who generally guard me, I have the most respect for Michael Cooper.

The Lakers as a whole played great defense during the finals. After they beat us in the sixth game, I told Pat Riley he had coached a perfect series. He made so many minor adjustments that kept us off-guard. They ran different guys at me from different places and had me off-balance.

They were not the same L.A. team I had known. In the past, I thought I knew exactly what they were going to do against us, but in that series they crossed us up.

They stopped us from running. We just couldn't get started and they took advantage of us. We had always known that we had to be physical, move the ball and play good defense to beat the best teams. In the past we had always had good success on the offensive boards against L.A. That's how we won the championship in '84. But this was a different L.A. team. They got a nice series out of Mitch Kupchak, a physical player, but it was more than just Kupchak. The Lakers had learned their lesson. They were *all* more physical. They were a completely different L.A. team than the one we had beaten the year before.

If you throw in all their defensive adjustments, they really frustrated me. I said to Riley, "I don't know what you did. I've got to look at those films and figure it out. You guys really had me pegged in this series." He just smiled and said, "Thanks a lot."

There was no question that we had lost to a better team. Some of our players didn't seem to be into it anymore. We got plenty of chances in the series, but we just weren't up to it. We were nowhere near as sharp as we had been the year before, especially after Max got hurt. Something wasn't there. We used to be a happy team all the time and we were always ready to play. That all changed.

Saying the Lakers were better didn't make it much easier to take. But once I decided that this was the case, the next question was: "What can I do to get better?" The first thing I decided was that I needed to work on my left hand. Whenever I'm trying to improve my game, I analyze my weaknesses first and work on those relentlessly. When Cooper made all those subtle changes on me, I knew I needed to come up with something new.

While I was still trying to figure out how I could improve

my game for the next season, I was notified that I had been selected as the league MVP for the second year in a row. Even though everyone around me was so excited because I was the only forward to ever accomplish that feat, I can tell you that, after losing the championship series, I didn't feel as if I had accomplished anything. I still felt terrible about the loss and I had to be talked into going out to Salt Lake City to receive the award at the NBA meetings. I flew out there on a private plane with Mr. Woolf and my friend Tom Hill, but losing the championship that year sure interrupted any feeling of joy about winning the MVP and I'm afraid that's how I'll always remember that season.

2 5

I PAID RED A VISIT IN HIS OFFICE right before I went home at the end of the '85 playoffs and he said, "What do you think of Bill Walton?"

I said, "Get him if you can. Robert was fatigued in the L.A. series. We couldn't control Kareem. We've got to get Robert some rest. He's had to play too many minutes every game."

As I've explained many times, I wasn't much of a fan when I was growing up, but the one player I was aware of was Bill Walton. In 1974 our high school coach took us up to see the Indiana state finals and while we were up there we watched the UCLA–North Carolina State NCAA semifinals on TV. Tommy Burleson was having a great game for N.C. State, but the player who got my attention was Bill Walton.

He was doing everything he could to be a team player. I loved the way he passed and rebounded and his technique was flawless. He did everything exactly the way Coach Jones had taught us to play. He was just so sound, right by the book. I said, "That's the way I always wanted to be. I'll bet his coach is proud of him."

I loved the way he held the ball up high and I loved the way he used the glass on his turnaround jumper. If you can say I had anything close to an idol in basketball at the time, that player was Bill Walton.

I can remember when Bill came to Boston with the San Diego Clippers and we were both shooting around before the game and I said, "Are you playing tonight?" He said, "I don't think so. Not tonight." I was so disappointed. I still idolized him as a player and I sure wanted to play against him. Now I would have a chance to play *with* him, something I could really look forward to.

As the world goes—and especially in the basketball world—you never get something without having to give something up and so the Celtics had to give Max up in order to get Bill Walton. As much as I realized how unhappy Max had been the year before and as much as I realized the truth was that he just didn't want to play with the Celtics anymore, the thought of not having Max around was tough to take.

When Max was on, he was a pleasure to play with. Anytime he played up to even three quarters of his ability, we'd have no problem. That seventh game in '84 against the Lakers was proof of what he could do. Most of all, I was going to miss him on the road.

There were a million laughs with Max and a lot of great times—on and off the court. I knew we were going to miss him.

And you might know what was going to happen the next time we played against the Clippers. We were all looking forward to that first game in L.A. and when we got there the writers told us they didn't think Max was going to play because he had the flu. We said, "What?" We were planning on going right at him from beginning to end. He didn't play and we blew the Clippers out.

But now we had Bill Walton and that had me excited. My thinking was that I had already had the opportunity to play with some great players and this was another one. Also,

Kevin would become a full-time starter, which was probably overdue, and we knew we were going to have a good year.

It did take Bill a while to fit in. If we had judged him by his performance on opening night, we all would have probably voted to put him on waivers. We blew a nineteen-point lead in New Jersey and lost the game and Bill had a rough night.

He walked off the court and said, "I'm sorry. That was the worst exhibition of basketball anybody could put on. I'm disappointed and I can tell you it won't happen again."

I said, "Bill, don't let one game bother you. Just keep working and plugging. Everything is going to turn out all right."

Max wasn't the only guy I missed. We signed Jerry Sichting of the Pacers as a free agent because we needed another outside shooter coming off the bench. The eventual price was Quinn Buckner.

Quinn played less and less as the 1984–85 season progressed and he knew there was a good chance he was finished as a Celtic. He said to me, "I don't know exactly what's going to happen, but don't worry about me. We've always had a good time and we'll always be good friends. I understand the game of professional basketball. I understand this league and nothing that happens will get me down." He's always had that great attitude toward basketball and life in general.

In a way, Quinn reminded me of my grandmother. She always said that she wasn't afraid to die, that she was ready any time the Good Lord was ready to take her. She always said, "If He takes me, He takes me." Quinn was the same way with his career. Quinn felt good about going back to Indiana. He knew people there and he figured it was the best place for him.

I knew I was going to miss him. I learned more about the world from him than I ever learned in school. We'd go places and he could point out the historic or social significance of this or that. Quinn was the greatest teacher I ever had.

When Quinn left, I started thinking, "Everybody who hangs out with me gets traded." For a while, I was hesitant to get that close to anyone, but I discovered that Jerry and I were going to get along well.

After that opening game loss to the Nets, we won seventeen of our next eighteen. Once Bill kicked in, we were really in a groove, except for one person—me. My back was giving me severe problems and I wasn't shooting well at all.

I'd always had a little stiffness and soreness there, but things got bad during the summer of '85. I was home, running and playing ball and doing some work around the house, when one day—*bam-o.* My back went out. For two weeks I just stayed in bed. I had no idea what was wrong, but I hoped it would pass.

I was miserable for the rest of the summer. I'd go out to shoot for an hour and then I'd have to come home and lie down. I kept hoping I'd get better, but I was getting progressively worse instead. When I went to training camp for the two-a-day sessions during the first week, I was really struggling. In between practices, I would go back to lie down and then barely drag myself up for the next one.

Finally we played an exhibition against Philly at the Garden. I played well, but after the game I told the team doctor how much it was hurting me. I was flat on my back on the trainer's table and the pain was getting worse by the minute.

Red came in and I told him there was something seriously wrong with my back. I said, "I don't how much longer I can play like this."

It was at this point that I was introduced to a man who has made a true difference in my life. His name is Dan Dyrek and he is an orthopedic physical therapist. Without him, I don't know how I could possibly have made it through that season.

Dan did not provide an instant cure. In fact, he didn't say much at all that first night. He just told me to come into his office the next day. When he examined me, he said there were definite vertebrae problems. Although he didn't say much about the treatment, I knew instinctively that it was going to take a long time.

Dan simply told me to be careful and to be sure to do the

exercises he gave me. I'd even go so far as to say that if you had asked him whether or not I should have played at that time, Dan would have said no. To get it healed quickly, I shouldn't have played. But I could see we had a great team and I just *had* to play. I couldn't sit out.

It took me a good three months to get over the problem. Before I did get better, my game deteriorated badly. I just couldn't get rolling in any way and I was laboring to do everything. It was hard to score, hard to rebound and hard to pass. I didn't feel comfortable playing at all.

Along the way, Dan even managed to fix my elbow. One day when he was working on my back, I said to him, "Could you fix my elbow too?" Dan said, "I don't know. Maybe I can do a little bit, but I don't want to mess with your arm. We'll do a little and see how it reacts."

He grabbed my right arm and exercised it a little bit. As soon as Dan started stretching it, the feeling was the same as when I had it drained during the Detroit series. He was afraid to do too much because he didn't know how my elbow was going to react. In two days, it felt perfect. I walked out of there, saying, "This man's a genius. He works on my back and it feels great. He works on my elbow and that feels great."

I could feel progress in my back, but it was slow. While I played—or right after I played—it would stiffen up. The entire experience was a giant pain. All year, every day, I'd practice and then drive down to Dan's office for a treatment. I was spending almost all my time playing and going to therapy.

I'd come away from a treatment feeling good and then I'd have to play a game. Traveling was a major hardship. After every bus or plane ride, my back was really killing me. This kept up all year. Dan was with me throughout the finals in Houston and during that series I felt better than I had felt all year.

The team was carrying me through November and December. Walton hit his stride around Thanksgiving and with Bill, Jerry and Scott Wedman coming off the bench we were just wearing people out. Half the time we could just show up and win, especially at home.

The only snag was what came to be known in the press as the "Lost Weekend." It was the last weekend before Christmas. First we went to Philly and got beat by twenty. We were terrible. You often have trouble getting around in the winter and this trip was a classic. We got up at 6 A.M. to get to the airport and we wound up having two delays. We didn't arrive at the hotel in Milwaukee until 2 P.M. and the game was at 7. We couldn't play a lick. Everybody was upset about the weekend and right after that we *really* came together.

Except for Christmas Day.

We had to play New York in Madison Square Garden on Christmas Day on national TV. I don't think anyone should have to play on Christmas Day, but you learn to accept these types of schedules when you are a professional athlete. Anyway, we were leading by twenty-five late in the third period and wound up losing in double overtime. We took all kinds of bad shots. It didn't matter what kind of shots I took because I finished eight for twenty-seven. Even though we had that twenty-five-point lead, we weren't in the right frame of mind for the game. Everyone was grumbling about having to play on Christmas Day. Everyone with a family wanted to be at home. There wasn't any of what you would call dissension, but we weren't really pulling our oars in the same direction.

When we got back to Boston, Jerry came over to the house, since his wife and family were out of town. We sat around and said, "Wasn't that the most embarrassing situation we've ever had in our lives?"

We vowed that the Christmas Day game was going to be the last time all season that we were going to be embarrassed. That game stuck in our minds for a long time. As we hit January, we were starting to become an awesome team. Walton was doing everything for us that everyone thought he could. It was apparent that the only impediment to us being a truly great team was me and my back.

Despite my back, life on the team was fun again, the way it had been when M.L. and Max were carrying on. The focal point was Walton. Kevin and I would call him at home, just to bust his chops. I'm talking about *every day*. We loved to call Bill up and talk trash to him. We never let up. We even got his wife Susan involved. She called us up, asking us to let up on her poor Bill. He loved it.

I don't think Bill has ever been on a team in the pros where he was more comfortable. He knew he didn't have to go out there and play for forty minutes a game. He loved the atmosphere. We practiced hard. We played hard. We played together. What else could you ask for?

We never had so much fun in practice—before or since. Everybody wanted Bill on him in practice so he could shoot over him and talk junk. Robert would walk into practice and say, "Hey, big fella, I'm coming after *you* today." Before we even got out on the floor, they'd be going at each other.

All we wanted to do was scrimmage. K.C. had started calling the second unit the Green Team because they wore green while we wore white and the guys took all that to heart. Bill would start yelling, "The best team is down here!" Those practices were like games to him. After all those years he had missed, he was feeling good and he just wanted to play. Now he was going to make up for lost time. The funny part is, he even inspired Robert to start talking some junk. We just had everything in order and we were real loose as a team.

Robert was pleased to have a quality backup. Bill was apprehensive when he first came to town that Robert would resent him in some way, but M.L. brought Bill over to Robert's house and the two big guys hit it off right away.

Bill didn't want to put any pressure on Robert. He said, "I'm just here to try to help you out." Robert said, "I just want to win a championship. You're going to help me because I can't play all those minutes."

Those scrimmages were great. That Green Team thought they were just as good as we were. If you put them in a game situation against us, with a ref and the clock on, Bill was moaning on every call. They *were* good. After all, Bill Walton and Scott Wedman had both been All-Stars and Jerry could shoot with anybody. Those scrimmages brought the best out in everybody. We really started kicking it in at practice.

We had a much different attitude from the year before. Everybody was talking and laughing. We'd be up by ten or twelve in a game and we'd bring those guys in and we'd go up by eighteen or twenty. We weren't losing a thing when the Green Team came in.

ITHIN THREE WEEKS OR SO of that Christmas Day embarrassment in New York, the Celtics were starting to roll.

Walton was at the top of his game. First of all, with his great passing ability, we wanted the ball to be in his hands. His style of play fit perfectly with mine. The key was to keep moving, to set good picks, to cut off him and to be ready for the ball at any time. We were able to work at least one give-and-go every game. The entire Boston Garden crowd seemed to know when it was coming, but opponents never seemed to catch on.

With Bill in there, I just concentrated on boxing out on the boards because if the ball was anywhere in his vicinity, he was going to get it. I have never seen anyone with better timing on the boards. His style was all his own, the way he kept his arms up, the way he was able to keep his man off-balance and the way he could sweep the ball right off the rim without being called for goaltending. Someone said it was like watching a waiter sweep the crumbs off a table.

Bill wanted to get his points, just like everyone else on the team. We weren't afraid to go to him, but we never wanted him to get to the point where he felt he *had* to score. I think there was a time that season when he felt he should score eight or ten points a game. I remember telling him, "Don't worry about points. We'll take care of that. Just make your move if you have it. If not, give it to someone who can shoot it." Once he accepted that, we didn't have any problems.

The big breakthrough game was against Los Angeles. Bill came into the game in the first period and completely domi-nated the game. He blocked a Kareem shot. He threw down a tremendous dunk. He finished with seven blocked shots in sixteen minutes of play. He was hitting me. He was hitting Scotty. He was just very active. Bill was getting into it because he knew what kind of a team the Celtics were capable of being that year.

We had a great week. The previous Saturday night we had gone down to Atlanta and beaten them in overtime after they had us by twenty at the half. Some of the Hawks were mouthing off at halftime and that got us motivated.

When we got to the airport in Atlanta that morning, our bus wasn't there, so Bill, Kevin and myself jumped into a cab and the cabdriver says, "Are you guys ballplayers?" We said, "Yeah." He said, "Who do you play for?" We told him, "The Boston Celtics." Either Bill or Kevin said, "Do you know about a guy named Bird?" The cabbie said, "Yeah, that guy's a great ballplayer." Then Bill or Kevin said, "Watch out for Dominique Wilkins. The Hawks are tough this year. Bird's not that good. I don't know if he can handle Dominique." And the cabbie says, "I think he can. I have to give that boy credit."

Life is great when you're winning—and we were winning. We actually had two different teams to throw at people. Our first team did certain things and Bill, Scotty and Jerry did something else.

Our road attitude was much better. We never had a problem at home (we only lost one game there all year), but in order to have a truly great team you've got to win on the road. Losing those games in Philly and Milwaukee by twenty was one thing that inspired us, but the big thing was that loss to New York on Christmas Day, which embarrassed us much more than losing to the Sixers and Bucks.

We finished with sixty-seven wins. Any problems we had were overcome. When Kevin came up with an Achilles tendon problem that forced him out of eighteen games, Scott Wedman moved into the starting lineup and we went fifteen and three. That's depth.

The first playoff opponent was Chicago and that meant our first series with Michael Jordan. He had come in and beaten us once when he was a rookie and I had told the press that he was the best player I had ever seen. What he did against us in this series demonstrated what I was talking about.

He started off with forty-nine in the first game. We won by nineteen, but Michael kept Chicago close with thirty in the first half and it wasn't until Dennis Johnson shot seven for seven in the third period that we were able to break it open.

Game two was truly scary. I thought Chicago had played very well in the first game and I frankly didn't think they could play any better. Chicago didn't have a dominant center, but they had Orlando Woolridge—and besides, any team with Michael on it can beat you. We really wanted to sweep them. We didn't want to mess around with them.

It took us two overtimes and we had to sweat out sixty-three points by Michael, but we beat them on that Sunday afternoon.

Talk about a topper. That was one of the five best games I've ever been in. We couldn't do *anything* with Michael. I'll never forget seeing him wide open at the end of that first overtime. I thought it was all over for us, but he missed the shot and we came back and beat them in the second OT.

What was amazing about Michael's performance was that he scored sixty-three points *in the flow of the game*! When he scored forty-nine in the first game, he did a lot of isolations, but he hardly isolated at all in the second game and he still wound up with sixty-three.

Michael Jordan was—and is—a completely different type of player from anyone I had seen before. He's literally on a different level. Magic and I do all our stuff on the floor. When I first saw Michael play, I recognized there was a different era coming in. Ten years down the road, you're going to see a lot of Michael Jordans out there. A lot of them will be taking the ball from one hand to the other and switching it around, going underneath, spinning around and doing all this different stuff.

People asked me to compare Michael with Dr. J. and the difference was that Dr. J. usually did everything one-handed. He didn't use his left hand very much, but Michael doesn't care whether he's going left or right. And if you don't stop Michael before he takes off, there is no way you'll do it once he gets into the air.

Michael has the whole package. He can run, jump, block shots and play great defense. Most of all, he is a great competitor. It was great seeing a guy like Michael come into the league, but I don't want to see too many more like him, at least not while I'm still around.

In many ways, I wouldn't say Michael is better than Magic because Magic plays the game the way it should be played. Michael's style makes him a different story entirely. The word I keep coming back to is "different." He's ushering a whole new era—a whole new style of play—into the NBA.

When we went to Chicago for the third game of that series, we were determined that someone other than Michael Jordan would have to beat us. We trapped him with *everybody* and we knew early in the game that none of the other Bulls was going to step up. We won the game easily and got our sweep.

We didn't have any trouble with either Atlanta or Milwaukee. We really peaked in the third quarter of the fifth Atlanta game, outscoring them by an amazing thirty-six to six in those twelve minutes. Everything was clicking. We were all over them on defense and we were really moving the ball on offense. It was a fun game for us, but we couldn't help but feel at least a little sorry for the opponent because *nothing* was going right for them. Atlanta was a good team, but this was simply the most awesome quarter we've ever had.

We won that by thirty or so and we won the first Milwaukee game by thirty-two. It was pretty obvious that no one was going to touch us, especially since Houston had upset L.A. in the West.

The most memorable aspect for me of the Milwaukee series had nothing to do with basketball. After we had beaten them in Milwaukee on a Saturday afternoon to go up, three games to none, a season ticket holder who sits right behind the visiting team's bench—he's a lawyer who had stirred up trouble for people in the past—went to the authorities and accused us of using illegal drugs right there on the bench!

He was referring to the ammonia capsules we sniff sometimes to clear our heads. There's nothing mysterious about them. They've been an accepted part of sports for decades.

I walked into the locker room after the game and I was told someone wanted to question me. He mentioned the capsules and I said, "What are you talking about?"

I was so upset about being accused of having anything at all to do with drugs, I started yelling, "Just bring me a tube and you can test it anytime you want!"

When I got back to the hotel, I got a call from Dinah, who wanted to know just *what* was going on. We finally got it all straightened out, but I was still hot about it. I was so angry that I didn't sleep very much that night. I was determined to do whatever it took to *win*. I had nothing against the Milwaukee players, but now I was *really* motivated to play.

The game was close for three quarters, but we got a little daylight on them in the fourth when I hit a pretty deep three-pointer. Then I hit another one and then a third. Finally I held the ball for the last shot in the game, waiting for the clock to run down. I wasn't trying to rub it in to the players; I was just thinking about that guy sitting behind our bench. After I released the shot, I started walking off the floor. When the ball dropped through the hole, I was just about off the court. That was one of the most satisfying baskets I've ever made in my whole life.

We always want to play L.A. in the finals, but for the second time in my career we were going to play Houston. This was a much different team than the one we had played in '81, the team that was built around Moses Malone. The new Rockets featured the Twin Towers: Akeem Olajuwon and Ralph Sampson. The only two players remaining from the '81 team were Robert Reid and Allan Leavell.

But the most important new Rocket wasn't a player. We were all looking forward to this series because the coach of the Rockets was none other than Bill Fitch.

When the playoffs started, I wanted to wish Fitch well all throughout the playoffs, never really thinking we'd wind up playing against him. Now I couldn't wait to get out there and play against him. I wanted to see what strategy he would come up with.

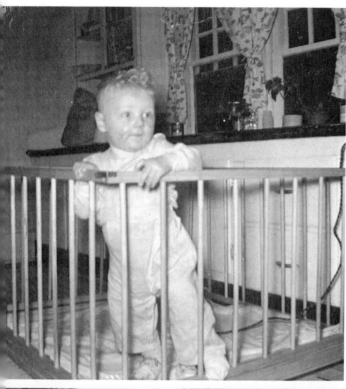

Me at nine months old.
(Courtesy of Georgia Bird)

Mike, Mark, Linda and
me at Santa Claus Land.
(Courtesy of M. L. Walters)

*Me, Linda, Mark and
Mike; in the back are
Grandma Lizzie Kerns
and Mom.*
(Courtesy of Georgia Bird)

*Me holding my
cousin Charles.*
(Courtesy of M. L. Walters)

*My seventh-grade
school picture.
(Courtesy of Max Gibson)*

*A family photo: Mike, Mom,
Dad and me in the back; up
front are Jeff, Linda, Mark
and Eddie.
(Courtesy of Georgia Bird)*

Springs Valley High School team, senior year. I'm in the middle and Coach Holland is on the left. (Courtesy of Max Gibson)

Coach Jim Jones and me at my basketball camp. (Courtesy of Larry Bird Basketball Camp)

With Coach Bobby Knight. This photo was taken the day I signed with Indiana University. (Courtesy of Max Gibson)

The Indiana State University team. Coach Bill Hodges is kneeling, second from right. (Courtesy of Indiana State University)

Zeroed in on the hoop.
(Courtesy of Dan Deem)

Making my move.
Note the canvas
high tops.
(Courtesy of Dan Deem)

It was a full house at the 1979 press conference announcing my signing with the Boston Celtics. (Courtesy of Bob Woolf)

Just getting a shot off against Michael Jordan. (Courtesy of Dick Raphael)

Still trying to make something happen, even though I'm down on the floor. (Courtesy of Dick Raphael)

Strong to the hoop in the Houston championship series. (Courtesy of Dick Raphael)

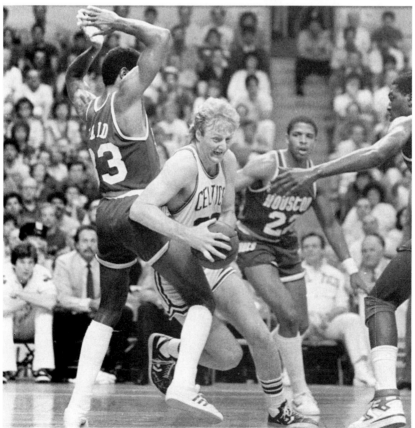

Getting the first step on Rodney McCray in the Houston championship series.
(Courtesy of Dick Raphael)

Celebrating the 1986 championship with D. J.
(Courtesy of Dick Raphael)

Everyone's waiting to see if my three-pointer goes in against Dominique.
(Courtesy of Dick Raphael)

Dinah and me going to
an awards banquet.
(Courtesy of Bob Woolf)

Bob Woolf and me
discussing the next
step in my contract
negotiations.
(Courtesy of Ken Regan)

*The unveiling of
Armand LaMontagne's statue of me.
Mom and Red Auerbach
are looking on.
(Courtesy of Fay Photo Service)*

*Giving instruction to a young member
of the Terre Haute Boy's Club —
crooked index finger and all.
(Courtesy of Max Gibson)*

Getting a shot off against the Knicks. (Courtesy of Dick Raphael)

Enjoying just being a fan. (Courtesy of Dick Raphael)

(Courtesy of Dick Raphael)

We won games one and two without any difficulty and we had a real chance to win the third game in Houston, but Mitchell Wiggins beat us with a tap-in. This was the second year the league used the two-three-two format in the finals, which meant if we could win just one in Houston we'd have two chances to win it back in Boston.

The fourth game was well played. The two big plays were a three-pointer of mine and a great follow-up by Walton, who was on the floor at the end of a close game for the first time all season. K.C. made a tough decision to take Robert out and put Bill in late in the fourth quarter, which is something he never *ever* did. But in this particular game, Robert was tired from battling Akeem, Ralph and Jim Petersen and Bill was fresh. That decision saved the game for us.

We were playing all right in the fifth game when a big fight broke out between Ralph Sampson and Jerry Sichting. They were both thrown out of the game and it helped Houston a lot more than it helped us because the fight really got their crowd into the game and we didn't respond very well to the situation.

After the fight was broken up, I looked over at D.J. and saw that he was bleeding from a cut above the eye. I knew this series would be over soon because D.J. was not going to put up with anything like that. But we would obviously have to do it back in Boston because the Rockets were killing us on the offensive boards and Akeem was blocking everything that came his way.

When the game was over, I walked off the court, saying to myself, "We'll get them at home."

I tried to concentrate more and probably prepared better for that game than any other game in my career. I asked Dinah to make sure no one came to the house because I wanted to concentrate completely on this final game. I couldn't afford to be distracted—by anyone or anything.

There was a lot of publicity back in Boston about the Sampson-Sichting fight. When the Rockets arrived in Boston, some Boston fans were there ready to greet them. When the Rockets arrived at the Garden for a little workout, there were more fans outside the building and they started getting on Ralph as soon as he got off the bus. I was home, watching TV with Dinah, and when I saw the look on Ralph's face I knew we weren't going to have to worry about *him* the next day.

I had a good feeling as soon as I got to the Garden. I went out early to do my pregame shooting and when I went back into the locker room I liked the atmosphere. Everyone wanted to finish it.

We jumped out on them quickly when the game started— and then Bill came in. Akeem Olajuwon stole the ball from him three times in a row and they were right back in it. I think Bill was *too* fired up. The truth is, it wasn't all Bill's fault. A couple of passes didn't lead him correctly and Akeem was quick enough to steal the ball.

K.C. did take Bill out for a couple of minutes and when he put him back in Bill went crazy with blocks, rebounds and dunks. We were playing real well and we went into the locker room with a big lead.

I changed my uniform during halftime and that's something I *never* do. I was playing so well and feeling so great that I just took that uniform off, stuffed it into my bag and got a new uniform out, so that way I would have two championship uniforms instead of one.

It was a great defensive game for us. Everyone was active early and I can remember getting my hands on two or three balls. When we weren't doing that, we were making the Rockets take bad shots and we were all getting out on the fast break. I was moving my feet well on defense, the ball kept coming to me on the boards and I was hitting my shots. I couldn't ask for anything more.

The play everyone remembers from that game came in the fourth quarter, by which time we were in complete control. I was going to the basket and Bill kind of got in my way, so I just turned around, dribbled by him and went back to the corner, right in front of the Houston bench. People behind the bench were hollering, *"Shoot it!"*, so I figured, "Why not?" The ball went in for a three-pointer and my heart started beating like crazy again, just the way it had in Houston five years earlier.

The crowd started surging toward the court with a few minutes left and K.C. pulled all the starters and had us taken directly to the locker room. In one sense, that was the best championship because we had those extra moments to ourselves.

I would put the 1985–86 Celtics team with any I've played on and I'd stack it up with any I've seen anywhere else. The Philly team that won it all in '83 was a very strong team and the Lakers teams that came later might have been better. But that was the best Celtics team I've seen.

That was my last MVP year. It had been a tough year for me in one sense because I had to deal with the back problem in the beginning of the season. But over all it was a fun year because the atmosphere was much different than it had been the year before. So I was pretty pleased about winning the MVP for the third straight year.

There is no feeling like that championship feeling. When you play for the Celtics, you hear about all the history and every night you look up at the championship flags that hang from the rafters in the Garden. It really can overwhelm you. Until we won our first title in 1981, we couldn't completely relate to all that.

You can't until your team wins a championship of its own. Until your team does that, you're not really a part of it. You can't put yourself into the history book with the old Celtic greats until your team can hang a banner of its own. The Celtics are all about championships. Unless your team has a flag up there, you can't really say you've played on the same court as Bill Russell. At least that's the way I feel about it. You don't know anything about Celtics pride if your team doesn't have a banner.

Now we had three and we also had the second pick in the draft. I thought for sure we'd be putting up a few more of those banners.

DURING THE HOUSTON SERIES, Red and K.C. asked me to watch some films of a college player. Thanks to the Gerald Henderson deal with Seattle, we had the second pick in the first round of the draft. I really liked the way the player looked. His name was Len Bias.

Len could obviously jump and run and he also had a tough streak in him. He looked like he really wanted to win and I thought he'd be a great addition to our team. Red even asked me if I would be willing to come to rookie camp in August to work with him if we drafted him. I told him yes, that I would look forward to it.

We drafted him. The next morning I was in the shower when Dinah came in and said, "I don't know whether or not to believe this, but someone just called and said Lenny Bias died of a heart attack."

I called the Celtics office and they told me he had collapsed and had been rushed to the hospital but hadn't made it. I issued a statement through Mr. Woolf's office, saying it was the cruelest thing I had ever heard. There's no question Len's death was a tragic loss to everyone and a sadness that we will all carry with us, but I have to admit, when I found out Len's untimely death was caused by drug use, I was filled not only with great sympathy for his family but also with a lot of anger and frustration. I will never figure out in a million years why anyone would get involved with drugs. How can anyone say they're looking for a good time when you are looking death right in the face every time you use them? I can't even imagine the extent of fear someone must feel deep down inside before they reach for those drugs. How many great athletes have to die or have their careers ruined before they get the message? I don't respect anyone who uses drugs. It's so obvious that drugs do nothing but debilitate your mind and your body and, no matter who you are or how old you are, drugs will destroy you sooner or later.

There has hardly been a day in the last three years when somebody doesn't make reference to Len Bias and what he would have meant to the Celtics. It's no secret we've had depth problems and when you consider the way Kevin and I have been hurt it's difficult not to speculate how much Bias would have helped the Celtics.

I can say that I felt he was the player who would be able to take my place. He wasn't Michael Jordan, but he was in that mold. He was a runner and jumper unlike anyone on our team and he was as tough as nails. I think he would have been a lot better in the pros than he was in college. I think he could do more things than, say, James Worthy. He had that Bernard King look to me and I've always loved Bernard as a player. We could have broken him in slowly—giving him twenty to twenty-five minutes a game—and we would have been an awesome team.

I was so excited when we drafted him. I thought, "Oh boy, here we go. We're on a roll now. We've finally gotten a player who can give me a break."

If you believe in omens, the Bias thing was a pretty bad one. Nothing that year really went right for us after that. I wasn't back in Boston very long when I heard that Bill Walton had broken his finger in a pickup game. That wasn't so bad, since he was only going to be out a couple of weeks, but that wasn't the end of the story.

One day Bill told us his foot was killing him. He was riding the stationary bike and something happened. It wasn't the foot that had been operated on, but the *other* one. That was something that could only happen to Bill. I still can't really believe he hurt himself just by riding on the stationary bike. I think something in the foot was ready to go and riding the bike aggravated it. But it's still a Bill Walton classic, isn't it?

We wound up waiting a long time for Bill, who didn't start playing until March. Even then, he was in, he was out; he was in, he was out. He helped us out in the first round of the playoffs against Chicago, but he hurt himself again in the next series and really struggled in the finals against L.A. The final game in Los Angeles was the last time he ever played in an NBA game.

Not having Bill anymore changed a great many things on the Celtics. We had gotten used to having Bill relieve Robert the year before and now that job belonged to Greg Kite. He had been a great eleventh or twelfth man for us and we all respected him because he worked so hard, but he wasn't Bill Walton, not by any means.

I always felt that Greg could help us—even with his limitations. The biggest problem he developed over the years was his foul shooting, which really deteriorated to the point where it became a big joke to the fans and the press. He asked me about it one day and I said, "Greg, all you have to do is have someone take a film of you in practice, as opposed to what you do in the games. You'll see for yourself what you're doing wrong."

But when Greg went to the line, he could hear everyone giggling and hissing. Once something like that gets planted in your mind and you keep reading and hearing about it, you can't forget it.

The press was really on him. We always tried to watch out for each other and we tried to protect him, but there was only so much we could do.

K.C. really stuck by him. I understand why. When you come to practice and the first thing you see is Greg Kite on the floor working on his game, you're impressed. An hour after practice, he's still out there. That's the kind of guy you want on your team. If Bill Walton were still here, Greg Kite would also still be here because he is an ideal tenth, eleventh or twelfth man on anyone's team.

But he had to become an eighth, seventh or even a sixth man that year and it didn't suit him as well. Robert needed his rest and Greg became the backup center.

Our problems that year started when Len Bias died and it seemed as if they never stopped. Bill got hurt. Danny hurt his back and wasn't able to start the season. Scott Wedman had a problem with his heel and wasn't able to play until the

end of November. He played in six games and then went
back on the injured list and never played for the Celtics
again.

The great Green Team that used to play us head-to-head
every day in practice the year before was down to Jerry
Sichting. We had picked up Fred Roberts and Darren Daye,
but without Bill Walton there was no Green Team to speak
of.

Once Danny got back in the lineup, we still had our starting five—and no one could match that. We were winning at
our usual pace and it seemed as if we were going to survive
all right.

The big story that year was Kevin McHale. He peaked in
the first three or four months of the season. He was absolutely unstoppable. No one in the league could stop him and
Kevin knew it.

We were all having a blast with it. We'd just go to Kevin
and never worry about it. Anytime we needed two points, we
just went to Kevin. He was scoring around thirty every
night, just doing whatever he wanted. I really thought at the
time he had a great shot at winning the MVP Award.

Guarding Kevin at that time was a lost cause. If you could
get the ball to him in his spot down on the blocks, no one
could do anything about it. I have always said that Kevin
could have been an MVP any year he put his mind to it. He
has every tool. He's got those long arms, he can shoot and he
can block shots. He can pass the ball a lot better than people
think he can. If he sees a double-team or if he sees people
moving without the ball, he can get it to them. If he wants to
get eight assists, he can get eight assists.

Kevin can do everything great except dribble the basketball. I've always told him he looks like a baby deer on ice
when he dribbles.

Kevin has the best low-post moves I've ever seen. He
really can't do much with his left hand, but it really doesn't
matter, since he can make all his right-handed moves going
either right or left. About the only person who could bother
his shot is Manute Bol, who's the first player I ever saw who
could block it.

Kevin has always liked to have fun playing the game. If

he's not having fun, he really isn't into the game. There's a lot of Maxwell in him. There were times he'd say, "Let's go out and beat them by halftime"—and we would do it.

Things were going great for him until one night in a game against Phoenix when Larry Nance accidentally stepped on his foot. Kevin tried to pull it out from underneath Nance's and he broke the bone. Things were never quite the same for Kevin after that.

We were doing all right as a team right up to our annual West Coast and Texas trip that takes place after the All-Star Game. We were basically doing it with the starters, plus some help from Fred, Darren and Jerry, but the starters were getting most of the minutes. We were still playing like the Celtics, though.

Then we suddenly stopped winning on the road.

I think everything just caught up with us at once. Teams had always been gunning for us, but we had always had enough weapons to get the job done. Now too many of our weapons were sitting on the bench in street clothes or weren't playing the way they could. That includes me because my back started to act up again.

It all came out of nowhere. We were playing the Clippers one night in Boston and after our morning shootaround at the Celtics' practice gym at Hellenic College, I went home to do some work in the yard. I had the leaf blower out and when I was done I put it back, then I swept out the garage. Then I got into my Jeep to pull the leaf blower back into the garage and—*bam-o*—my back started to hurt.

I knew I was in trouble. Dinah had cooked a big meal and all I could think about was getting upstairs to bed. The sweat was pouring off my head and I was in agony. I finally made it up the stairs and into bed and then I couldn't move at all. Dinah called Dan Dyrek. Dan came over to examine me and he said, "No way tonight."

I watched the game on TV. It was a typical Kevin game, in that we got them down by twenty right away. That made me feel a little better.

But from that point on, I was just not the same player for the rest of the season. I was always worrying: "What if my back goes out in the playoffs?" I worried about it all the time. I'm sure that the other teams sensed that we had lost it because we began struggling badly on the road. We kept talking about it and talking about it, but we just didn't have the ingredients to do anything to fix it. All the bad events that had begun with Len Bias's death seemed to catch up with us at the same time.

2 8

B Y THE 1987 PLAYOFFS, we just weren't comfortable playing on the road anymore. Since opposing teams now sensed that they had a chance to beat us, the teams approached each game with a different attitude, making it that much tougher on us.

We actually did very well to win fifty-nine games that year. Winning sixty is always one of our goals, but we still had the best record in the Eastern Conference, which would give us the home court advantage for the playoffs, something that turned out to be crucial to our success. We knew we weren't the same team we had been the year before—how could we be, with Bill Walton an uncertain factor and Kevin McHale struggling with what turned out to be a broken foot?—but we couldn't dwell on our problems. This was our team, period. We knew we'd have to put the home court advantage to good use.

We drew Chicago in the first round again, but it didn't turn out to be the scare the previous year had been. We got some important help from Walton, who had come back to the lineup for the last three games of the regular season, and we were even able to complete a sweep in the third game without Kevin, who had come up with a sprained ankle on top of his already broken foot.

Bill looked a lot like his old self in the third Chicago game, but that turned out to be his last major contribution to the team. His foot started bothering him in the next series and at no time in the remainder of the playoffs was he ever able to play the way he wanted to.

We were going to play Milwaukee next and I knew we weren't going to have any trouble getting up for that series, not after what had happened in '83. Robert, Kevin and myself had never forgotten how it felt to be swept. If a team is good enough to do that to you, the respect is there. Always. We respected Milwaukee as a smart team, a team that was well coached by Don Nelson. We wanted to get rid of them as quickly as possible.

Right. We needed seven games to do the job and we had to come from eight or nine down in the final five minutes to win the seventh game in the Boston Garden. It turned out that we had *every reason* to respect Milwaukee.

The key game was the fourth. We were up, two games to one, but we still had this road thing hanging over us and we really needed that game.

Game four was one of the greatest games I've ever been in. Both teams played well from start to finish. We were tied after regulation and tied again at the end of the first overtime. We got a huge lift when Darren Daye came off the bench and made some big plays. We were up by a point after Darren hit two clutch free throws, but with nine seconds left Dennis Johnson missed a jumper and suddenly I found myself back on defense with John Lucas leading a fast break against me.

Lucas is a lefty all the way and when he takes it to his left he can kill you with a variety of shots. I saw Kevin kind of taking his time getting up the court and I yelled, "Get back! Get back!"

Kevin did make it back and now here came Lucas—full-blast. I figured he wanted to take it to the basket and draw a foul. I was thinking, "I've got to get him to go right." I was just inside the free throw line and I was hoping that Kevin would block the shot. Lucas did go to his right and he forced up an off-balance shot. I don't know whether or not Kevin got a small piece of it, but Lucas missed it. There was no time left on the clock. Meanwhile, Kevin came right down on Lucas and twisted his ankle, only we didn't know that at the time. We were all very busy celebrating an important victory.

We were now up, three games to one, and should have wrapped it up at home in game five. Instead, the Bucks took it right to us and beat us. There was more bad news to come out of that game. Now it was Robert with a sprained ankle. Now we had Kevin hurting, Robert hurting and, in effect, no more Bill Walton at all.

When we got to Milwaukee for the sixth game, there was a big news story coming out of Phoenix that had an effect on both Milwaukee and Boston players. A very dubious investigation of alleged gambling and drug use on the part of past and present Phoenix and Milwaukee players included the names of Jack Sikma and Paul Mokeski from the Bucks and our own Dennis Johnson, who had spent four years in Phoenix. In D.J.'s case, the only thing they could dredge up was supposed marijuana use about seven years earlier. D.J. denied everything, but the damage had been done. It always is, once your name is out there.

I went to D.J. and said, "I really feel bad for you. Don't let it bother you." But you know it does and it really upset D.J. To get accused of doing drugs is the worst thing that could ever happen to someone. When you know you are not guilty and they bring up stuff like that, it just destroys you. It really hurts.

All these stories came out on the morning of the game. Things were bad enough for us, since we had left Robert back in Boston so he could have treatment for his ankle. It's not that we were conceding the game, but you had to be realistic. We were better off taking our chances on a Friday night in Milwaukee without Robert and having a somewhat healthy Robert Parish at home before our great fans on a Sunday afternoon.

We went down with dignity, however, and our best player that game was Dennis Johnson. It might tell you all you need to know about him that on this trying day he went out and scored thirty-two points, more than in any previous game all season. (He would get thirty-three in our final game with L.A.)

As I said, we were down by eight or nine with five minutes to go on Sunday. Everybody was looking at each other and saying, "Let's just give one more big effort." We were in trouble. Robert and Kevin were still in severe pain. Then in the middle of the fourth quarter we also lost Danny Ainge when he banged up his knee in a collision underneath the basket.

All day long we had been doing the job on the offensive boards. It's probably the only reason we were in the game because Milwaukee was outplaying us in every other phase of the game. In this situation, we believed our best chance to win was to get the ball inside as much as we could and then crash the boards. That way, we would either get easier baskets or go to the line.

Paul Pressey was guarding me and he was in foul trouble. I kept taking him low because I knew he didn't want to foul out. I'm four inches taller than he is and should have an advantage in the low hole. He had no choice but to foul me in that situation and eventually he fouled out of the game.

The biggest sequence came when Sikma tried a turn-around from the left baseline, Robert blocked it and D.J. saved it for us by making a great hustle play, knocking the ball off Sikma out of bounds and getting it back to us.

Under all the circumstances, it was a great win.

We had survived that series, but we now had to face a Detroit team that was rested and healthy and we were going to be starting the series without Danny. Kevin and Robert weren't getting any healthier either. No one knew how much longer we could hang on.

With Jerry Sichting replacing Danny, we won the first two games at home. Then we went out to the Pontiac Silverdome, where I, for one, had *never* felt comfortable, and played two terrible games. They blew us out both times.

Let me clarify my feelings about playing in Pontiac. I never liked to shoot there. But I did like to play there because I love their fans. You'd go to Pontiac and they might have twenty or thirty thousand fans at the game. Once we played there before sixty-one thousand, the largest NBA crowd ever. The Piston fans are great. They're up on their feet, hollering, all the time. I've never had any problems in Detroit. I respect fans who support their team and the fans do just that in Detroit.

The writers all had plenty enough to write about after the third game on Saturday afternoon because Bill Laimbeer and I got into it—big-time.

The incident started when I was trying to score in close with Dennis Redman on me. I made a fake with the ball and got him up in the air. I knew the clock was winding down and I was trying to go around him. But his leg got caught on my shoulder and then Laimbeer grabbed me and took me down hard.

In my opinion, Bill knew exactly what he was doing. Any player respects another player who plays as tough as he does, but if someone takes that aggressive effort too far, any respect you have flies out the window and you feel as if he's crossed the line. I felt that Bill was deliberately trying to hurt me on that play and out of sheer frustration I threw the basketball at him. Even under those circumstances, I shouldn't have done that and of course I was kicked out of the game. When I got to the locker room, Robert was already sitting in there. K.C. had taken him out because his ankle was bothering him.

He said, "Is the game over already?"

I said, "Yeah."

I started taking my clothes off and he said, "Where are the other guys?"

I said, "I don't know. Maybe K.C. is having a meeting with them."

Then he catches on and says, "What did you do?"

I told him I got thrown out.

He said, "Laimbeer."

I said, "You got *that* right."

Robert just laughed.

The next game was more of the same, except this time instead of me fighting Laimbeer, Robert got into it himself.

It was in the second quarter and I really didn't see much of what came down.

Going through the lane one time early in the quarter, I saw Laimbeer plant an elbow in Robert's gut. I heard Robert say something to Laimbeer, something like: "Keep your elbows down."

Well, anyway, late in the second quarter I was going for the basketball when out of the corner of my eye I saw Robert punching Laimbeer and Laimbeer going down. Referee Jess Kersey was standing right there, but he didn't do anything about it.

Robert wasn't thrown out or anything. In fact, I believe a foul was called for something else that happened on that play. But after the game the tapes were sent to the league office and Robert was suspended for the sixth game. Jan Volk, who has a way with big words, said, "The consummate provacateur is still roaming the hardwoods." I took that to mean *he* didn't like Bill Laimbeer very much either.

Everyone remembers this game for the steal I made at the very end. We were definitely in trouble and Detroit was leading us by one. If we lost that game, we'd have been down, three games to two, going back to Pontiac, where we had absolutely been *pounded* twice the weekend before.

I had the ball in an isolation situation with Rick Mahorn on me. I was thinking, "Shoot or drive either way." I could make a quick move and then get a pull-up jumper or else if I saw a little daylight I could go all the way for an easy two.

I got around Mahorn and then I saw John Salley sliding over. Then I saw Rodman making a move, but I figured he'd never get there in time. I was thinking about just getting the shot up on the glass and then maybe getting the rebound. Well, Rodman got there and he blocked it cleanly and the momentum knocked me to the floor.

He didn't knock it off me, but they got the ball back when Jerry Sichting wasn't able to save it for us. He and Isiah were racing toward it and maybe he stepped out of bounds or something. But it was Detroit's ball, with a one-point lead, in any case.

The primary thing I was thinking was "Get up!" Because there was still time to do *something*. Jerry was still trying to extricate himself from the stands (his momentum had carried him out of bounds) and everyone seemed to be scattered all over the place when the referee handed Isiah the ball for the throw-in. The Pistons could have called time—I believe their bench was screaming for one—but they didn't.

I saw Laimbeer open down low and I automatically headed toward him. Isiah lobbed one to Laimbeer. At the last instant, I reached in and just barely tipped it. I was trying to get control of the ball while practically falling out of bounds on the left baseline and I was just getting ready to throw it up when I saw a blur, a white jersey streaking down the lane.

The blur was Dennis Johnson. I passed it to him and he laid it in with Joe Dumars on his back. If D.J. hadn't made the cut down the lane, we would have been dead ducks. I couldn't get my feet positioned right. I didn't really want to shoot it, but there wasn't much time left, so I would have had to. D.J. reacted perfectly. A lot of players would still be standing there. I *might* have made the shot, but who knows?

I felt very lucky and very grateful. We couldn't shake those guys. The Pistons played us with a lot of confidence in that fifth game. They felt they were definitely good enough to beat us. I don't think they honestly believed that when the series started, but by that point things had changed.

The sixth game was a formality. We didn't have Robert and we weren't playing well enough on the road to win a game in a place like the Silverdome. They took us apart once again, setting up our second consecutive seventh game at the Boston Garden.

The seventh game with Milwaukee was tough, but this one was even tougher. It seemed as if neither one of us could ever go up by more than three or so the whole game. We couldn't put them away until Danny hit a jumper to put us up by three with twenty-five seconds left, but the big play had come around the three-minute mark when we were really pounding the boards and got *six* shots in one sequence before Danny hit a three-pointer to break the last tie.

Detroit may have been just plain unlucky because they were hanging right in there late in the third quarter when Vinnie Johnson and Adrian Dantley banged heads while going for a loose ball. A.D. went to the hospital and Vinnie was virtually useless after that.

With Dantley out, the Pistons put Dennis Rodman on me in the fourth quarter. I didn't know much about Rodman, but he got our attention with his hot-dogging.

I remember fooling around against Detroit during an exhibition game before the season. I was standing out at the three-point line with the ball and Rodman, who was supposed to be guarding me, was switched up on somebody else. I hollered at Isiah, "When are you going to come after me?" But nobody did. Finally Rodman came running at me and I shot the ball and it went in. I said to Isiah, "Does that rookie know how to play defense?"

After the game I was talking to Isiah and he said, "Rodman is going to be a good player, Larry. He just has a lot to learn."

The truth is, I have always had a lot of respect for Dennis. I could tell right away there was something different about him. He had a great attitude toward the game. He had that streak of hot dog in him, but he also had a way of getting his crowd into the game and there's nothing wrong with that.

I felt Dennis might be two years away. But I knew he'd make it because he has the tools, because he's got good coaching and because playing with Isiah would help him. He's gotten where I thought he'd be much quicker than I anticipated.

Now Rodman was guarding me in the fourth quarter of what was the most important game of the year. Earl Strom was refereeing and Rodman was all over me. I turned and looked at Earl and said, "You'd better get him off me or I'm just going to have to score on him." Earl just smiled.

When the game was over and we had won by three, I thought it was a typical postgame situation for an important playoff game, no more and no less. The press crowd began to fade away and as things were winding down I can remember heading toward our training room when four or five writers came up to me with reports of things Rodman and Isiah had said about me.

Apparently Rodman had said I was overrated because I was white and Isiah, when asked to respond to that, had laughed and said if I was black, I'd be just another "good guy."

That didn't mean anything to me. I said, "Hey, this isn't Russia. They can say whatever they want. It's a free country."

I really didn't think anything of what Isiah said. I knew he was upset because he is a great competitor and he had come out on the losing side of a very tough series. I knew how he felt. It just went in one ear and out the other.

Having had reason to think about it a lot, the whole thing just demonstrated some immaturity on Rodman's part. Rodman had no clue what was going on, since it was just his first year in the league. He was just mouthing off.

When I walked out of the locker room that day, I wasn't thinking about any of that. We had a little celebrating to do after beating the Pistons and we had to start getting ready to play the Lakers. The important thing to me was that we were getting a chance to defend our championship, not what I considered to be the irrelevant remarks of Dennis Rodman and Isiah Thomas.

That's why I was astonished when this thing became the biggest nonplaying sports issue in the country. Here we are, trying to prepare for the finals against Los Angeles, and all anyone wanted to talk about was what Isiah Thomas said about what Dennis Rodman had said about me. All over the country, writers and broadcasters were taking sides. *Rodman's a jerk. Rodman's not a jerk. Isiah's a racist. Isiah's not a racist. Bird's overrated. Bird's not overrated.* Sociologists and political columnists were jumping into it. It was completely crazy.

We were having a team meeting in the hotel in L.A. when the phone rang. K.C. picked it up and it was Isiah, wanting to apologize! He said it was all taken out of context. At this point, I *still* didn't know how big it was.

I should have. Everywhere we went we heard it. But I couldn't believe it because it didn't mean that much to me. To me, it was just something said in the heat of battle.

But when Isiah called me at the hotel in L.A., I *knew* he was in trouble. I said, "Don't worry about it. If there is anything I can do to help you out, I will because I know how it

is." He said, "I'm sorry." I said, "One thing you'd better do
. . . you'd better call Mom." Mom has always been an I.U. fan
and she always loved Isiah and thought he was the neatest
little guard.

The league brought Isiah to L.A. for a press conference
and they asked me if I would go out there with him. I said,
"No problem." It was no big deal to me.

Isiah and I met and we entered the room together. I had
never seen so many people crammed into a room. Right then
and there, I finally realized how big this thing was.

They started asking questions and a lot of them were
pretty good. I began to sense how intense this whole thing
was and I thought, "This is getting *serious*."

I told the press once again that what was said didn't
bother me and if it didn't bother me, it shouldn't bother anyone else. It was directed at me, but it did not bother me or my
family. A guy was beaten in a big game. He was disappointed. He said something. He says he was misquoted, so
why not leave it at that? I told them that everything was
squared away between Isiah and myself, so what more was
there to say?

The questions started coming at Isiah and the press
wouldn't stop. Poor Isiah was getting in deeper and deeper. I
thought, "I've heard all I need to hear." I said to everybody
that I had said everything I had to say on the issue and that I
had to start thinking about playing the Lakers. That's when
I got up and left.

The key element in the whole affair was that Isiah should
never had gotten sucked into commenting on what was said
by a rookie. Rodman can blow off steam and nobody will notice. But a player of Isiah's stature should have known better, in the sense that everyone will pay attention to a
superstar's quotes. The bigger you become in this league, the
more careful you have to be. I learned that lesson the hard
way a few times and Isiah just wasn't careful enough.

But that wasn't the only controversy. By this time people
were well aware that Kevin was playing on what was technically a broken foot. Kevin had gone for an examination
during the Chicago series and they told him he had a broken

navicular bone, but he could play on it and have an operation following the season.

Writers and people with microphones and cameras were running around talking to Kevin and to Dr. Silva, our team physician, and Dr. Silva tells them it is up to Kevin, whether or not he wants to play. He actually said, "I don't know whether Kevin should be playing or not."

The press came to me for a comment. I always try to say what I feel and I said, "They should have told Kevin that back in Chicago. I don't think he should be playing. There is too much of a risk." I really felt bad for Kevin.

By this time it wasn't easy to concentrate on the job, which was to beat the Lakers. I'm not saying I didn't think we could win, but it was difficult to get in the right frame of mind, given all the distractions.

But I *was* very proud of the team. After all we had been through, the team was still together. Kevin was hurt. Robert was hurt. Danny was coming off that sprained knee. I told myself that maybe one good thing would finally happen and we would be able to pull together and win the championship.

We had come off two very emotional series in which our fans were absolutely the greatest they had ever been. We wouldn't have won the seventh games against Milwaukee and Detroit without the home court advantage. The fans really did their job. It had been a very frustrating year because it had begun with Len Bias dying and there had been injury after injury after injury, but it was also the most gratifying year because guys were falling down and being picked up by someone else. Everything seemed to be going wrong the whole year, but the fans were really behind us and that gave us an extra incentive to keep going and going. I was really hoping we could reward them with a title.

We were tied, one game apiece, in the championship series against the Lakers. At this point, Magic Johnson and I had each won three championships and there was nothing I relished more than having a chance to go head-to-head with him for the big prize.

This was the year Magic won his first MVP, which I

thought was long overdue. I had always felt while I was winning my MVPs that I wasn't any better than he was. This particular year Magic was asked to provide more scoring and he did. He was putting up fantastic numbers and doing whatever he wanted. He was always improving—and he's still improving. Just last year he improved his three-point shooting and he won the free throw championship.

We had been linked in the public's mind ever since the 1979 NCAA final, but we really didn't know each other until he came to French Lick to do a Converse commercial with me. Now we understand each other a lot better.

We messed around that day. I got him to drive the four-wheeler around and he had never done anything like that before. Our relationship really blossomed that day because it was the first time we had ever really sat down and talked.

If we had grown up together or if we were teammates, I think we'd have been best friends. I have always admired the way Magic handles himself. I feel he's the greatest all-around team player in basketball. I have always looked up to him because *he knows how to win*. I've always put him a step ahead of me. (I never include myself in the "best player" discussion because I can only watch myself play on films. I always feel: "I practice so much. I'd *better* be good.")

Magic plays basketball the way I think you *should* play basketball. We think the same way about the game. We look at such-and-such a player and say, "If he was on my team, I could make *him* a great player." Well, maybe not *make* him one, but sort of bring out the best of his abilities. We've reflected on that experience when we played on the same All-Star team in college.

Both of us want to bring out the best in our teammates. We also want the fans to be involved in the game. Without them reacting, it just wouldn't be as much fun.

Magic plays to the strength of every teammate. The Lakers have a great team and they would be very good without him, but he is the special ingredient that brings them championships.

Magic and his teammates have also benefited from having Pat Riley as a coach because they are always very well prepared. They're a lot better when they've had time to prepare, which is why they're so good at playoff time. Riley makes subtle changes to keep you off-guard.

If you have a good playoff game against the Lakers, the next game isn't so easy. Riley makes a few key adjustments. I've always worried about coaches like Pat Riley. You hear people say, "In this league, you don't even need a coach." Not true. Pat Riley is the type of coach you have to watch out for. But it is also true that there are certain coaches you never have to worry about. You could score fifty points against their team every night.

The Lakers learned a lot from the loss in '84. They've developed the attitude we *used* to have. When we had our great teams, we remembered every loss. The next time we played that team, we wanted to bust 'em. If we lost a game, the players would say, "What went wrong tonight? The next time we play them, it won't happen again." And it wouldn't.

The Lakers are that way. They learn from their own mistakes. We beat them by being physical in '84 and all of a sudden L.A. was physical in '85. Now they can play either way. If you're a finesse team, L.A. can beat you that way. If you're a physical team, they can get *very* physical with you.

When we played them in '87, they were a better team than the year before—if only because they got Mychal Thompson. He put them over the hump, the way Bill Walton had put us over the hump the year before. Mychal also had one very big added extra value—he plays Kevin McHale as well as anyone. They had two key matchups where they weren't losing anything. They had Michael Cooper to play me and they had Mychal Thompson to play Kevin.

We played hard and we had our chances—we should have won the fourth game—but they beat us in six games and won the 1987 championship.

They won the first two games and made us look bad. When the Lakers are going well and everyone on the team is fast-breaking, every rebound seems like a steal. It seems as if you're *always* trying to get back on defense and there are guys flying at you from every direction. I think they had us feeling a little sorry for ourselves when they destroyed us in the first two games at the Forum.

We won the third game and it was a special game because it was the highlight of Greg Kite's career. Robert got in foul trouble during the second period and when we put Greg in to replace him everything seemed to turn in our favor.

He never scored a point, but that didn't matter. He put his body on Kareem Abdul-Jabbar and made Kareem take shots he didn't want to take. Greg didn't really take Kareem out of his game, but he harassed him and that was enough to help us. Greg was all over the boards, he was setting picks and he even blocked one of Magic's shots, which really excited the crowd.

He was the player of the game and when it was over he was standing out in the middle of the Garden floor, holding court for the press, and he was all smiles. If ever a guy worked hard and deserved a moment like that, it was Greg Kite. I was really happy for him.

We blew game four. We were up by sixteen in the third and we knew they'd make a run at us because they always do. We were still leading by two when I hit a three-pointer and when Kareem missed the second of two foul shots with seven seconds left, we should have been in good shape. But Kevin couldn't quite control the rebound. The ball went out of bounds and back over to L.A.

Wouldn't you know, Magic gets the ball, drives across the lane and throws in a hook shot over three of us. I had the last shot—a three-pointer from the corner—and it looked good. But it wouldn't stay down and they had beaten us to go up, three games to one.

I'll always remember that shot. I had gotten by James Worthy and I had a pretty clear shot at the basket. Just when I released it, I heard Wes Matthews on their bench and he was yelling, "Don't! Oh God, don't go in!" The ball went in and out.

We won the fifth game at home, but I can honestly say the Lakers were only thinking about getting back home and having two shots at wrapping it up in the Forum. If we had won game four, they might have approached game five differently. They didn't seem to have the desire to make the kind of effort that got them back into the fourth game.

When we got out to L.A. for the sixth game, they were just too much for us. They put it away with an eighteen to two run in the third quarter. D.J. went out with his head high, scoring thirty-three and getting ten rebounds, but the rest of us weren't up to his level.

I certainly didn't help the team at all. I had some good shots, but I couldn't get the ball to drop. We actually had a ten-point lead in the first half and we would have been way ahead if I was doing anything at all. I figured I was due to hit in the second half, but I was never a factor in the game.

Everyone said, "With all the injuries, you never really had a chance to win the title," but anytime you are in the finals and you lose, you feel you've given the championship away. I thought about game four and how we would have won if we had gotten one more rebound. Earlier in the year we lost a game in Atlanta because the same thing happened. We lost another one in Cleveland the same way.

I remember walking into the postgame press conference and saying the better team had won. I thought our team had shown a lot of character and guts because we had battled back from so much adversity.

But we still had a decent chance to win a championship, which is all you can ever ask for. I just wasn't happy with the way we had played. How could you get that far and lose by missing the rebound of a free throw? The *way* we lost the finals took away a little of the satisfaction we had gotten from beating Milwaukee and Detroit. Yes, over all it was a good year and yes, we had a lot to be proud of, especially without having a healthy Bill Walton. We felt good about our team, but it's not the same feeling as winning a championship.

29

I WAS LOOKING FORWARD to the 1987–88 season. I had a new body and a fresh outlook. I couldn't imagine we'd have the same trouble with injuries we had the year before. I'm usually optimistic about the Celtics before a season starts and I had every reason to think we'd be back in the finals, competing for another championship.

Like every athlete, I learned about the value of real conditioning the hard way. When I was younger, I could snap back from an injury like *that*. If I had sprained my ankle, two days later I was ready to go again. As time goes on, you sprain an ankle and it's still stiff a month later.

Every off-season was the same. I'd go home, eat a lot and worry about getting in shape when training camp arrived. I'd go up to 240 pounds or more. I'd be in pretty good shape because I'd run every day, but I wasn't doing myself any favors. In the back of my mind, I knew this would have to change someday and Dan Dyrek was the one who convinced me that the time had come. Looking toward the summer of 1987, he said to me, "You've *got* to change your lifestyle. Once you get to thirty, it is hard to get that weight off."

I knew the day was coming when I'd have to pay attention to my body. When I was sixteen, seventeen, eighteen . . . who needs to stretch? Even when I went to college, I noticed that it would take just a little longer to warm up. Now I'll ride a bike or jog awhile and be stiffer than heck. But a lifestyle is hard to change.

If I was going to listen to anyone, it would be Dan Dyrek. He had already saved me from missing a lot of games by helping me with my back and elbow. I was heading for all kinds of trouble in both those departments.

Dan set up a diversified summer program for me. It was designed so I wouldn't get bored. One day I'd concentrate on weight lifting. The next day I might be running distance. Another day might be a combination of the two. There were strenuous exercises. After I got into it awhile, I really enjoyed it.

I was very faithful to the program that summer—I still am—and there was a definite change in my body. Dan came to Indiana in August of '87 to check me out and as soon as he walked in he said, "I can't believe the difference."

When I started playing serious basketball in August of that year, I could tell the difference on the court. I just felt better all around. I was quicker and I could jump a little better. I felt lighter on my feet. I've always said, "If I feel good, I'll play well." That's the way it was for me at that point.

When the exhibitions started, I was shooting the ball well. When people came up on me, I was able to get around them easier. I was driving better and more often.

If anything, I was *too* light. I weighed around 213 and I decided I'd have to gain a little weight for the regular season.

I felt good about the team, but I would have felt a lot better if Kevin was in uniform. The broken foot had been operated on in June. The doctors had put a pin in it and he wasn't ready to return. Fortunately we did have Fred Roberts and we also had three rookies who could help us in Brad Lohaus. Mark Acres and Reggie Lewis.

We played well in training camp, but there was a mild shock in store before it was over when the Celtics traded Sam Vincent and Scotty Wedman to Seattle for a draft pick and money. Management had a numbers problem and felt that this was the best way to solve it.

Scotty had never fully recovered from the heel injury. Sam had shown some promise, but he was never a favorite of K. C. Jones, who appeared to think Sam wasn't prepared to work hard enough to become a solid NBA player.

Very often a young player must be very patient and this

was hard for Sam. K.C. wanted Sam to work extra-hard and make sure that every day at practice he was the first one to arrive and the last to leave, but that just wasn't Sam's style.

I tried to show the young big men what to expect, particularly Lohaus. Everyone was teasing Lohaus about this and that and sometimes he took it to heart. Brad's a seven-footer with more of an outside game than an inside game and he initially encountered some defensive matchup problems. But I really believed in him because he can run, shoot and catch the ball. He can also block some shots.

I would take him out to eat and tell him to keep working hard. I'd say, "When you guys see K.C., Chris and Jimmy leave after practice, don't think they don't know who's staying around. Stay out there and show them you're willing to work hard."

The one thing I tried to stress with Brad was how to make the most of his time. The reason I get to the arena very early and do my shooting before anyone gets there is simple: I accomplish more by myself, just me and a rebounder who isn't into chitchat. It's hard to establish a routine when you're a rookie because you've got so many new thoughts on your mind.

It's just like off-season practice. I get so much more accomplished by myself. My theory is that if two people can work out together for an hour and take maybe two hundred shots apiece, one person can put up four hundred shots if the other player just rebounds. Even if you're by yourself and have to rebound your own ball, you can put up three hundred.

The season started well enough without Kevin, but I knew that once he did come back there would be problems with whoever took his place with regard to playing time.

The effects of the new Bird body were evident immediately. I scored over forty twice in the first four games and I don't know how I could have played much better in general. We had a terrific double-overtime game in Washington the second night of the season. I had forty-seven points, including a twenty-foot runner at the buzzer to win it.

It's a good thing we won that game because a very unfortunate yell by K.C. could have lost it. It was real late in one of the overtimes and I was coming upcourt with the ball when I decided to pull up for a three-pointer. As I was shooting the ball, I heard a whistle and what had happened was that K.C. had called a time-out. The shot was good, but it didn't count.

K.C. went, "Oh no." He was just trying to set up a good play and it really wasn't a good shot, but I was hot all night long. I was open and I felt it. Really, what can you do in a situation like that but laugh?

Even without Kevin, we were doing well. Fred Roberts and Darren Daye were playing well (as soon as the exhibitions ended, K.C. stopped playing the rookies) and we won our first six games.

Then we arrived in Cleveland—or should I say Richfield Township? It was the second quarter and we weren't playing very well, but it was still too early to think we couldn't win the game.

All I remember is coming upcourt on a fast break. I was at midcourt when someone on the Cavaliers went for a steal and I tried to avoid it by dribbling behind my back. As soon as I turned, *both* Achilles tendons popped.

It felt worse than a sprained ankle. I knew I was in very serious trouble because, after they had calmed down a little bit and I was just standing around, the tighter they got.

Here I had done all this off-season work in order to avoid injury to my back and to just generally make myself a better athlete and now something freaky like this had happened. It was scary. By the time I got to the locker room, it felt just as if someone had stabbed both my heels with a knife.

I did try to start the third quarter but after a couple of trips up and down the floor I couldn't continue. I would miss four games, but the heels wouldn't really loosen up and permit me to play the way I wanted to for the next three months.

I've only seen the replay once. My body was going one way and my feet were stationary on the floor. I really didn't get to pivot. I sort of stopped dead on a dime and then I tried to take it behind my back and go the other way. I could see my whole body just twist and my ankles just staying there. It was just a freak play.

It seemed to take forever for the things to heal so I could

play. For the next couple of months, I'd be out on the court and I could feel the tendons tightening as the game progressed. The pain never really went away. I couldn't get up on my toes and take off running. I fought that until the middle of February.

I am not a very good interview when I get injured. The press wants to know how things are going on a daily basis, but I don't deal very well with the situation.

I am just not into talking about injuries. My mood changes completely. It's not easy going from being able to play this game—and play it well—to a situation where you're struggling all the time. You want to play and you want to do the best you can, but you can't perform up to your capabilities.

Kevin came back in the beginning of December and it only took him a few games to become "Mr. Automatic" in the low post again. Things kind of settled in. Danny was going wild with three-pointers, D.J. was having his normal year and I was scoring all right, even though the injury wouldn't let me be the kind of player I wanted to be.

I was in the All-Star Game again and early in the season I said there was no doubt about who would be the MVP of the All-Star Game that year.

That's exactly what happened. Michael Jordan scored forty points and got the MVP Award to go along with the slam-dunk prize he had won the day before.

I never had any intention of trying to score much in that game. I saw my role as that of setting picks and helping distribute the ball. We were all trying to help Michael put on a great show for his hometown fans in Chicago, which he did.

The All-Star Game has come a long way since I started out. They used to have a banquet where we all had to stand on a big stage. It always made me feel like some kind of animal in a zoo. Now the All-Star Game has been turned into a whole weekend of special events, which gives a lot more players the opportunity to participate, such as the three-point contest, the slam-dunk contest and the Old-Timers' Game, where players such as Calvin Murphy and John Havlicek show us they've still got it. The All-Star Game is a lot more fun now. The league has done a great job with the whole concept.

Guards ought to be the All-Star MVPs, since they control the ball. It generally comes down to whomever scores a lot of points and that always bothers me. Of the nine games I've played in, Magic probably should have been the MVP in six of them. And he hasn't won any!

It still bugs me that after all this time so many people look at basketball and all they see is points. I have seen players have great games and wind up scoring ten or twelve points. I have always been partial to players with a total game and I'll always believe that the best players are the well-rounded ones.

The one thing lacking on the Celtics that year was depth. We thought we had solved the problem to a degree with the addition of the rookies, but K.C., like many coaches, wouldn't give the rookies much playing time. Meanwhile, the Celtics had waived Greg Kite and we had a definite hole at backup center.

One day Red came in and said we had a chance to get Artis Gilmore and what did I think? I said, "We've got to get *someone* who's experienced who can come in and play ten or twelve minutes behind Robert." I felt that Artis could be that person because I knew he was good at setting picks and getting rebounds.

I knew Artis played a stationary game, a lot more so than most people. I was prepared to adapt to that. The key, to me, would be explaining to Artis exactly what we needed from him—no more and no less.

I have always liked Artis. I had met him years before at a camp one summer and he just kind of took me under his wing.

The first time I ever ate oysters was with Artis. He had six dozen as an appetizer! He said, "My record is nine dozen. Or maybe even a dozen dozen." The guy is seven-feet-two and weighs 240, but wow, six dozen oysters for an *appetizer*?

I was really impressed because at the time he was a big star and I was just a nobody. Artis taught me a lesson once.

He told me how he had once picked out new tires for his car and when he went to pay for them the guy said, "No, that's all right." Artis said, "I don't operate like that. If some poor man comes in here and needs tires or some gas, you wouldn't give it away to him. So I feel I should pay too." I felt that if I ever made it big and got to his stature, I'd want to be the same way.

When Artis joined the Celtics, I did my best to motivate him. He wanted it real bad; I'm sure of that. And he liked being with us. One day after practice Artis said, "I haven't had the ball this much in the last five years."

He had this little dip-in move he loved and it was hard for us to get used to it. As far as we were concerned, all Artis had to do to be effective was take a power hook or just move in and stuff it.

I said to him, "You'll have an opportunity to score on this team. Just make sure you try to stick to our style of play. You do that and miss, nobody will say anything. If you start taking the ball and dipping under people, they're going to slap it away."

I thought Artis could be a dominant force and I tried to get the ball to him as much as possible.

You had to concentrate on what you were doing when playing with Artis. People thought his hands were bad, but they were okay if you followed some basic rules. It wasn't the same as passing the ball to Robert or Bill. You had to throw it right at him—nothing fancy. You had to look at him and the ball had to be right on target. If you threw a bounce pass, it had to be an easy one, so he could get the ball and go to the basket. If you passed it right to him, you had to make sure he didn't have to jump to get it (something Robert is particularly good at). Everyone in this game has their own style of play and anytime a new player joined us it was up to us to identify their individual moves and make appropriate adjustments.

3 0

SOME PEOPLE SAY THINGS always even up in this league, so maybe that's why I've spent so much time getting injured in the past few years after going along playing eighty-two games a season for so many years earlier in my career.

Just about the time my heels were starting to loosen up and stop hurting so much, I came up with a broken nose.

It was just one of those things that happen now and then in the NBA. We were in Denver during our annual trip following the All-Star Game. I was coming off a forty-nine-point game in Phoenix and in a basically good frame of mind when I was driving along the right baseline in the second quarter at McNichols Arena. Blair Rasmussen came over to help out and he accidentally got me on the nose with his elbow.

I *knew* my nose was broken. It was all pushed over and my head was all fogged up. My eyes were watery. I had no animosity toward Rasmussen because you've got to take your shots in the NBA every now and then. There are lots of accidental injuries sustained in the normal flow of any game and this just happened to be one of them.

About two and a half weeks later, we were playing Cleveland at home on a Sunday afternoon when I was driving in around the same spot. Dell Curry came into the play and as he was jumping up to get the ball his elbow caught me in the face.

I knew there was something seriously wrong with my eye. He had caught me directly in the socket and I just couldn't see. When I looked up, I saw two baskets. One of them was just a little higher than the other. I went to the locker room, trying to shake it off. For the rest of the game, I was seeing two baskets.

I played the second half and scored more points than I did before I got hurt. I just tried to shoot a little higher to get it over the rim. The two baskets didn't look side by side to me. Instead, they were on top of one another. I aimed at the top one and things worked out okay.

The pain was intense and when I looked into the mirror there was an egg-sized bump on the outside of my eye and my eye was swollen shut.

I went to the doctor, who gave me some pills and said, "There is no way you can play until this thing starts to heal." Then we started discussing the goggles situation.

Nobody is ever wild about wearing goggles, but if I was going to play at all I had no choice but to wear them. I tried them at practice—I took maybe ten or fifteen shots—but right away I knew I hated them. I've got a lot of respect for the guys who wear them because I don't know how they can stand it. Goggles just get fogged up too much, plus they feel strange. I've never liked wearing glasses of any kind. I never even wore sunglasses until two years ago.

Ed Lacerte, our trainer, ordered the goggles for me. I walked into practice one day and he had them ready for me. They did make the basket look bigger, but since the ball looked bigger too, that was a wash. There was a constant glare and things looked brighter than normal.

I had to learn the ins and outs of goggle-wearing. I noticed that Moses Malone put his up on top of his forehead while shooting free throws, so I tried that. Occasionally I'd forget to put them back down while running down the court. Once Kevin had to yell to me, "Put your goggles down!"

Another time I threw them to Kevin when I got to the line. I had to run back over to get them and then take off the other way. There was one game when I was hitting everything from the field. I got to the line and forgot to push them up. I made the shot, then I pushed them up and missed the next one. A fan yelled. "Put the goggles back on. You can see better!" I'm just glad the experiment only lasted for four games. The funny thing is, as much as I hated them, I had four good shooting games, scoring thirty-six, thirty, twenty-eight and thirty-four while shooting fifteen for twenty-seven, twelve for twenty-four, thirteen for twenty-one and twelve for twenty-two from the field. The first game after I took them off, I shot eight for nineteen, for which I had no decent explanation.

The Celtics were essentially operating the same way we had the year before. The burden was mostly on the starting five. We went all the way to the finals in '87 by playing five men most of the time and it looked as if that was the way we'd have to do it again.

Fred Roberts started off well and he was a valuable player while Kevin was out. But Fred played consistently better as a starter than as a reserve and he wasn't as good a player for us after Kevin returned and he had to come off the bench.

Darren Daye has NBA ability; there is no question about that. But he was waived late in February of '88 after we got Jim Paxson from Portland in exchange for Jerry Sichting.

Despite our continuing depth problem and our so-so play on the road, we were still strong enough to dominate in the Garden and finish the regular season with the best record in the Eastern Conference once again. We figured that with the home court advantage in the conference playoffs we'd get to the finals for the fifth consecutive year and for the sixth time in my career.

For one brief period late in the season, we even thought we'd have Bill Walton back for the playoffs. When Bill first came back as a practice player, he was completely out of rhythm for a couple of weeks. Then he had a very good practice while we were in Chicago and we began to get excited. There was great speculation that he was going to be activated for a home game with New Jersey. But Bill walked into practice one day and said that his foot was hurting again.

Everyone on the Celtics was down again. We hoped Bill was going to give us that extra boost we needed, but it just didn't happen. (Little did I know that a year later I would be the one the team would be waiting for in exactly the same way.)

*   *   *

We were again seeded number one, but we didn't know who we'd be playing in the first round until the last day of the season when New York defeated Indiana to clinch the eighth spot. To be honest, I was hoping the Pacers would win, not only because it would have been fun to go home for a playoff game or two but also because the Knicks were coming on as a team and I knew their style of play would give us trouble. Rick Pitino had them pressing all the time and with the big minutes our starters would be playing, I thought we might be worn out by the time we got to the next round.

That's pretty much what happened. We beat the Knicks badly twice at home. (They didn't even press in the first game.) They won the third game in New York and we wrapped up the series by winning the fourth game with D.J. making the big fourth-quarter plays.

The big news in this series broke between the second and third games. We had just finished practice at Hellenic College the day before game three. After we had showered, K.C. asked us all to come into his office. I thought he was going to make us go down to New York that night instead of the day of the game and before he said anything I spoke up. "We don't want to go to New York tonight, Coach," I said. "Let's go tomorrow."

He said, "It's not that. It's something else." Then K.C. told us he was retiring from coaching after the playoffs and that Jimmy Rodgers would be taking over. We were all happy for Jimmy, who had been paying his dues as an assistant coach for over fifteen years, but the news that K.C. was retiring took us all by surprise.

From that point on, the Celtics had an extra incentive. We wanted to win the championship for K.C. Everyone on the team looked up to him and enjoyed playing for him.

I had always felt that K.C. stood back too much from the spotlight and allowed himself to be bypassed for many of the honors he should have received. K.C. was never voted Coach of the Year and I thought he deserved it a couple of times. In 1986 we had a great year, but they gave it to Mike Fratello. Not only that, but it was announced while we were down in Atlanta for a playoff game. I always respected Mike, but when they did that, I felt as if we were stabbed in the back. I reached over, grabbed K.C.'s hand and raised his arm in the air. We knew what kind of a coach he was. We had won two championships with him and were in the finals four straight years. What more can you say about the job he did?

I was very pleased to get by New York. I told people it was like being let out of jail on offense and I meant it. I never could get into a shooting rhythm against the Knicks and I believe I proved my point when I shot nine for nine and had twenty-four points in the first quarter of the first Atlanta game.

I've said before that when I think of certain teams I think in terms of an individual and in Atlanta that player is Dominique Wilkins. I first discovered what he was made of in 1983. He was a rookie and was thought of exclusively as an offensive player, but in our three-game miniseries he did a good job of guarding me. Dominique worked hard during that entire series and, believe me, he earned my respect.

Meanwhile, Dominique had become a much different—and better—offensive player. He's a better rebounder and passer than he used to be and he's also broadened his offensive game.

When Dominique gets hot, there's nothing you can do to stop him. People say he takes bad shots, but so do I. He definitely doesn't take as many as he used to and he has much more range than when he came into the league. He has become a three-point threat, whereas when he came into the NBA he was strictly a guy who would hurt you close to the basket.

As an acrobat, Dominique is even more interesting in many ways than Michael Jordan. While Michael takes the ball straight to the basket, Dominique loves to spin. He comes right at you and then does a 360-degree spin, right off the dribble. It's a totally *different* type of basketball than anything I've seen before.

The Atlanta Hawks had gained a great deal of poise and maturity since we had played them in 1986 and they proved it by beating us in the fifth game to take the series lead, three games to two, heading back to Atlanta. Given our depth situation and age, most people thought that was the end of the year for the Celtics, but we still had a little left in the old reserve tank because we went down there and won that sixth game to tie the series.

It was a great atmosphere in the Omni. There was a man walking around with a sign saying: WELCOME TO K.C.'S RETIREMENT PARTY, but we weren't quite ready for that yet. We had been in tough situations a million times and we still thought we could win—even if no one else did.

When the game was over, I did some talking. The Hawks had done some talking after beating us in the fifth game and now it was my turn. I said that they had "guaranteed" this and "guaranteed" that, but that they had blown their chance. When you can wrap it up at home, you should win. I said that now we were going back to Boston and it was *our* turn and *we* weren't going to blow it.

I think I can safely say that, considering the stakes, the seventh game against Atlanta in 1988 was one of the greatest games ever played in the history of the league. That's a big statement, but I think I can back it up.

There were only forty-two possible defensive rebounds in the entire game. Why? Because we shot 60 percent from the floor and the Hawks shot 57 percent. There were only fifteen turnovers between us. In the fourth quarter, each team scored on seventeen of twenty-two possessions. And if you think all this means the defenses weren't very good, you couldn't be more wrong. The defense was aggressive, both ways. It was just a high-level game from beginning to end and when it was over I had more respect for the Hawks than I ever had before. I was very grateful the final score was Boston 118, Atlanta 116.

In the fourth quarter, I got hot. Thank goodness. In a situation like that, what you *don't* want is everybody standing around watching you. You want everybody involved in the game, no matter how hot you are. I was looking for my shot first, yes, but I was still checking around to see if anyone else was open. Kevin also had a couple of key baskets down the stretch. He had a great game, scoring thirty-three and blocking four shots.

Robert was setting great picks. Dominique was guarding

me and whenever Robert would set a pick, Dominique would be trailing, which enabled me to get some shots off. We just kept running the same kind of plays until they reacted differently.

We had to keep scoring because the Hawks weren't letting up. Doc Rivers had come out firing, but the guy we couldn't do anything with was Dominique. In that fourth quarter, I wound up with twenty points and he finished with sixteen. That's sixteen out of forty-seven in a very big game. The game wasn't secure until Dominique went to the line with a couple of seconds left, trailing by three. He made the first shot and then deliberately missed the second, hoping the Hawks would get the rebound and an easy shot for the tie. But Robert knocked the ball over to D.J. and the game was over.

That's why I do all that shooting, in order to be able to have games like this. You want to feel in *control*. There is no better feeling than to be in control of a basketball game and know your shot's going to open up every other aspect of your game, as well as help other players. I remember thinking during that fourth quarter that with the way Dominique was shooting, I had to make *every* shot. I came close, since I was nine for ten.

That set up a rematch with Detroit for the Eastern Conference championship. We had the home court advantage and that gave us confidence, but we knew this was a better Detroit team than the one we had played the year before.

When we played Detroit back in '84, we had some trouble with them, but we never really worried about them because we always felt we could score whenever we had to. By '88, the Pistons had a completely different style and mentality. They were as deep as any team in the league and they had players who could really play defense. Players such as Joe Dumars, Dennis Rodman and John Salley gave them a new look and now they had added James Edwards, a seven-footer who could shoot and who had lots of experience. They had nine legitimate NBA players.

We were basically in trouble from the word "go." They beat us in the first game at home and put us on the defensive for the entire series. We did get even in the second game, 119–115, but it took two overtimes and a miracle shot by Kevin to put us in a position to win. We were down by three with five seconds left in the first overtime when D.J. passed me the ball. I was cutting the wrong way and it sailed by me, but it went right to Kevin, who was standing at the edge of the three-point circle, looking straight down the gut. He let it fly and it went in for his only three-pointer of the year!

We couldn't believe it. Kevin messes around with threes during practice a little, but not much. He had only hit one other three-pointer in his entire career. He deserved to make that shot more than any of us because he was playing great.

We lost the third game in the Silverdome and by this time there was one media and fan issue in the series: *What's wrong with Bird?* I shot eight for twenty in the first game, six for twenty in the second game and six for seventeen in the third game. Everyone in Boston wanted to find an excuse for me—back? elbow? ankles?—but injury had nothing to do with it. I was being defensed very well and I couldn't get into a good shooting rhythm. And when I did get a good shot—which wasn't often—I was just missing.

I knew my lack of offense was hurting the team, but in situations like that I've always prided myself on being a complete player. Knowing that I was having trouble on offense, I really concentrated on the boards and I had good assist totals.

The Pistons would start the game with Adrian Dantley on me. I am four or five inches taller than he is, but he was working very hard and he knew he would get help if I took him inside. Then I'd get Salley, a seven-footer, and then Rodman, who is about six-feet-seven and a very good defensive player (the second-best, in my opinion, behind Michael Cooper). They kept me off-balance all the time. You must give the Pistons credit.

It hurt me, of course. I'm looked upon as a scorer and I wasn't scoring. I have to take the blame. But I try never to worry about missing shots. When you're a shooter, you always have confidence that the next one will go in. I didn't lose self-confidence and I didn't get frustrated. I tried my best to be an all-around player who could help the team in as many ways as possible, which has always been my goal anyway.

From the beginning of my high school career, people said I couldn't run, couldn't jump and didn't play against strong competition. I still can't run or jump, but I can play. If I wasn't practicing my shooting, I would have felt guilty about it. But I knew I had done my work. It was just one of those things that happens. I was really pleased with the other aspects of my game (I averaged twelve rebounds and six assists a game), but my shooting was way off. I finished the series shooting 35 percent from the floor.

We didn't hand this series over. In fact, we won the fourth game in Pontiac by a bizarre 79–78 score. D.J. won it for us with a free throw, but what I remember most was Bill Laimbeer passing up an open shot and giving it to Dumars, who had to take a tough rainbow jumper that Parish rebounded. They asked me about the Laimbeer shot and I said that even if I had been zero for twenty-seven I'd have taken that shot. But I knew there was no way *he* was going to take that shot. It just isn't in Laimbeer's makeup.

We have always felt game five is *our* game. That's one reason I don't like the two-three-two format in the finals because the fifth game should be in the building of the team with the home court advantage. The old two-two-one format was much better, as far as I am concerned. Things looked great for us when we went up by sixteen in the third period, but the Pistons slowly got back into the game and we began to have more and more difficulty getting good shots against their defense.

I had two good chances to win the game for us in regulation, but Rodman stopped me both times. With thirty-four seconds left and the score tied, I thought I had a shot going down along the right baseline, but the ball didn't drop. The next time K.C. wanted me to pop out, get the ball, fake and drive. I made the fake, but Rodman didn't go for it. I started driving, but he cut me off. I was trying to keep track of the time in my head and I took a bad shot. Those were two great defensive plays by Dennis Rodman.

We lost in overtime and the series might as well have been over right there because when we went back to the Silverdome for the sixth game very little went right. We played all right for a half, but we lost Robert to a knee injury in the first quarter and eventually their bench killed us, which has been the case for the entire league for the last three years. Detroit's second team is equal or superior to most people's first team.

K.C. threw Brad in there and he played very well. That, at least, made me feel good because I had believed in Brad all year. Meanwhile, I closed out my miserable offensive series with a four for seventeen performance.

We weren't able to win that last championship for K.C. When it was over, he called us together and said, "Thanks a lot. I feel bad because we lost and I'm sure you do too, but I want to wish you all the luck in the world." I liked his style. He didn't go out with a bang.

There aren't many pro coaches like K.C. Jones, a true "players' coach." He always respected the wishes and feelings of the players. He played us a lot of minutes, so when we'd come to practice he'd say, "Are you tired? You don't feel like practicing today? Okay, you can rest. But don't take advantage of me."

He was completely different from Bill Fitch, whom I also admired. Fitch was demanding, while K.C. was laid-back. The atmosphere was more relaxed. There was more joking than ever. We always had a lot of fun. But when we stepped onto the court, we knew it was time to work.

K.C. didn't get angry very often, but there were things that irritated him. When he wanted your attention, he knew how to get it. But he was always conscious of not embarrassing anybody. He felt you should know when you were goofing off too much. We always had mutual respect and that's why things worked so smoothly on the Celtics when K.C. was the coach.

Technically speaking, the one thing K.C. hated the most was turnovers. And that's about it. He knew how we liked to kid each other, but if one player was getting on another too hard, K.C. would tell him he was going too far. His main objective was to keep everybody on the team pulling in the same direction.

The one thing he harped on me for was to get closer to the basket more often. At the same time, he gave me great offensive freedom. Once I was coming down on the break and the other team had two or three men back. I pulled up from about eighteen feet and as I was getting ready to shoot he yelled, "No no, wait for the guys!" Just as I released the ball, I said, "Too late, Coach." The ball hit nothing but net. K.C. just sat down.

K.C. welcomed player input. You could go to lunch with him and talk things over whenever it was necessary. We all wanted to play for him and win for him. Everybody on the team just thought so much of him.

I've always respected coaches anyway. I give them total respect because in basketball they are the law. To me, they're just like police officers. This all goes back to when I was starting to get interested in the game and I came under the influence of Jim Jones. Every suggestion he made to me paid dividends in the end. I found that if I worked at something, I'd get good at it and I figured that the man must know what he's talking about.

Coaches all have their own individual styles. You probably couldn't play for two people more diverse than Bill Fitch and K. C. Jones, especially back-to-back. Coach Fitch wanted to have his finger on everything. That was fine with me when I was starting out. I didn't know anything about the NBA. When K.C. came in, the atmosphere was different.

In general terms, you can't find a nicer man than K. C. Jones. You can't get more down to earth. The sequence of Celtic coaches was good for me because I learned a great deal from Bill Fitch and I was given the green light to put that knowledge to use by K. C. Jones.

31

I F THERE WAS EVER A YEAR I'd like to have back to do all over again and have it come out better, it was 1988–89. It was the most useless season of my career. I can't even call it a season. I played in eight exhibitions and six regular season games.

I'd been having problems with my ankles and heels for a long time, even before I wrenched both Achilles tendons on that freak play in Cleveland the year before. I hurt my left one around December or January of the 1986–87 season in a game at the Garden. I made a hard cut along the baseline and a sharp pain went through my ankle. It was stiff and sore and I struggled with it for about two weeks. I hurt it again at the end of that year while making another cut and it seemed to stay with me through the playoffs.

I knew something was wrong down there. When it was stretched properly to get it loose, it was all right. But it seemed as if that was taking longer and longer to happen.

Then came the accident in Cleveland early the following season. I was playing exactly the way I wanted to play, but when that happened I never really got over it all year. The tendons started to feel almost passable during the February West Coast trip and I was able to play through the pain. They'd hurt all day, but when the game started I'd run a little bit and put it out of my mind. But there was always the fear that one sudden cut might tear them or jar them.

But I never even considered having surgery done. I just saw the ankles as something I had to deal with. For the last couple of years, I haven't been able to practice or prepare myself the way I used to five or six years ago. Still, I assumed I could live with the situation.

*   *   *

By the time I got back to training camp in 1988, I was concerned about my new contract with the Celtics. The team and Mr. Woolf had been talking about it all summer, but it was still up in the air. There were some major problems in settling the contract because of the salary cap situation. I had meetings with Mr. Cohen, the owner of the team, while Mr. Woolf was talking directly to the league to work out some complex language that would abide by the salary cap rules but still allow me to receive a contract comparable to Magic's and Michael's. It took a long time, but thanks to everyone—Mr. Cohen, Jan Volk, Red Auerbach, Mr. Woolf and the legal counsel at the league office—an excellent contract was finally agreed upon that will take me through the 1990–91 season. I'm always happy at that point because I'm the kind of person who likes to know where I'm going to be for the next few years; security is very important to me.

In our first couple of exhibition games of the 1988–89 season, the ankles felt pretty good. When we went to Madrid to play against the Yugoslavians and Spaniards in the McDonald's Open, I began to have more problems. I wasn't able to loosen them up in our second game against Real Madrid.

I knew then I was in for real trouble. By the time I could get the left one stretched out and loose and then start on the other one, the first one would stiffen up again. There was also some swelling.

I still thought it was a matter of "playing through it," until we opened the regular season with a Friday night home game against New York, followed by a Saturday night road game in Philadelphia. We beat the Knicks in overtime and I had twenty-nine, but the only thing I could do was shoot and I don't even know how I was able to do that. The next night was a nightmare. I was running stiff-legged and my ankle never loosened up the whole game. Basketball was no longer any fun and I *knew* something had to be done.

The left was the one I had hurt originally, but in time the right one became the bigger problem. Before I left Boston in 1988, I had X rays taken of the ankles. When we took new X rays the following fall, you could see how much bigger the bone spur in the right one had grown. The difference was enormous. The final decision to have surgery came about after CAT scans were taken. That's when the doctors knew how serious the problem was.

The operation was performed on both heels on November 19 and there was talk of a March 1 return. I never made March 1—or any other date—last season. I came close. If we had made it to the second round of the playoffs, I could have played.

I did everything I possibly could to return. I was riding the stationary bike with my casts on two weeks after the surgery. I was swimming. I was weight lifting every day. It was all with an eye toward returning March 1—or as near to that as possible.

After a while I had a routine. I'd go to practice and have my ankles worked on by a therapist. Then I'd lift weights for an hour and a half. Next I'd shoot a little bit. When I was done with that, I'd go over to use the Boston University pool and swim for an hour or so. Then I'd go to the therapist again to have them stretched out. It consumed four or five hours a day. Here I was, putting in all this time and not even playing ball.

My left one healed quicker than the right. I tried to come back in the beginning of March, but the right one wasn't ready. There was pain and swelling and I had to back off.

By the end of the regular season, the left one was fine. If the right one eventually catches up to the left one—and there is every medical reason to think it will—the entire ordeal will have been worth it.

My problem in getting ready to play was not only the pain and swelling in the right heel but my conditioning. I was in good shape, but I was far from being in basketball shape. There is a huge difference between the two.

I knew from experience that whenever I missed as few as two days of practice, it was horrible coming back. It does not take much time to get out of proper playing shape. Even taking off two days means that when you come back you're completely dead in a short period of time; you're sucking air. If that's the case, can you imagine what it's like to sit out for months? It's unbelievable.

Working out with the team that week in March was revealing. I was rusty. You can work on your ballhandling, but when somebody is guarding you, it's completely different. The physical contact . . . the movement . . . nothing is there. Your skills are just not there when you're not in condition.

If you take a pretty good high school basketball player and put him out on the floor with nine NBA players, he'll be lost. He won't be used to the contact. The pace will be different. Coming back to a team in the beginning of March, I felt like that high school guy.

I now understand why they have training camp. I used to think training camp and exhibition games were a bunch of baloney. I know better now. Even after you start the season, it takes you six or seven games to *really* feel as if you're in shape. Trying to come back for playoff competition is even harder. If I had tried to play in the first round series against Detroit, I wouldn't have been of any real use to the team, but I would have been ten times better by the second round.

At first I was resigned to the reality of the situation. I knew that my return was a long way off and so I was able to go to the games and feel comfortable—if not exactly happy. But at the end it was harder and harder. The fans were expecting me back. I wanted to play and I couldn't. We had a big stretch of home games late in the season and going to those was very difficult.

I tried to be a vocal presence on the bench. That was my job: to offer encouragement, to give the team all the moral support I could. I know being there was the right thing to do, but it wasn't any fun. It's just too hard to watch when you can't play. At the end, it was taking a toll on me.

It was even tougher watching the Celtics play on the road because the team really had a difficult time. I *know* how tough it is out there and it's getting tougher all the time. When you're L.A., Boston, Detroit or another top team, people are always gunning for you. Road games tell you who the best players are. You've got to play twice as hard as you do at home. I believe you can tell a great player by his stats on the road. *Anybody* can play at home.

*   *   *

With me out, Reggie Lewis got a chance to play and he proved he was a great scorer. I was a Reggie fan from the day he joined the ball club. He's got a great scorer's mentality, he's very quick off the dribble and he's going to be a great player in this league for many years. Whether his immediate future is as a big guard or swingman, Reggie's going to be a star.

We still hadn't solved the depth problem we've had for three years, especially with me not being able to play. The Celtics tried to remedy that by trading Danny Ainge and Brad Lohaus to Sacramento for Ed Pinckney and Joe Kleine.

I hated to see Danny go. People on the outside never fully appreciated how much he meant to the team. Danny was one person who *always* came to play. He meant so much to our defense and he was a great threat with the three-point shot.

Danny was probably our greatest competitor. Jimmy Rodgers tried to utilize him as a sixth man for a while, but Danny didn't like that very much. Coach Rodgers needed some scoring off the bench and he hoped Danny could give him some, but Danny wanted to be out there all the time. He's just too fierce a competitor.

I didn't like the idea of trading Danny at first, but we had to get some depth up front, which Ed and Joe will now give us. After seeing what they did for the team after we acquired them, I'm very anxious to play with them this coming season. Danny also seemed to be very happy in Sacramento, so this looks as if the trade worked out well for both teams.

Robert Parish had a great year, which didn't surprise me a bit. He knew he'd have to score and rebound more with me out. People made a big deal out of the fact that his numbers were up, but I've always known how great Robert is.

Kevin's scoring was down a little. He didn't get the ball exactly where he wanted it often enough and when he did get it the ball was arriving a little late. But nothing has really changed: Kevin's still impossible to stop one-on-one. It might not have been a great year for him, but it was hardly a bad one. Kevin's never going to have a bad year. He's just too good.

Dennis Johnson was hurt all year with his own Achilles

tendon problem, so he wasn't able to take the ball to the basket the way he usually does. He has said that 1989–90 will be his last year and I'm sure he'll work hard to show people he's serious about having a good last year. He's not the type of guy who will sit back and let somebody else do it. He wants to be a part of it.

The best thing that happened to us last year was the development of both Reggie and Brian Shaw. Brian has great potential. He's already very dangerous in the open floor and he's a good student of the game. Brian needs somebody out there on the court who can coach him a little bit and this year that somebody will be me.

So it wasn't a totally lost year for the Celtics—even if it was for me personally. I really thought I'd be back by March. When that didn't come to pass, it became a very frustrating thing to deal with. Dave Cowens used to talk about this or that being something for his "portfolio of basketball experiences." My own portfolio would have been very complete without this particular experience.

PART III

OBSERVATIONS

THE THREE-POINT SHOT

THE FIRST YEAR I CAME INTO THE NBA, the league instituted the three-point shot, but at first it meant nothing to me. I never thought I'd be shooting one. The distance looked to be just too far out. I didn't even *like* the rule because I felt that a two-point lead at the end of the game should at least be enough to get you an overtime unless a player fouls you in the act of shooting.

I later discovered that referees sometimes mistakenly give you three when you've made a two and two when you've made a three. Once we were in New Jersey and I got the ball late in the game. I was way behind the three-point line and I hit one. The referee signals a two. After the game he came up to me and said he was sorry he had missed the call. But that one point can make a difference in the outcome of a game.

I must admit that the three-pointer has been *very* good to me—and to the Celtics. Chris Ford was probably the first player who took great advantage of the shot. We were involved in a close game in Atlanta early in the 1979–80 season when Chris hit a set shot from the corner for three. When we got the ball back, we ran another play for him in the same spot and he hit another one.

I didn't really take that many three-point shots in the beginning. No one in the NBA knew exactly what to make of the strategy. I made the first one in the history of the All-Star Game, but it still took a few years before it began to play a large part in my overall game.

When the NBA announced there would be a three-point contest in conjunction with the 1986 All-Star Game in Dallas, I didn't know what kind of setup they had devised. I thought they might be planning to mix in some old-timers with active players. I couldn't quite picture the format until the league sent out a demonstration tape to the competitors.

I've always been a team player, but if you put me in a one-on-one contest for *anything,* there's no question my competitive juices start pumping and I'll definitely do everything I can to be the best.

Danny Ainge and Scott Wedman helped me to get ready for the first three-point contest. They'd set the balls up in the rack for me and give me encouragement, but I wasn't hitting many three-pointers in my practice sessions.

This was a whole new territory and I figured I'd need every edge I could find. We were in the locker room before the competition and I decided to start working on Leon Wood because I figured he'd be my biggest competition. I knew he went out and shot about two hundred three-pointers before every game. The man just loved to shoot.

Leon mentioned something to me about the red, white and blue basketballs being slick. (The red, white and blue balls count two points, while all the others count as one.) I said, "Yeah, Leon, I can't hold them. There's no way we can shoot *these* things." The truth is, the red, white and blue basketballs *were* a little slick. I said, "Leon, if we can't make one of *them,* we're never gonna win."

I was trying to psyche him out, of course—and anyone else who was listening. I didn't really know any of the other guys very well—I remember Norm Nixon and Trent Tucker were there—and finally I just said, "Who's going to get *second* place today?" None of them said anything, although they all laughed. I kept going. I said, "Well, that's what you're all playing for because I'm going to finish first."

One of my concerns was the time limit. You have to get off twenty-five shots in sixty seconds. After I got through the first round, I knew that wouldn't be a problem. I didn't shoot very well in the first round, but it was enough to advance. The second round was better and by the third round I was in the groove.

The crowd was a big factor. They swing over to the shooter who gets hot and in the third round that was me. I hit something like eleven in a row. Rhythm? I had two basketballs in the air at once and everything was flowing.

When I first walked out there, I was nervous. I really wanted to win that contest. You just knew there were thirty-four thousand eyes looking at you. I had my warm-up jacket on for the first two rounds and I was so nervous and pumped up that I didn't even know it! When John Havlicek, who was down there, came over and said, "Take off that jacket," I just whipped it off and handed it to him. I had arranged all the balls I was going to shoot with the seams in the same position, so I wouldn't have to look down when I picked them up. I wanted to make the process of shooting as automatic as possible.

I was ecstatic about winning the three-point contest. Kevin, Danny, Robert and those guys had been kidding me that I didn't have a chance and I couldn't wait to get back to the team to start talking some trash. M.L. always used to say he was the "Three-Point King," and that was on my mind when I walked into the press room for the interview after the contest. "*I'm* the 'Three-Point King'!" I shouted. Winning the contest meant a lot to me.

The one common factor in my three-point championships is that each contest was held in an arena where I like to shoot. I've always liked Dallas and I felt confident there. When I heard the next All-Star Game was in Seattle, I was worried because I don't like the Kingdome. Fortunately, the contest was going to be in the Coliseum.

The problem that year was my elbow. It was flaring up and I needed to have it worked on. I wasn't sure I was going to be able to get in enough practice. I told Dinah and my family that if I could win this one I'd *never* lose the contest. I just figured that if my arm could get me through this, it would survive anything.

Danny had been jabbering that if he had been in the contest the year before he would have won it. "I'm the real three-point shooter," he said. "You can't shoot from distance as well as I can." He got his chance because when someone

dropped out of the contest they called him up as the replace-
ment.

He lost in the first round. I was sitting on the bench, giving him all kinds of baloney. "You're gone, Danny," I said.
"Now I only have to worry about these other guys."

The truth was, I had *myself* to worry about. I struggled in
the first round and my second round wasn't all that great
either. I got to the final round against Detlef Schrempf and I
had a pretty good third round but nothing he couldn't beat.

I was counting off his shots in my head and Detlef did not
start well. Just when I was thinking I had it wrapped up, he
ran the rack in the fourth station and he came to the last
shot with a chance to beat me. If Detlef made that red, white
and blue ball from the corner, he would have won.

I was on my knees watching him take that last shot and I
knew when he let it go that it wasn't going in. I had survived.

By the third year, everyone knew exactly who was the
man to beat. Chicago Stadium is another building where I've
always liked to shoot and I went in with a lot of confidence. I
repeated the line about the other guys "playing for second
place." I couldn't use it in Seattle because I was too busy
worrying about my elbow.

It was the same pattern. A so-so first round, but good
enough to advance. A fair second round. Then a good third
round. I was shooting last and I needed to run the final rack
in order to win it. The first one I put up there was all net and
I just tried to recapture that same rhythm. They all swished
and now it was the red, white and blue ball. The worst that
could happen was an overtime, so the pressure was off. As
soon as I shot it, I knew it was going in, so I started to walk
off and held up my index finger. I sure enjoy being the three-
point champ.

It's still interesting to me what's happened with the three-
pointer because I thought so little of the shot when I first
came into the league. It's a great weapon and I'll tell you
when it is a particularly good time to use it. You're the road
team, you've got maybe a five-point lead with a couple of
minutes to go and you're wide open. That's when I love to
crank that thing up there because if you make it you simply

destroy a team at that point. That's when you need your concentration.

The three-point shot demoralizes an opponent; there is no question about that. You're working very hard on defense and all of a sudden there is a three-pointer and you feel so deflated. If the deficit goes from two to five with a minute to go, you're dead in the water. It's really a killer.

There was a big difference in my approach to the three-pointer when the Celtics changed coaches. I was making a name for myself as a three-point man right from the start, but it wasn't because we emphasized it in our offenses. Chris Ford and I would have little contests between ourselves in the beginning, but it was more for fun than anything else. Chris and I were just messing around.

We really didn't have the green light to shoot the three under Coach Fitch. That, combined with the fact that I was somewhat opposed to the rule philosophically, meant I didn't shoot all that many. Fitch was more interested in getting the ball inside. I was concentrating on getting to certain spots on the floor, so I wasn't drifting behind that line very often.

I could see an immediate difference when K.C. took over. He never really said anything one way or the other, but you just *knew*. Oh, every once in a while he would caution us to take better shots, but he never directed the comment to an individual. You always felt comfortable out there, taking the shots you felt you could make. The game was opened up for me. If I came down on a break and was open, I could throw up a three. I started drifting toward the corner and shooting them. We made it a much bigger weapon.

The corner shot is a lot easier. The three really isn't a very long shot from the corner and I've always considered myself a good corner shooter anyway. I feel very comfortable from either side.

The key, of course, is the footwork. When I'm over there, I always shoot a standing set shot and try to make sure my feet are together. When I float over there, I always hope I'm behind the line when I catch the ball because I don't want to start fumbling around after I get it. If my foot's on the line, I don't worry about it. The shot will just have to be a two. I never look down; I just shoot it.

Incidentally, this is one area where having the third official should help. Presumably, there is better coverage now, so referees can tell the difference between a two and a three.

There has been a lot of discussion in the past few years about changing the distance. Some people want to bring the line in a foot or so in order to keep the defense from sagging on people inside. That would help a lot more people become three-point shooters, I'm sure, but it wouldn't make that much difference to me.

Besides, if you're hot, you find you can make *anything*. Back in the 1985–86 season, I had the hottest three-point streak of my career, making twenty-five out of thirty-four in one stretch. I was in a groove and everything was going my way. When Dirk Minniefield joined our team in 1987, he told me a funny story. When I was in the middle of that streak, we were playing Cleveland one night in the Hartford Civic Center and I was really on fire. Keith Lee was guarding me and I hit about three in a row. Dirk said the Cleveland bench was yelling, "Get that sucker!" When Keith came up on me, I drove around him. The next time Keith was kind of caught in the middle and I stepped back behind the line and hit another three.

We were in San Antonio during that same streak. I've always loved to shoot in the Hemisfair and I was having a good night. I was over in front of their bench and had already hit two or three and nobody was on me. But I was standing a good two or three feet behind the line. It was a ridiculous idea, but I put a little extra arc on it and the ball went right through.

One thing you have to do is learn not to listen to the home crowd. As soon as you even *look* as if you're thinking about shooting a three, you can hear the murmur. And when you let it go, they start yelling, *"Threeeeee!"* Sometimes it's hard not to get caught up in that, especially if you think you're hot.

It is great fun when you're hot; I won't deny that. We were playing Dallas two years ago and for some reason Mark Aguirre wouldn't come out to guard me. I said, "Well, if he's not coming out, I might as well keep shooting them." Danny was also hot that game. It was a real three-point festival.

After a while, Hank did start coming out and then it was worth shooting them just to see how hot I was, since we were way ahead in the game. I hit six or seven and went to the bench with about three minutes to go. Some of the guys said I should go back in to get some record or other. I said, "The heck with that."

One thing about the three-point shot: It's either going in or it isn't. There's none of this "shooter's roll" you hear about. It's not going to hit the rim, bounce around and fall in—at least not very often. It also leads to a long rebound and that can work either way. It might be an easy offensive rebound for a teammate standing fifteen feet from the basket or it might turn into an immediate fast break for the other team.

The normal key to shooting a three-pointer is rhythm and balance. When you're feeling good and you catch the ball just right and let it go, you can get it up there pretty easily. But if you're tired and you come down on a break without really having your feet under you and then you throw one up there, you've got to heave it and you don't have much of a chance. Anytime you're off-balance, you've got to throw it up there harder.

It's amazing how good some of those little guys are. Mike Evans, who used to be with Denver, among other teams, was very good, going either way off the dribble. Evans was a drifter, always shooting off the dribble. Michael Adams is very good shooting straightaway. One year we were killed by Frankie Johnson. He's one of the good ones, as long as he is shooting straightaway.

Kevin figured out a great way to utilize the three a few years ago. We use it as an in-bounds weapon. I'd pass it in to him, move to the spot in the corner and then he'd throw it back to me and I'd put it up for a three. For some reason, people did not catch on. If they don't now, after reading this, I suppose they never will.

Since I missed the 1988–89 season with my Achilles injury, I wasn't able to defend my three-point title in Houston last year. Dale Ellis is the new "Three-Point King." Well, I'll be in Miami this coming year and I'll just have to get my title back.

RED AUERBACH

F ALL THE GOOD THINGS that have happened to me in my career, one of the best has been my association with Red Auerbach, who is definitely one of a kind.

The first time I met him was when I was playing in a college All-Star Game in Atlanta. We were on an escalator. He introduced himself and that was it.

The next time we met was when he came to Terre Haute to see me play. He came back into the locker room, where nobody is allowed to smoke, and naturally he was smoking a cigar. He was flipping ashes everywhere. This was after I had been drafted by the Celtics. There were four of us in the room, I believe. It was Red, Tom Heinsohn, Coach Hodges and myself. Red made a little chitchat and said he was looking forward to working with me the next year.

The third time I met him was the time in Cincinnati when he made the offer to join the team immediately after the 1979 NCAA tournament. As I said, I wasn't very pleased with the way he made that proposal, since he seemed to think we'd be losing our next game.

The immediate impression you get from Red Auerbach is that he thinks he's pretty good. You know, the "I've been there and I am Red Auerbach." Well, he's right. He has done it all—better than anyone else has ever done it. People think that Red is real tough and he can be, but I know another side of Red, the side that instructs, supports and motivates young players. He's always pushing us in his own way, trying to make us a little better every day. He expects a lot from us and never wants to hear any excuses as to why we can't play or why we didn't play well in a game. In that regard, Red has always been tough, but his attitude always makes us want to play harder and be better. I've learned so much from Red over the years, both on and off the court.

I never go near his office. I've been a Celtic for ten years and I bet I haven't been in that office ten times. A lot of players go up there, but I stick to the basketball court.

I've always had friends who were older because I believe you are never too good or too smart to learn something. Even in college, I picked out the older guys to hang around with. I try to learn from other people's mistakes. A lot of people learn things the hard way. If I can use that to benefit myself, why not?

Jim Jones always told me, "If you surround yourself with good people, good things will happen. I've always tried to do that, whether it's the Committee or business relationships or anything else. I always try to learn something from a new person.

So picking Red's brain was a natural. He's always ready with advice, little hints to help you out. You might even call them secrets. Sometimes he'll bring up a move someone used in the past that might be good for me. Many times we've just talked about opponents, how to stop this team or this guy.

Red isn't around as much as he used to be and I miss him. He's spending more time at his home in Washington, D.C., than when I first came to the Celtics. K.C. always looked in the stands to see if Red was there and I do too. There is something about the man that makes you want him to be there if you do something good. If you win, you want him there.

It's especially important during playoff games. He usually doesn't go to the early round games on the road. But if we're in trouble, all of a sudden he'll show up and it means a lot to the players. You look at him and you know you're looking at "Mr. Basketball," in a sense. It's an inspiration.

People wonder if a man in his seventies is in step with the modern NBA and in Red Auerbach's case I can tell you the answer is yes. Red has changed with the times. I know he always tells people he doesn't live in the past and I can verify that. Sure, he'll tell a story about the old days, but as long as I've known him he has always been able to visualize the future of the league, whether it's player abilities, salary structures or anything else. I believe the older Red gets, the better he sees things in the future—not the reverse.

When Red's at a game, he'll come into the locker room afterward and he always has something useful to say. Sometimes he'll kid. Say we've won and Danny did something wrong in the middle of the game. Red might look at him and say, "That's the dumbest play I've ever seen anybody make." Danny would have to laugh. Red would only do a thing like that if we won—never if we lost.

In that case, he would offer encouragement. Then he would come around and say, "You doing all right? Keep your head up. You've got another game tomorrow."

Red doesn't interfere with the coach. I only remember him addressing the team as a whole once. He came in before a New York game at a point when we were losing on the road. He gave us a talk and straightened us out.

I played tennis with Red for a while and I learned he has a different method of keeping score than most people. I was keeping score in my head one day and I knew I was up in the set, five to two. We switched courts and when we got to the other side he announced *he* was up, five to two.

Tennis is one of his loves and Red is pretty good for his age, even if he does have an odd way of keeping score. When I first came to rookie camp, we used to play. He wouldn't play me on hard surfaces, only clay. It always had to be clay.

One hot and humid day—it had to be ninety or more out there—we were playing and Red kept calling time out to get his breath. I said I'd kill him if he didn't get back out there and play. He was over against the fence and he was breathing hard.

I said, "Are you sure you can play?"

"I'll make it. Just give me a little more time."

So we go back out to play and every time he'd hit a bad shot, he'd take a time-out. After a while, Red was beating me and then he was laughing at me. It took about two and a half hours just to play a set. He knew what he was doing, all right. Red was conserving his strength he beat me that day.

Jan Volk is the Celtics' general manager now—and a good one too—and Red is supposed to be in some sort of semi-retirement, but he's still Red. When there is a decision to be made, he'll make it. I remember they had a party for Red to announce this "retirement" a few years back and Red was walking around shaking everyone's hand and then he looked at me and said, "Heck, I ain't goin' nowhere." I just started laughing.

There's one keepsake I'll always treasure and that is the instructional video I made with Red. It's not every day Red Auerbach comes to you and asks if you want to do a video with him. I know that twenty or thirty years down the road I'm going to have it and it's something I'll always be proud of.

WALTER, HOWIE AND DAVE

THE CELTICS ARE A LOT MORE TO ME than just the players and coaches. Some of the most interesting Celtics during my career have been people the public may not even be aware of.

Walter Randall and Howie McHugh were two of them. Each of them had been around forever by the time I came along. Each was a character unlike anyone else I've met.

Walter Randall was well into his seventies when I was a rookie. He was the Celtics' equipment manager and, like Vince Lombardi, he treated everyone the same way—bad. Until he got to know you. Then he couldn't do enough for you. But you must understand that we were all transients to him. They tell me he started working for the Bruins when they opened the Garden in 1928.

I remember clearly the first day I met him. I was talking to Red when Walter just broke into the room and started complaining about something or other. I liked him immediately because I find people who are like that interesting.

After a while we got pretty close. He usually referred to

players by their numbers only, but I was "Birdie" to him. I got to know his wife and kids; they're great.

Walter, whose clubhouse nickname was "Randy," also doubled as a masseur. He gave absolutely great rubdowns and he would massage my back and neck before a game. He had short, stubby, powerful fingers and they could really do some good work. He was a very important part of our locker room atmosphere. The players loved having him around and they always did their best to tease him—one way or the other.

He was always accusing players of stealing supplies. Once we got Wayne Lebeaux, who is now our equipment manager and traveling secretary, to get six or eight new pairs of socks and stick them in Rick Carlisle's bag. We told Randy that Rick was stealing socks. Randy went over to Rick and grabbed his bag. Rick said, "What are you doing?" Randy said, "You're stealing stuff." Rick said, "I'm not stealing anything, Randy." Then Randy opens the bag and finds the socks.

Randy raised the roof. He went to tell the coach that Rick was a thief and naturally we're all laughing like crazy.

As crabby as Randy was in the locker room—he acted as if it was his living room—he would change like *that* if his wife came there. He was always mad at something and he was always grousing around. I liked to get there early, just to see what he'd be complaining about. Then his wife would come by and it was day and night. "How're you doin'? Can I get you anything?" As soon as she'd leave, he'd go back to cussin' everybody out.

We all knew Randy had cancer and was dying. He'd taken to napping in the locker room. I'd ask him if he was all right and he'd always say yes, but we knew how weak he was. But when the game started, the pain seemed to go away. After the game, he'd admit to being sick. Randy fought that thing all the way and he reminded me of my father. He never gave in. He was a tough, tough man.

I'll never forget my first playoff series in Chicago. Randy never went on the road, except during the playoffs. We were in the lay-up line at the Chicago Stadium when up walks Randy. He comes right on the court while we're still shooting. Nobody in Chicago knew who this old guy was—what with the suspenders and the pants hiked way up—shaking hands with the Celtics. It's a wonder nobody knocked him over.

The stadium security people came over to grab him and we said, "It's okay. He's with us."

"He's with *you?*"

I told him yes and the guy looked at me and just said, *"Man."*

I said, "Randy has been with the Celtics since they started."

Coach Fitch came over and took the one and only Walter Randall to the relative safety of the bench.

A few years ago, they put cardboard cutouts of each player at his locker and they even made one of Randy. One day after he died somebody wanted to take down the one of Randy. I said, "No way." He's up there still, looking over the locker room and watching for anybody daring to steal a pair of socks.

Howie McHugh was another old man I loved. He was the Celtics' first publicity man back in 1946 and he was still on the job when I came around twenty-three years later.

Howie had all the stories. We were always curious when we came in to see what Howie would be up to, if he'd be on the prowl.

He was another tough cookie. He had been a great athlete when he was younger; He was a catcher, a goalie and a football center. How much tougher than that can you be?

He used to sit on the floor between the scorer's table and midcourt and get on the officials. He was even thrown out of a playoff game once by Jack Madden for things he was yelling. I remember once when Jack made him move his seat. Jack said, "You've got to move. I'm not listening to any more of your crap."

Well, once Howie got sick and was in the hospital. When he came back, I said, just kidding him, "Jack Madden is here tonight and he's ready for you."

Howie says, "I learned a lot. When I was in the hospital, guess who called me? Jack Madden." Howie was just about crying when he told me. He never said a word to any of the officials after that.

*   *   *

The Celtics must breed these types. Take Dave Gately, who used to run the twenty-four-second clock when I first came up. We'd get into a fight or something on the court and Dave would be ready to get into it himself! I mean, if somebody blew on Dave, he'd fall over.

Dave and I would get into fake arguments and we wouldn't talk for weeks. I loved to tease him. He was always looking for me to sign something and once when we were supposed to be feuding I said to him, "Don't bother me in the locker room before a game!" Just to get something started, you know. Oh, he fumed over that.

Dave used to bring doughnuts to practice. I told him that he was trying to make the team fat and lazy and that I wouldn't eat his lousy doughnuts. Sooner or later he'd leave one by my locker and I'd eat it after practice.

People like that are fun to have around. They are part of what makes the Celtics organization special.

I wouldn't mind growing up to be a Walter Randall, to be that tough and never want to give up. You need people like that around, people who won't take excuses. *Why did we get beat? What's wrong with you? Why didn't you play harder?* When you're in the locker room and you hear some of their stories about the old days, it makes you want to be tougher.

You need a good shaking up every once in a while. You don't mind hearing it from men like that, people you respect. That is true constructive criticism.

ROBERT PARISH

I LOVE PLAYING WITH ROBERT PARISH because he is probably the most unselfish basketball player I've ever played with in my life.

K.C. would sometimes say to him if we were up by fifteen

or twenty, "You want to go back in?" And Robert would say, "No, let the rookie play." It's not that he doesn't *want* to play, he just wants the rookie to get some playing time. He'll do the same thing at the All-Star Game. If the coach asks Robert how much he wants to play, he'll say, "Five minutes. Let the younger kids play."

A Robert Parish goes from eighteen points a game to sixteen and then fourteen. His shots go down to about nine a game. He never says a word. Last year, when I was out, his numbers shot back up again. I knew they would.

He runs the floor, he rebounds, he is a much better passer than he used to be and he is a great defensive player. Our defense starts with Robert Parish. He is always talking, helping you out with picks. He contests shots inside. Every time we have a great defensive game, the defensive star is Robert.

People have the wrong impression of him because he's so impassive on the court. We'll get on the bus after a game and often it will be just the two of us in the back because the other players may be playing cards. We'll be talking about things and he'll sit there and say, "Can you believe we do this for a living?" He's a lot more emotional than people think he is.

He'll do his share of locker room joking. He's got a very dry wit. Everyone knows I like to stay after practice and shoot, but once in a great while I want to get out of there. One day Robert came out of the shower and saw me in the locker room. "Where are *you* going, Mr. Practice?" he said. I said I was going home. "Oh, are you getting a little *tired*? Three years ago, you wouldn't do that." And then he laughed that great laugh of his.

Robert rates very high among the all-time centers. He is so reliable. Over the years, I've missed practices. Kevin has missed practices. Robert *never* takes off. And he practices hard.

After thirteen years in the league, he is still outrunning younger centers down the court. You can tell in the beginning of the game how much he is going to run. You can get a rebound and if you look over and see him with those arms pumping, you know that sooner or later you are going to catch him with a long pass.

That jump shot of his is an amazing thing. It still fascinates me after all these years. We're always talking about that shot in the locker room. Sometimes he'll take that turnaround and his momentum will carry him right off the court. If he misses, he just shrugs it off and runs downcourt. If it goes in, he throws those shoulders back and he kind of struts along. He doesn't even come back onto the court until about the midcourt line. He knows that we're all watching him and that we'll be talking about it later in the locker room.

He is the most underappreciated Celtic of them all. He probably should have spoken up for himself a long time ago, but he'd never do that. Once in San Antonio he was hot. He had about twenty-four to twenty-six points and we were up big. He just said, "I've had enough tonight." He never wants to embarrass anybody. Robert's just great.

CITIES AND ARENAS

FTER TRAVELING AROUND THE NBA for nine-plus seasons, I've formed a few opinions about the cities, arenas and fans. Here's what the other NBA cities mean to me:

NEW YORK

I don't like to go there the night before a game. I'd rather get there the same day because the hotel we stay at is too noisy. There is a fire station across the street and it's just too noisy in general.

I love walking into Madison Square Garden itself. To me,

it's something out of the movies. Everybody just looks rough and tough. You ride up on the elevator and every time the door opens somebody wants to get on with a big pushcart and they're always mad when the elevator is full.

I like to go out and shoot early and many times when we get there the workers are still putting the floor down. As soon as they get one basket up, you can start shooting. The ushers are always talking junk. You hear them talking and you know they're talking about *you*.

"Aw, he'll tear us up."

"Nah, Gerald Wilkins will eat him up."

My first NBA exhibition game was in New York. We played the 76ers in the first game of a doubleheader. Sometimes I think about that. I love playing in New York and everything that goes along with it.

PHILADELPHIA

I love their fans and I love the rivalry. It's another rough city. I love to see their fans up and jumping around. There's a red-headed guy who sits in the first row and who's always kneeling on the floor. I love him. I used to talk junk to him, but he got so he wouldn't talk anymore. I don't know why.

Philly had the late Dave Zinkoff—the only PA announcer I ever paid attention to. He'd always have a story to tell you when you came in. I love old guys anyway and the 76ers have a lot of old-timers around who can teach you stuff. They're nice people and in my opinion they've got the best stat crew in the NBA. Those guys know *everything*.

I love going to Philly when Harvey Pollack, who's in charge of the media information, puts out the big copy of the pregame notes. I can't believe all the trivia he keeps, but it's fun to read. I can't imagine how he keeps track of it all, but I do love to read it.

Sometimes I like to have fun with ball boys and one of the best of them was Tony in the Spectrum. He was supposed to be working for us, but Dr. J. would make a great move and you'd see Tony over there cheering for them. The year we came back from being down in the series, three games to one, to beat the Sixers, I can remember us walking into the locker room before the game and Tony saying, "Tonight's the night. It's all over tonight."

We beat the 76ers to tie up the series and when we get back into the locker room Tony has got his Sixers jacket on inside out. He was in there high-fiving everybody. "I can't *believe* you guys beat them," Tony kept saying.

I like to have some rapport with the ball boys. I used to tell one of the kids from the Pacers to go break his piggy bank and we could shoot for pennies.

NEW JERSEY

I don't like playing in New Jersey. I knew I wasn't going to like it the first time I walked into the building. The Brendan Byrne Arena has too much open space and too much glare. I've never liked to shoot there.

And you don't have to worry about the home team giving a boost. It's no fun to play there because their crowd is *never* into it. It's as if they're not even there. It seems as if we have more fans in the building when we play there than they have. You want to hear it go both ways when you're on the road. It's nice to have some backing, but there's something wrong when you hear more noise for one of your baskets than for one of theirs.

WASHINGTON

Not a bad place. It's very dark in there, but I've got some pretty good memories of the Capital Centre.

My first three or four years, we never lost there. You don't forget a thing like that. It's also the place we know Red will show up, since it's his city. If you haven't seen him for a couple of weeks, you can count on seeing him in Washington.

There's a little old man, always well dressed, who sits near midcourt, yelling at everybody and waving a cane. I love that man and I always make a point to say hello to him. I'll say, "You're not dead *yet?*" He'll say, "No, I cheated it."

There's another man there I don't think anybody says hello to. If there was an open season on fans, he'd be the one I'd bag. He's mouthy the whole game and I mean he never lets up. He doesn't even watch what's really going on; he just hollers all the time.

I should make it a point to spend more time in the city because from what I've seen it's beautiful down there. I remember being impressed the first time we went there, just looking at all the buildings. I was never what you'd call a history buff, but I am curious about some of it. When we played the Bullets in the playoffs, all the flowers were out and the city looked great.

CLEVELAND

The Richfield Coliseum is twenty miles outside of Cleveland and I love that building. I hate the long ride out there because we have to leave so early just to get there. But it's worth the ride because I really like the building. It's just a great setup.

It's a good eight or nine hours from French Lick, but for some reason when I go there I feel like I'm close to home. It's the same with Chicago.

I had a lot of fun with their fans in 1985, the year I had the bad elbow. I thought we'd really have something going between us after that, but when I went back in the next year it had all died down.

We used to stay at a different hotel out closer to the arena, but we had to get out of there. The place was a mess and you couldn't get anything to eat after the game.

The one good thing about staying out there, however, was that it was a good place to jog. It was a perfect place to run distance. You take off running a bit and you are out in the country.

Back in the '85 playoffs I went out running one day and I came across a man fishing in a little lake. I was talking to him and you could tell he was half scared to death, since I had my Celtics gear on. I don't think he knew who I was, but I guess I looked intimidating.

He let me borrow his pole and I made about five or six casts. I caught these itty-bitty bass. I said, "What else is in here?" He answered, "That's all. Just those itty-bitty fish." I tried to show him a technique with worms, where you've got to do it very, very slow.

Later on that afternoon, we went riding by in the bus on the way to the game. There was that same old man, trying to fish with worms the way I had shown him. That made me feel good.

INDIANA

I like the lighting of Market Square Arena, but I don't particularly like to shoot there. It's a tough trip for me because of all the attention. So many people want your time and you're trying to get ready for a ballgame.

It's different than any other trip and I've had to establish a firm routine in order to keep things under control.

We get in relatively late on the morning of the game, which is good. I'll have lunch with friends and then I'll go back to the hotel and go take a nap. I will take the phone off the hook, which is something I do just about everyplace.

If people want to see me, they can come around four-thirty. The bus to the arena is around five-fifteen or five-thirty. That gives them their forty-five minutes or an hour. After the game, it's pretty hectic, but it's not as bad as it used to be because people now know I just don't have time for *everybody*. There are always people I knew at college or people I know from French Lick, Jasper, Orleans or Paoli and sometimes the best I can do is give them a wave. For some people, that's enough. I'd like to accommodate them better, but what can I do in a limited amount of time?

The Indiana fans have changed since I came into the league. At first I'd get the big native son ovation. You know: *He's our boy. He's going to Boston and he's going to do well.* That sort of thing. Then as the team got competitive, things changed. They started wanting to beat me more, which is the way it should be.

I always had a good relationship with Jack Ramsey when

he coached the Pacers. He's a man I really respect. I've always had an interest in competing in a triathalon someday
and he said he'd give me some pointers in swimming and
cycling.

DETROIT

I never liked the Silverdome, but I always liked their fans. I
like the places where the team was down and people really
got into it as the team improved. That would sum up the
Pistons, wouldn't you agree?

I've never liked playing in the big domes, but I did like the
size of the locker rooms in the Silverdome, since they were
constructed with football in mind. No matter how many reporters and TV people are in there, you've still got some
room.

Detroit probably has, next to Jack Nicholson, the most famous fan in the league. *Everybody* knows "Leon the Barber,"
whose real name is Leon Bradley. He is loud and he is funny
and he is impossible to ignore. He doesn't get on me much
and people have said to him, "Why don't you get on Bird?"
He says, "You don't really want me to make *him* mad, do
you?"

Leon is an example of a good fan because he says clever
things that prove he really knows what's going on in the
NBA. His lines are good and he loves basketball. You don't
care what a fellow like that says, as long as he loves the
game and is *halfway* decent.

We used to stay at a hotel I hated. It was always cold in
there and the rooms seemed like they were half a mile from
the elevator. You'd be walking to your room and you'd keep
looking at your room key to see if you were getting close. You
couldn't believe how far away the room was.

They've got a skinny ball boy in Detroit who looks like
Michael Cooper. I love to kid him. I say, "When *you* come
into the league, I'm going to dunk on you and walk off the
floor. I don't care what part of the season it is or if it's the
first quarter or the last quarter. I'm going to dunk on you,
raise my arms and just keep walking. That is going to be my

last dunk and it's going to be on *you* because you look like Michael Cooper."

I'm not sure if he knows what to make of that.

ATLANTA

Sort of a middle-of-the-road place. I like the Omni and I don't like it. I've had real bad games there and I've also had some good shooting games. As far as I'm concerned, you can pretty much flip a coin.

I don't know much about the city, but the little bit I've seen has been all right. The locker room is very small, but in the last couple of years some of the guys have been using an extra room next door, which helps a bit.

The fans are about average, but they are better than they used to be. They've followed a pattern, in that they've gotten more and more into it as the team has gotten better and better. When fans sense something and they see they've got a competitive team that really has a chance to go somewhere, it's completely different. But there are still a lot of Celtics fans down there.

MILWAUKEE

I can't say I ever cared much for the Mecca. It was too dark and I didn't like the dressing room much. The one thing I've sensed is that a lot of their fans come a long way to see the game, at least during the regular season. The Milwaukee fans, especially the older ones, are nice people.

I like the city itself. You walk around a bit and you get a strong smell from a chocolate factory not far from the hotel. I love that smell. Every city should have it. They should take that smell to L.A.

CHICAGO

It's second only to Indianapolis for me in terms of seeing people I know. I've always been treated very well there.

The security people there are the best in the league. They always make sure you get where you want to go—without a fuss. I always feel comfortable there.

I've had good and bad games in the Chicago Stadium, but in the playoffs I've had more good than bad. It may be the noisiest building of them all. I'll never forget that playoff game in '81 when the fans were raising the roof and Coach Fitch said, "Will somebody please do *something* to shut them up?" So I went out and I drilled that three-pointer on the first possession of the fourth quarter.

Chicago now means Michael Jordan, of course, and you can't overestimate the impact he has had on basketball. I knew he would have an impact on the franchise, but I never dreamed it would be as big as it's been. It's even bigger than the impact Magic and I had when we came in. Chicago is now an ideal NBA situation, one anyone would want to be in.

HOUSTON

We've won two championships there and I've always enjoyed playing in the Summit. For some reason, the floor itself appears bigger than it really is. I really don't know why. It's a very neat and clean building. The fans are so-so. They can make some noise and get into it, but not like other places.

DALLAS

It's been fun to see the change in Dallas. Once the team became competitive, the fans got very good. This is one trip I look forward to. It's generally good weather when we go there and we stay right next door. You walk over to the arena and there always seem to be fans lining the walk. It gets you in the mood to play.

We were the last team the Mavericks had never beaten

and when they did it two or three years ago they got so excited they made a highlight film out of it and sent it to their season ticket holders. I think Dallas is a very well-run organization and the arena is very nice to play in. The locker rooms are spacious and comfortable.

I've been around a little bit and I like the city. We stay very close to the site of the Kennedy assassination, so you feel a sense of history when you go there.

SAN ANTONIO

I love the city. I love the food. I love the arena. I love everything about San Antonio, including the fact that we haven't lost there since my rookie year.

I love going there and seeing all those Air Force guys up in the balcony. When I was growing up, I always said I wanted to go in the service and I wanted to be a police officer. It reminds me of playing overseas. Whenever Americans play overseas, there are always military people at the game. I've talked to these men, and it's always "U.S.A.-this" and "U.S.A.-that," which I love.

It's a great place to shoot. The lighting is perfect and you seem to get every roll. I even like the type of basket supports they have. The basket never shakes when you shoot. You hit the Boston Garden basket and it shakes a bit. It's the same in L.A. But these baskets have supports on both sides. They're the best.

When the Spurs first started playing there, the building only held about ten thousand. They expanded it to around sixteen thousand by raising the roof and putting in new seats. Everytime I go there, I look up at that building and shake my head. You can see the old brick and the new brick and see where they raised the building. I say to myself, "How can you lift a roof and raise it up and put all these supports under it and the whole thing stays up?" It amazes me.

I have been very successful there. I have always shot well there and played well there. I believe I've had two thirty-point halves there and I know I once made my first ten shots there.

I've got to be the biggest fan the Hemisfair has. If they ever leave that building, I hope it's after I retire.

The other thing that sticks in my mind about San Antonio was playing against George Gervin. He was an amazing player. Once he had about twenty-eight in a quarter against us before he got hurt. We were really ribbing Chris Ford about that. I remember the way he banked and the effortless finger rolls he had. I never saw a smoother player. Reggie Lewis reminds me of him a little.

DENVER

It's always a tough game in Denver, both because of the Nuggets themselves and because of the altitude.

In the first period, you just try to get your wind and generally get straightened out before you really start to think about playing. You try to get out and get a good run. Once you get your second wind, you're fine.

McNichols Arena is a pretty good place to shoot. It just seems to me we're always playing them without our full squad. Someone on the Celtics always seems to be injured when we go to Denver.

I never really got to know Doug Moe until I was on his TV show a couple of years ago. It was pretty neat. After about two minutes, you're relaxed with him. He didn't even ask many basic basketball questions. We just sat around and talked about different things. I like doing coaches' shows. I like hearing their opinions.

Denver is a pretty city. I like the mountains. I also like going to a restaurant called the Broker, where you can eat shrimp as an appetizer until you burst. I wonder if Artis could get enough to eat there.

SALT LAKE CITY

I like what it stands for—the Mormon tradition. There is something special about that city.

They used to have a great love-hate relationship with us

because of Danny, Greg Kite and Fred Roberts, three ex-
B.Y.U. boys. I also had a fondness for the city because that's
where we played the 1979 NCAA finals, although that was
held at the University of Utah and not the Salt Palace,
where the Jazz play.

Utah means Karl Malone now and it also means Mark
Eaton. It's a challenge to score over him.

I always liked Frank Layden. I remember playing—and
losing—a tough game in Philly once and for some reason
Frank was in town. He came in and we talked for a while.
He's a very easy guy to be around. Like Doug Moe, he makes
you feel at ease and I think the NBA will miss him.

SACRAMENTO

I haven't played in the new Arco Arena yet, but I have a very
positive feeling about the old one. Sacramento's all right
with me.

I'll never forget our first game there after they moved from
Kansas City. The fans gave me a standing ovation during
the introductions and it was one of the nicest things that's
ever happened to me. I had never even been in Sacramento
in my life and I found that welcome very touching. That city
will always have a place in my heart.

When we first went there, the people were half there to
cheer the Kings and half there to gawk at the other team.
That changed very quickly. Now they just want to see their
team do very well and they could care less who the opposi-
tion is, which is fine with me. I can understand that.

I like going there to play against Jerry Reynolds, who is
also from French Lick, and to play against a team run by Bill
Russell, who is, well, Bill Russell. When we lost to the
Lakers in '87, the year we beat Milwaukee and Detroit despite all our injuries, Bill Russell called me up to say how
proud he was of us. Boy, did *that* mean a lot.

Sacramento is one place I like to have a little fun with the
equipment manager. A lot of places I'll say, "What's the
arena record?" as if I'm going to go out and break it. Sacramento is one of those places. I'm always asking, "What's the

record again?" and the guy will tell me. I think Alex English has it now with about forty-six.

The last time I was there I had a good game—something in the thirties—but not that good and when I came back in the guy said, "Well, you didn't get your record tonight." I said, "Next time I'm bustin' it." When I get back out there, I'm coming in and asking, "Hey, what's that record again?"

PHOENIX

I'll tell you how much I love Phoenix. I'm going to spend my winters there when I retire. I've already played a lot of golf there and I just love the place.

I've always done well in the Veterans Coliseum. It's a great building to shoot in.

LOS ANGELES

The Forum is another place I just *looove* to play in. I just like being out there and I like the building. It could be a little brighter, but you can get by. I can't blame the bad games I've had there on the building, the way I could the Silverdome and the Kingdome.

No crowd has changed more in my time in the league. When I first came in, the fans really were laid-back. You wondered why they even came. Here they had Magic Johnson, Kareem Abdul-Jabbar and this great team—and no real enthusiasm.

That's all changed now, especially during the playoffs. They get into it as much as anybody. They're really high on their team now. When you take the floor, they're playing Randy Newman's "I Love L.A.!" on the loudspeaker and people are really getting charged up. Magic is there and nobody gets me up to play more than he does. And speaking as a Celtic, I can tell you what a great rivalry is all about.

But as much as I like to visit there, I honestly don't think I'd like to play for L.A.—or for Phoenix. Why? The climate's *too* nice.

Basketball weather, to me, is cold weather. I would have a hard time going to work every day in that constant heat. You play basketball when it's *cold* outside. (I know, I know. What about the playoffs?) If I woke up every day and it was 75 or 80 degrees, I don't know if I could get into it. I admire the Lakers for overcoming this and winning all those championships.

Yes, I've even met Jack Nicholson. He came to Boston in '87 for the finals and he even came to one of our practices. I was shooting around afterward and not really paying attention to the four or five people standing over on the sidelines. I was walking off the court when somebody hollered to me. It was Jack Nicholson.

We talked awhile in the locker room, then he asked if there was a place around where we could go to lunch. I said, "Sure." We went downtown and we sat around and talked basketball all afternoon.

He is a legitimate fan. There is no question about it. The game is *serious* to Jack. If he's working on location, as he was when he was making *Ironweed,* he has tapes of Laker playoff games sent to him. Jack is definitely involved. When we beat the Lakers in '84, he came down to congratulate us as a group. Jack said, "You guys played a great series." He's a legitimate fan. Absolutely.

The Los Angeles Sports Arena is completely different from the Forum. I don't like shooting there at all. To me, it doesn't even seem like L.A. in there. You're only six miles away from the Forum, but you know you're on the *other* side of town when you play the Clippers.

I guess the fans who can't get tickets to the Laker games go to Clippers games and they're not very passionate. There's just nothing very inspiring about playing there.

OAKLAND

Strange place. I like the rims. I like to shoot there. But I've had some bad games there, including my zero for nine game during my second year. (You can imagine how the guys busted my chops after that one.)

I've had some good games there, but more in the rebounding and assists departments. They like to hand out assists there and that's where I had my career high of seventeen. But I've never really put everything together there.

Oakland makes me think of scoreboards. When you go to an arena, one of the first things you have to locate is the scoreboard. That can be very important. Oakland used to have kind of a weird-looking round scoreboard hanging over midcourt. I'd prefer scoreboards that cannot be blocked out by fans. Oakland should have the time and shot clock above each basket, so the players have a better idea of what's going on.

Oakland has always had one of the great collections of Celtics fans in the league, but I think that's going to change now that Don Nelson has rebuilt that team.

PORTLAND

Another good place for me. I may shoot as well here as anyplace, including Boston. It rains all the time, but I don't mind that. Walter Randall always said, "When it rains out, the Celtics are going to win."

I never have any trouble getting up to play a game in Portland. People are always coming around, looking for tickets. It seems as if everybody there is into the Trail Blazers. The whole atmosphere is great and the building is a nice place to play.

SEATTLE

There are few places I hate more than the Kingdome. Those domes are all terrible for basketball. The Seattle Coliseum is another matter. That's a good basketball building.

But the one bad thing about the Coliseum is that everything is so far away. I thought it was a long walk after a game back to the locker room until somebody said to me,

"You ought to see how far it is to the *other* room." No thanks.
I went there once for treatment and I couldn't believe how
far it was. I said, "How do you guys make it from game to
game?" They said, "You have to be in *good shape* to play
here."

The fans in Seattle are great and I'm comfortable there
because everyone seems to be wearing green.

THE IDEAL ARENA

I've always been a student of arenas. Even as a kid, if someone said, "Come on over and play some basketball," the first
thing you did when you got there was look at the baskets, the
rims and the backboards. In high school and college, it was
the first order of business to check out the visiting gym.

Size wasn't what interested us. We weren't as interested in
seating capacity as we were in playing conditions. That
meant the floor, the baskets, the rims, the nets and the backboards. One time when I was at Indiana State, we walked
into somebody's gym and fell in love with it. It wasn't that
big—held maybe six thousand or seven thousand—but everything was just right and it looked as if the fans were right
on top of you, something I like because it makes the game
more exciting. We thought, "Oh man, this is just like high
school. We're going to kill 'em." I ended up getting forty-
seven or forty-eight points. I remember walking into the
gym at Southern Illinois. The floor was hard as a rock and I
knew I was going to hate it. I was right. I hated that place for
three years.

A lot of people hate artificial floors, but I really liked the
one we had at Indiana State. You can make some passes you
can't make on wood, things with backspin. People in the
NBA would be very interested if they knew some of the stuff
you can do on those tartan floors. But most people say they're
a killer on your knees. The Celtics used to have their training camp on one of those floors at the Massachusetts Mar-
itime Academy, but the veterans hated it and they moved it
to our regular site at Hellenic College. I'm sure there were
other reasons for the move.

There's no floor like the Boston Garden parquet floor. I've been used to it for a long time and I like it because it's to our advantage. But if Red ever went somewhere else and had to see his team play on a floor like that, he'd raise a very loud ruckus.

There really are dead spots where the various boards intersect. Once I was dribbling and the ball flew away from me like there was a rocket on the bottom. You see some funny things happen out there, but I'd never want to change it. They're putting up a new building and I bet that once they get a regular floor, they'll probably wish they had the old one back.

If you were constructing the ideal arena from my experience, I'd say, "Duplicate the Richfield Coliseum." Take Cleveland's arena and Portland's baskets. But put the combination in a city somewhere—not a suburb. There is nothing like having an arena in the city. I love it each year at playoff time when people start camping out to buy playoff tickets in Boston. I love to ride down there after practice and see all the people standing outside. It gets you pumped up to play.

I love knowing people will buy obstructed view tickets just to be inside the building. Knowing that people are happy just to *be there* means a lot to me.

REFEREES

I TRY NOT TO GET CAUGHT UP in worrying about officials the way some other people do.

After I had been in the league for a while, I started rating them in my mind. Every player does. You've got the ones you think are the best, the ones who are average, the ones who are homers and right on down the line. But I don't like to dwell on it very much.

You'll hear people talk before the game. They'll say, "Ooh, we've got so-and-so tonight." I could care less. I just know how good the referees are in general and I can't complain.

It's amazing to me the things they pick up on, the things they see you do. A lot of times I'll complain about something that was or wasn't called, but when I watch the replays I see that the referees might miss something once, but they usually won't miss it twice.

There's a lot of conversation out there, depending on who's officiating. Some refs you can talk to and some you can't. There are refs who'll listen if you make a legitimate point. They'll say, "Okay, I'll watch out for that." You appreciate a referee saying that.

The best game I've ever seen officiated was game four of the 1986 finals with Houston. It was a well-played game (we won by three) and when it was over I said, "I don't even remember the officials *being* out there." The refs were Darell Garretson and Earl Strom and they had such firm control of the game that it was a pleasure to play in.

My most celebrated ejection came at home against the Bucks in 1986. This one really hurt me because the next day I learned that Wayne Gretzky had been sitting in the front row. The Oilers were in town to play the Bruins the following night and he had made a special trip to the Garden to see me play. If I had only known that, the whole thing would have come out differently. *That* I can guarantee.

I started the game and I wasn't playing too well. Then something happened and I was complaining a little bit and I got hit with a T. I threw the ball up in the air and the *other* official, who was Billy Oakes, called a second T and I was out of the ballgame.

Man, I was *hot*. Oakes said he heard something, but I wasn't even talking to him. He turned around and saw the ball up in the air. When it came down, I got it and tossed it to Jack Madden, but it was too late. I was kicked out.

I was upset because it was the first quarter and nothing had happened yet and I really wanted to play. The last thing you ever want is an ejection in the first quarter at home. For me, it was ten times worse because Gretzky was there. I really admire him and I couldn't believe I was stupid enough to get myself ejected the night he showed up to watch me play.

To this day, I feel bad about that incident because people didn't get their money's worth. And finding out Gretzky was there killed me. When I saw him the following summer, Wayne said, "I came to see you play last year, but you didn't last very long." Believe me, if I had known Wayne Gretzky was in the building, I wouldn't have said a word.

My only consolation was that I hadn't hurt the team. That's the night Fred Roberts came in for me and went crazy. We won the game easily.

The referees have a very tough job. I know that. They're trying to concentrate on the game and they're getting flak from everywhere. I believe they're all trying to be fair. It's hard to imagine a tougher job in sports.

I'll tell you what makes me laugh. It's when people—coaches, mainly—make a big deal about an official blowing a goaltending call. It's often a very difficult call to make, as everybody knows. I love it when these coaches keep running the tape back about ten times and then they freeze the tape and say, "See, *there* it is!" That burns me up. When they're out there working, the referees don't have a videotape machine available to run the tape ten times and catch the freeze frame at exactly the right moment. There's all this action going on and the referees have to make quick decisions. These coaches are unbelievable. Two days later, they're still upset and they're saying, "That wasn't goaltending. Let me show you." It's ridiculous.

A lot of people think rookies get a raw deal and I won't argue with that. I'll give the officials the benefit of the doubt and say that they may need time to adjust to the styles of the new players. Then someone like Brad Lohaus comes into the league and he's kind of big and lanky and they make certain assumptions. They see him block a shot and they figure he must have fouled the other guy—even if he didn't.

The referees must adjust to the new players, just the way we must adjust to a new referee. A rookie is a rookie, whether he's a player or an official. Coaches get into it too.

They'll say, "That kid's a rookie and he's going to make mistakes." I'll have six turnovers and the poor rookie, who played the same amount of time, will have two. But he made "rookie mistakes." I guess I just made *dumb mistakes*.

You've got to pay a certain amount of dues and a young player must show respect. If you're a Magic Johnson or a Michael Jordan and a rookie comes in and jumps all over you and starts talking trash, no one is going to respect him. But if a guy comes in and plays good, solid basketball and acts properly, he'll fit right into this league.

It's the same with officials. If a kid comes in and says and does things to aggravate veteran officials, they're going to say, "Look here. That's not the way we do things." Earl Strom has been around for thirty years. If you think you're going to come into the league and give him baloney, you're only kidding yourself.

TRIPLE-DOUBLES

PEOPLE MAKE TOO MUCH OF TRIPLE-DOUBLES, which is usually defined as a game when a player has double figures in points, rebounds and assists. If that's all anyone wanted me to do, I honestly believe I could get a triple-double in at least forty-one of the eighty-two games played every year. How many games we'd win while I was concentrating on getting these triple-doubles is another matter.

I believe if a coach wanted me to go out and make sure I had ten rebounds and ten assists in a given game, I could do it. Just don't ask me to score thirty points the same night. It's all according to the opponent and how the game is going. If other guys are playing well, you could do it and it would be to the team's benefit. If they're not, what does it mean if you get a triple-double and we get beat? It's like scoring fifty points and losing. (I did that one night in Dallas.)

Assists are a questionable stat anyway. I believe it's generally easier to get one on the West Coast. It's just the way they interpret it. To me, an assist should be given when a player gets the ball and scores—period. He can make a fake, *but he can't put the ball on the floor*. You also can't pump it three or four times and then put it in. There's a limit to what should be allowed to be called an assist.

You hear the Celtics complaining at home that they are stingy with assists at the Boston Garden. I think they're closer to being on the money at the Boston Garden than anywhere else. It's all subjective. You can get them on three-pointers or on in-bounds passes now. It doesn't mean what it did when Bob Cousy and Oscar Robertson were playing, that's for sure. You've got to be playing with good people—guys who can *score*—to get a lot of assists. Magic has had Kareem Abdul-Jabbar, James Worthy and Byron Scott. I've got Robert Parish and Kevin McHale. A lot of players would like to be passing the ball to those people.

And while we're on the subject, there are triple-doubles and there are triple-doubles. When I see Magic have a game with fifteen points, thirteen rebounds and seventeen assists—*that's* a triple-double.

FREE THROWS

ONE THING I'VE NEVER REALLY UNDERSTOOD since I began playing basketball is why more players don't make the effort to become reliable free throw shooters. It just takes practice and hard work. And concentration.

Some guys seem to take missing free throws for granted.

They'll say, "I'll take my chances when I get there." Or "I don't get fouled much, so why worry about it?" I can't understand that type of thinking.

It's an easy two points and a lot of games come down to what happens at the free throw line. I've already told the story of our Springs Valley High School team losing in the sectionals because Beezer Carnes missed three consecutive one-and-ones. That never should have happened on our team, since Coach Jim Jones had us up in the morning before school shooting free throws. Every guy I know who did that became a good free throw shooter. Of course, Beezer didn't feel like getting up at six-thirty in the morning just to shoot free throws.

When I teach foul shooting, the main thing I tell kids is to make sure that whatever style you decide upon, make sure the ball goes straight. You can't make free throws if the ball is bouncing off to the right or to the left. If you're missing them short or long, at least you're on the right track. That's an easy adjustment. That's why I always thought Greg Kite could have been a decent free throw shooter. He gets the ball up there straight every time. All you've got to do is bend your knees a little bit, get square with the basket and shoot the ball the same way every time. Do that and you're *guaranteed* to have success.

Concentration is absolutely necessary. You can't go up there and take it for granted that you are going to make the shots. You've got to concentrate *every* time. You've got to go up there, take your time, relax and think about what you're doing.

When I go to the line, I am always thinking, "All net." No rim or anything else, just "All net." When I don't think that and I get too cocky and just walk up there, I'm likely to miss and every miss troubles me.

I don't miss two straight free throws very often, but it does happen every once in a while and when it does, you're thinking, "What's *wrong*?" I'll have little slumps and that's when I go back and practice hard. I'll really work on free throws.

I've never air-balled a free throw—not that I remember. I can see it happening, though. You bring the ball up and get ready to shoot and then hesitate just a second and it'll happen. What I can't comprehend is people shooting it far enough and missing the rim!

If you're very bad on the line, you are a detriment in close games; there's no doubt about it. Karl Malone obviously realized it because he's made a big improvement since his rookie year. Buck Williams has gotten a lot better too.

I always feel I should go to the line more. I only average about five free throws a game. I figure if I averaged ten or eleven free throws a game, the way some guys do, I'd be ten or eleven points ahead. But I don't want to get caught up into jumping into people, trying to draw the foul. To me, that's just not basketball. I believe you should just go out there, play a good, hard game and get to the line on merit.

I've won three foul shooting titles, but I needed a little help from K.C. to get one. In the 1985–86 season, we came down to the last day of the season with me leading in free throw percentage. The only other player who could beat me was Danny Ainge and it didn't appear he had much of a chance since he wasn't close enough to the requirement. You needed to make a hundred and twenty-five and he went into the final day against New Jersey needing to make about twelve or thirteen and Danny never got to the line very much.

The game starts and Danny is just trying to get fouled from the word "go." He's telling everybody he's going to win this free throw thing and at halftime he announces that he's going to win it and knock me out.

Danny keeps picking up fouls in the third quarter. He's taking it to the hoop and throwing his body at everybody and as a rule he doesn't drive twice in a season. The officials are giving him every call and it's all making me sick. And, of course, everybody on the bench is laughing because they all know what's going on.

Now Danny comes within two! That's where K.C. thought the joke had gone far enough. Almost before K.C. could say anything, Kevin got up to put himself into the game. Danny was getting ready to in-bound the ball from the sideline when K.C. got him out of there.

Kevin said later he never would have allowed it to happen.

"If Danny had gone to the line," Kevin said, "I would have stepped over it so they'd have to call a violation."

I'll say this for Danny: He must have gotten up early to shoot his free throws when he was a kid.

NBA MUSINGS

THE PRO GAME and the college game are two completely different things. It's funny. When I was playing college basketball, I thought it was the greatest game on the earth. I didn't pay attention to any pro games, nor did I feel any attraction to the NBA style of play. Now that I'm in the NBA, I love our style of play and wouldn't want to go back to the college game. Really, each level of game is exciting and fun, but there are different aspects in each of them. For instance, compared to the NBA, the college game is slowed down by the zone defense factor.

It still bothers me that critics of the NBA don't understand what kind of defense is played in our league. Players are making tough, tough shots with opponents hanging all over them and people seem to take it for granted. Down low, guys are scoring in heavy traffic. It's difficult just to *catch* the ball down there, let alone shoot it.

People will sit up in the balcony and look at the game one way. But when they get closer to to the floor, they get blown away because it's a completely different game down in the trenches. The players in the NBA are so much more talented than most people realize.

The college game has some things I like better than the NBA game. The NBA "continuation" rule is too loose. Players are taking two dribbles after the whistle and getting credit for the basket. You can get hurt that way. They'll take extra shots at you to make sure you won't get the basket.

The other things I like about college ball are the one-and-one foul shot rule and the alternating possession on the jump balls.

I do wish we could do something about the schedule so we could be fresher when we play. People look at the schedule and see, for example: BOSTON AT PORTLAND. They come to the game expecting the Celtics to be at their best. They don't take into consideration that you've been on the road for two weeks and this is the last game or you went into double over-time last night. They expect you to put on a good show and you should. Goodness knows, we're being paid enough. The true professional is the one who comes prepared to play every night, but sometimes it's very difficult to be ready for that kind of effort.

Sometimes people suggest playing a shorter game, but I think the forty-eight-minute length is ideal. The first half just flies by. To me, it doesn't even seem as if it's twenty-four minutes long. But the second half drags out because of all the time-outs when the coaches are conducting their "strategy."

A lot of times people will say that you don't need a coach. That's a bunch of baloney. Sometimes I think there is a little bit too much coaching, but you still need a coach. And there is more studying and more tape watching going on in the NBA than in the colleges. We fly somewhere for a game and the first thing a coach does is set up the VCR and watch a tape of the team we'll be playing. Sometimes they put in ten- and twelve-hour days.

You look at the clock in the first quarter for the first time and there are seven or eight minutes left. The next time you look, it's down to two or three. The first quarter is over and if you get a little break, you go back into play the final eight or nine minutes of the half and it's over. Forty-eight minutes sounds like a lot of running up and down the court, but the first half doesn't seem like anything at all.

Fifteen minutes is plenty of rest at halftime. Actually, it's too much. Ten minutes would be adequate—more than enough time to go in, get a drink of water and get ready to come back out. I *hate* going back out on the court too early. You're out there shooting around and then you're just standing there. It drives me crazy. *That's* what makes the game seem long to me.

The ideal is to get out there with five minutes to go. Let everybody go through the lay-up line twice, shoot a couple of jump shots, go in the huddle and play.

The essence of the pro game is defense. To play good, sound pro defense takes five guys playing and thinking together and you can't have that on *every* possession, every game, even in the playoffs, when the overall intensity level is at its peak. Somebody is always going to miss an assignment, not think the way he did the possession before or not react quickly enough.

You can only reach the maximum defensive level as a team for a certain percentage of those forty-eight minutes. Good teams know when and how to pick their spots. Obviously the end of a game is one of those times. You're playing along and everything is smooth and then you just *know* the time has come. All of a sudden, you think, "We've got to dig down. Everybody has got to get the job done *now*."

Sometimes the big stand is taken in the first quarter. You get out there and suddenly the ball is just flying around. You deflect a pass, one of your teammates picks up the ball and off you go. Everything starts going your way. There's luck involved. A lot of times I'll get my fingers on a ball and it goes right to someone else on the other team or the ball goes out of bounds. But other times you bother a guy to make him do something he doesn't want to do and there is a snowball effect for the next four or five minutes. Everybody gets into it and everything starts clicking.

Those moments when everybody is working together on defense are the best times you can have in this game. It's what team play is all about. On offense, a man can go one-on-one and get the job done, but in order to have a great defensive sequence or game *everybody* must be doing it.

It's great to see everything you practice happen in a game. We've had those moments when the ball is coming down off the boards and people are filling the lane and the right player gets the ball at the right moment and everyone is thinking together. We had a lot of that in the 1985–86 season. But as great as those moments are on offense, there is even more satisfaction when they happen on defense.

I've played on teams where our defense in crucial moments was nearly perfect. What we did in the final five minutes of the seventh Philadelphia game in 1981 was that kind of an effort. We were down by nine with five minutes to go and the 76ers only scored one point in their final ten possessions. Now that's *defense*.

THE PLAYOFFS

THE PLAYOFFS *are* different. The intensity level is way up. I have never lost sleep over a regular season game, but in the 1986 playoffs against Houston I had that experience. I think it was before game six. I woke up, thinking about the game the next day. I said, "This is crazy. It's just a basketball game." I tried to relax myself, but sometimes in the playoffs you can't do it because it's just too emotionally draining.

You lose a game in the regular season and say, "Hey, it's over." But during the playoffs, you're way up one day and way down the next. When you win, you're up. When you lose, you're down. The human body is just not made to take that.

Weird physical things happen. I never go *into* a playoff game tired, but I always come out of one completely drained. After a game, you feel totally exhausted. All you want to do is sleep and it carries over throughout the next day.

Preparation is more intense. It's a constant game of adjustment and a coach figures if he can cut off this one thing or eliminate one basket, it might make the difference in a game and, therefore, the series. You're watching more tape than ever before and after every game it's back to the drawing board for more.

THE STATUE

I 'VE HAD A LOT OF NICE THINGS happen to me in my life, but one of the more interesting was to be the model for a statue without even having to die first. The sculptor's name is Armand LaMontagne. This all came about because Dave Cowens asked me if I would do it and I'll try to do just about anything Dave asks me.

I was skeptical at first. Dave took me down to Armand's studio in Rhode Island and I was fascinated. I always admire people who are skilled with their hands and I expected to see some nice stuff, but nothing prepared me for what I saw. I was told Armand had done a statue of Ted Williams that is now in the Baseball Hall of Fame, but somehow the whole thing didn't register for me until I got down there.

I thought it would be tough to pose, but it was very simple. Armand had me stand up on a pedestal while he took photographs of every part of my body. The whole thing only took two and a half hours. After that, I just kept in touch with him so he could be sure of the details.

Once I showed up with a new haircut. Armand said, "Oh no," and changed my haircut. He added a scar that's on my thumb. I lost fifteen pounds in between the posing and the completion of the statue, so he had to reflect that.

The statue was unveiled at a nice dinner in Boston. The proceeds from the dinner went to the New England Sports Museum, of which Dave Cowens is the director. Then the statue was shown to the fans at the Garden the next night. It's currently on display at the New England Sports Museum in Boston.

I have to tell you, I wasn't sure about this whole thing when it started, but when he was done with the project I loved it. The detail on the statue is truly amazing. Since then he's made a statue of Bobby Orr. Twenty years from now, I'll be able to go over and look at that statue and say, "Man, have I put on weight!"

THE FANS

I PLAY FOR THE FANS, but they don't come first. The owners come first. Without them, none of us would have anything. Then come the Celtics, which means Red. He gets me more fired up to play than any other individual. My high school and college coaches were great, but Red's "Mr. Basketball" to me. Then come my teammates and somehow in there I include myself.

That might make it sound as if the fans are unimportant, but that's not true at all. The fans pay the money and they provide a big source of inspiration during a game. I love doing things for the fans.

I've seen the fans take players out of a game. Some players just aren't tough enough to stand up to them and play hard at the same time.

Ralph Sampson in 1986 is a good example. When he came out to shoot his lay-ups before game six of the finals, I had a feeling that he wasn't going to have a good game. He had had that fight with Jerry Sichting in the fifth game and the fans were on his case the minute the team plane set down in Boston.

But the biggest effect a crowd has is to pump up the home

team. When we had our great rivalry with Philadelphia, the fans in both buildings were up for every play of every game. It makes you give an extra effort. If there's a rebound or a loose ball, *you* want to get it. The crowd keeps every player mentally in the game.

If you're hot, you might make it a little more spectacular. Somebody will cut backdoor and you might put a little more zip on the pass. You might dive for loose balls you don't have much of a chance for, just for the fans.

We used to have a boisterous bench. Everybody was into cheering except Max, who used to tell me that if Red wanted a cheerleader, well then, he should have *drafted* cheerleaders. But if it was a big game, who was the first one off the bench, screaming and talking junk to the other team and doing stuff to get the crowd into the game? Max. He knew how important it was. We had M.L. and his towel waving. Quinn was another good guy on the bench. Walton was very, very good on the bench.

The worst thing you can have is a deadhead bench. One of the favorite photos I have is one where I'm standing up and waving a towel on the bench. Kevin had just thrown Max a great pass and Max had made a three-point play and I was up screaming and hollering. I was so into the game, even though I couldn't play, and I'm very proud of that picture.

I've always been conscious of having the fans involved. I'll use the press, if I can, to send a message to the crowd that we really need them in the next game. They all read the papers. I did that before the sixth Houston game in '86 and I'm not ashamed to admit it. Sometimes the fans need a bit of prodding. People ask if I can personally relate to being a fan. Yes! If I was going to a lot of Red Sox games and people were getting into it, I'd be into it. I've never had much experience going to basketball games. I've gone to some of my brother Eddie's basketball games and I'm nervous. I can relate better as a baseball fan. If I had season tickets to the Red Sox and I was going there every day, I'd be up cheering.

I can tell you this: I was standing next to Bill Walton during the 1986 playoffs while the crowd was going crazy over something and I said to him, "I wish somebody else was out here playing and I could be up there with the fans." They seemed to be having such a blast. When I'm retired later on and if the Celtics make the finals, I'll be up there in the stands going crazy, just like everybody else.

THE "BEST PLAYERS"

EVERY PLAYER WHO IS PLAYING at the NBA level is exceptional and, believe me, you realize that very quickly when you have to play against these guys night after night. Players develop too, as time goes on, into even better players. Look at how Joe Dumars has improved every year until he became an integral partner with Isiah Thomas in the Pistons' long-awaited championship. I can't wait to play the Pistons this coming season.

On any given night, any player in the NBA can get hot and be the star for that game—every player is that talented. So, if I'm going to mention just a few of the best, I guess I mean the *best* of the best. I'm not qualified to judge players from other eras. In my time, I believe the best all-around player has been Magic Johnson. The best defensive player has been Michael Cooper. And in a few more years Michael Jordan will be the best player there ever was.

Michael is on another level. Nobody can do the things he can do with his body. Karl Malone is another awesome player. He just gets it, puts his head down and goes. Nobody can stop him any longer. In a few more years, *he* might be the player I'd want on my team.

People seem to have short memories. There have been some great players in recent years. Now that we have Michael Jordan, everyone is forgetting about Dr. J. I didn't catch the Doc in his early years, but after looking at him in his later years when he was awesome, I can only imagine what he was like.

If you're building a team, you need role players. M. L. Carr would be on my team somewhere. I always loved being around him as a teammate. He might not have been the most skilled player, but you knew he had worked hard to be what he was. I'd like to have Buck Williams. And give me Charles Barkley. He's six-five and he just *dominates*. If you're talking about a smart all-around player who can play several positions, you'd want Craig Ehlo. You need a player like that on your team.

It is very hard to pinpoint who is the best, but if I were selecting a team I would take Magic first because he makes it so much easier for everyone on the club.

KAREEM ABDUL-JABBAR

I don't know the man personally at all and I probably never will get to know him. I just like his style.

I have all the respect in the world for what Kareem was able to do. Playing twenty years in this league is almost beyond comprehension. Just think how hard he must have worked during those off-seasons.

I missed out on his earlier years, I guess. I have seen some clips and he was scary. He rebounded better and blocked more shots than anyone. He's the all-time leading scorer too.

Nobody could stop the sky hook. I think everybody knows that. What I didn't realize when I first played against Kareem was how well he could pass. He never seemed to miss a backdoor cutter.

The range on that sky hook of his was awesome. In '85 he was shooting that thing from the corner like it was a lay-up. It didn't matter how old he was, when you needed a basket, you'd want Kareem shooting that sky hook. There was nothing you could do except hope that he missed it.

How did he do it for twenty years? The travel. The beating. The pounding. Kareem must have the greatest body imaginable.

MOSES MALONE

I've always liked Moses Malone as a player for one very simple reason—he works for his money.

Moses plays hard every day and he has ever since he came out of high school. And he's competitive as can be.

RITUALS

PEOPLE HAVE NOTICED that during the national anthem at home games I am always looking up to the Boston Garden ceiling. There are a couple of reasons for this.

First of all, I'm ever conscious of standing still. When I first made the B team at Springs Valley High, the coach said, "When they're playing the national anthem, don't look around." So a lot of times I just focus on the flag.

Early in my Celtic career, I became fascinated by Bobby Orr's retired number 4. Ever since I arrived in Boston it was "Bobby Orr this" and "Bobby Orr that" and I never got tired of hearing about him. I decided he was someone I could model myself after. I want people to talk about me with the same kind of personal respect after I retire.

It seemed to me his number shined more than the others up there. There was just something about it that made it stand out. I was able to see some game clips of him—they're always the very best stuff—and I became very interested in him. Looking at his number helps me get fired up for the game.

The other thing I look at up there are our championship flags. I focus on the three championships my teams have won and I always look at them in order. I start at 1981, move to 1984 and shift over to 1986. I try to capture how I felt when we won each one and play the championship through my mind. It doesn't take very long to zip through that, then I go back to Bobby's number and then back to the flag.

On the road I just find the flag and zero in on that.

*   *   *

The other thing people always want to know about is the habit I have of wiping my palms on my basketball shoes. I always let on there was some great mystery to it, but there isn't.

I first saw my brothers Mike and Mark do it. Everybody at home did it. The school got Converse shoes and we did it simply to clean off the soles of the shoes. People say, "Is it for traction?" The answer is yes, but it's traction for the shoes, not for the hands, which is what people seem to think.

There was nothing deep about it. Our floors were kind of dirty, so we just wanted to keep the shoes clean. You put a little water on your hands and clean them off. After you do it, the shoes feel new. Now I just do it without knowing it.

I usually do it when we come out of a huddle. The only time I know I'm doing it is if I'm hurt somewhere, if my knees are hurting or I've pulled a groin or something. Once I reached down there and I felt a pain. I said, "Oh man, this hurts." I hadn't been aware I was doing it.

I'm not that aware of individual fans. Rick Robey was amazing. He knew there was an aunt in this seat and an uncle in another. He had a vision of the whole place; he took in everything. I just take in the court. I don't want to get to the point where I'm checking out the crowd. I need to concentrate on the game.

I've had people come visit me in Boston who have good seats and who will slip down to courtside and I'll never notice them. As a rule, I prefer not to talk with people when I get to the Garden. I'm there to work.

I leave the house around four o'clock for a seven-thirty home game. I get down there around five, or quarter to, and I'm on the floor around five or five-fifteen.

It doesn't take me long to get ready. I come in, change into my practice gear, stretch my back, tape my right pinky and get out there. If my back is tight, I get it worked on.

At home, Joe Quatato, the assistant equipment manager, usually rebounds for me. I don't have any set order of shots; I just want to get my rhythm.

I have revived one other ritual. I used to take the shadow practice free throw when I was in college, but I got away from it in the pros because Max did it and it was one of his trademarks. Once he left, I started doing it again.

Finally for quite a while I would give the same man a high-five when I walked onto the court—he was the father of one of the ball boys. One night he wasn't there and I was terribly sad to learn that he had died. Someone else stepped in his place at the next game, so even though it's not the same, the tradition keeps going.

LEADERSHIP

L EADERSHIP IS GETTING PLAYERS to believe in you. If you tell a teammate you're ready to play as tough as you're able to, you'd better go out there and *do* it. Players will see right through a phony. And they can tell when you're not giving it all you've got.

Leadership is diving for a loose ball, getting the crowd involved, getting other players involved—no more, no less.

It's being able to take it as well as dish it out. That's the only way you're going to get respect from the players. I'll say something about somebody on this team and he might say something back to me. Then you'll hear, "How could he say that about Larry?" Hey, I'm open to criticism too. I probably don't get into that stuff as much as I should. Maybe I'll start doing it more. I wish D.J. and Robert would speak up more often. People would listen because of the respect they all have for D.J. and Robert.

You'd just better be able to produce. You can't say, "I'll go out there and beat that sucker," and then go have a lousy game.

THE PRESS

THE INTERESTING THING TO ME is how easy it is after a game during the regular season. The playoffs are another matter.

I always look at the clock when I come out after a game and very seldom does the questioning take more than ten or fifteen minutes. I dress back in the trainer's room and before I come out I take a peek through the curtain to see if Kevin is out there or if the coach is still talking to people. I always wait until they appear to be done because I know what will happen if I come out while they're being interviewed. The press will all come over to get me two cents' worth.

In college when I played a game, it was over and I was only thinking about the next one. You didn't play enough games. I wasn't that interested in reflecting back. Even if I had decided to talk to the press, I wouldn't have been very enlightening.

In the pros, you tend to savor that game awhile before you discard it. Who knows? You might not like the next one.

By this time, I know what the questioning will be like. They'll want to know what happened in the third quarter or what the coach said to get us going. He might not have said a word. Maybe we just got a little rest and then we went out and played much better. I don't analyze that much.

Things get more involved during the playoffs and the first thing you notice is that the press corps grows with every round. I don't usually like to talk before a practice or shootaround, but when you're the visiting team that's the format and you've got to deal with it. I don't like it because you get caught up in it for fifteen or twenty minutes and then the whistle blows and you've got to think about the game. I don't think I've ever had a good road practice after talking to the press. My mind gets completely out of whack.

I don't mind giving them what they want, however, because I really do enjoy the give-and-take.

When I first started out, I never made eye contact with the press. I'd hear the questions, but I'd always look down. After a while, I started looking around and trying to remember the faces. I also started putting a little two and two together.

I learned that if somebody asks you a question and they start writing down your answer and then they all look up at you real quick that you'd better cut it off. Then you know maybe it's going to get too deep. You can tell when they *really* want you to spell it out and then you know it's time to move on to something else.

I like the process a lot more than I ever thought I would. Being in the finals all those times and meeting the national press on that basis was actually kind of fun. Sometimes they'll ask really good questions and you find yourself very interested in the interview.

When I first started, I preferred the one-on-one interview. Now I like the big group sessions. They're fun because you get all kinds of different questions thrown at you and sometimes it's a little challenging. They get a little cocky with you and then you've got something going. The turning point was 1984. I've learned to enjoy the whole thing a lot better since then. You win a couple of championships and you relax more. You've been there, you know what it takes to win and you can go out there and say anything you want. Of course, you always realize you've got to go out there and win the game.

WEST COAST TRIPS

THE CELTICS HAVE TO LEAVE the Boston Garden each February for a circus or ice show. We are out of there for about eight games and we always play the Western Conference teams during that time. I've had some of my better games on that trip.

I really look forward to going West. There's the warm weather, of course. As a change from the cold in the East, it's great. Another big reason I like the trip is that they play a different type of basketball. There's more running and gunning and you get to pass the ball more. I can do more of what I do best, which is move, cut, come off picks. There's less of the clutch-and-grab defense you get in the East.

I've liked this trip since I was rookie. I had some good games then and I got it in my head I could tear up the league if I ever got to play out there. Believe me, it's all in my head. And like I said before, playing in that climate all the time would be difficult for me.

The timing of the West Coast trip is good. I'm ready for it because it comes right after the All-Star break and I've had some rest. You go the game and you feel better when you come back. You haven't seen the guys for three days and you're really in the mood to play with your team again.

Some of my favorite arenas—places like Portland, Phoenix and Los Angeles—are out there. I tell you, I just love that West Coast trip.

PART IV

WHERE I STAND

WELL, NOW YOU'VE READ MY STORY. Believe me, I had no idea that my fascination with basketball would lead me to where I am today. I'm proud of my image because hard work has never scared me. Of course, I'm lucky that I grew to be six-nine, but I also know that there are a lot of seven-footers out there who can't play basketball at all.

I've worked hard because I *had* to. I always worried that I couldn't run and couldn't jump, so I tried to be a great shooter and passer and I learned how to box people off the boards—all things that I hoped would compensate for any shortcomings I might have. I learned how to get good position and use my body correctly. Some people are natural shooters. They pick the ball up and they automatically get great rotation. They are true "natural" athletes. Danny Ainge is one of those people.

I had great training from Jim Jones. Some of the things he taught me have never left me. Even after I became a Celtic and I'd go back to French Lick after the season, I had the same drive to excel. One day we played for about four hours and then I stuck around, shooting for hours afterward.

As a kid, I *always* thought I was behind and I needed that extra hour to catch up. Jim Jones once told me, "No matter how many shots you take, somewhere there's a kid out there taking one more. If you dribble a million times a day, someone is dribbling a million and one." Whenever I'd get ready to call it a day, I'd think, "No. Somebody else is still practicing. Somebody—*somewhere*—is playing that extra ten or fifteen minutes and he's going to beat me someday." I'd practice some more and then I'd think, "Maybe that guy is practicing his free throws now." So I'd go to the line and practice my free throws and that would take another hour. I don't know if I practiced more than *anybody,* but I sure practiced enough. I *still* wonder if somebody—somewhere—was practicing more than me.

Practice habits were crucial to my development in basketball. I didn't play against the toughest competition in high school, but one reason I was able to do well in college was that I mastered the fundamentals. You've got to have them down before you can even *think* about playing. When I went from high school to college, I was so fundamentally sound that I fit right in with everybody else because I knew how to do all the basics.

There are many times when you're better off practicing than you are playing, but most people just don't understand that. I love to play, to scrimmage against other players. But if that's all I ever did, I wouldn't know the game of basketball as well as I do.

I still adhere to these principles of practice. When we played the Knicks in 1988, I decided to go back to Hellenic College for more work. It was the day before a game and I assumed the Knicks would do what we normally do, which is practice on the day of the game.

Coach Jim Jones was visiting Boston that week and he and I were in the gym. Jonesie was helping me out by throwing me the ball in the low post as I was turning and spinning, turning and spinning, getting a move down. Coach Jones still loves to help me out with things like that. We were really working up a big sweat—just about to die—but we wouldn't quit.

Mike Saunders, the trainer for the Knicks, happened to come in because he needed to get something set up for the next day's practice. "What are *you* doing here?" he said. I was sure that he went back and told the Knicks that I was in there and that really fired me up for the next game. Practicing is something I will always be doing, I guess.

Basketball has brought so many great things into my life. For one thing, it's allowed me to achieve financial security for me and my family—something that's always been very important to me. I've always enjoyed sticking to my "roots," so the members of The Committee still offer me guidance in my financial affairs and help me manage the moneys generated from my employment and endorsement contracts, which are negotiated by Mr. Woolf and his associate Jill Leone. I know I make a lot more money now than I did when I worked for the Street Department, but I would like to think that I am still the same Larry Bird as I was back then. I still try to stick to what I believe in and not let the notion of having a lot of money sway me. That concept can crop up a lot in the endorsement area. I only endorse products that I believe in. Last year a company was going to pay me $250,000 to endorse their product. Sounds great, doesn't it? Only problem was, their television commercial campaign called for me to appear as a dancer. Can you believe *that*? I said, "Thanks but no thanks. Larry Bird will *not* wear a tu-tu!"

So I hope my friends from home still see me as being the same. Oh, your relationships do change over the years—no matter what. Michael Cox was probably my best friend growing up and he still lives in French Lick, but he's married now and has kids so I don't get to see him much these days. David Qualkenbush was practically a brother to me, but we've had few opportunities to get together over the years. However, I still get to spend time with my close friend Tony Clark. You're always looking for that one friend you can always count on and Tony's the one for me. Sam Sanders is another person that I'll always want around me. Deep down, I think I'm still Larry Bird of French Lick, Indiana. If I hadn't been a basketball player, I'd probably be a construction worker or in some other profession, using my hands, and I would have enjoyed that too.

Basketball has provided me with so many opportunities to travel to places I had only heard of. For someone who never thought of ever leaving French Lick, Indiana, it's been an unbelievable journey. In college I went to Bulgaria for the World University Games and in 1982 I went to Japan with

my friend Max Gibson. The Japanese people were great to
me and I was fascinated to learn about their culture and lifestyle.

In 1983 I traveled to Israel and Egypt with an All-Star
basketball team organized by Mr. Woolf, which included Pat
Cummings, Billy Paultz and Calvin Murphy, among others.
We played games in Tel Aviv, Haifa and Jerusalem. This was
also a great trip because I was able to go to Bethlehem,
which was a place that my grandmother told me about when
I was little. She always said she wished I could go there
someday. I almost didn't make it, though, because on the day
we were supposed to go sight-seeing in Jerusalem I got so
terribly sick with dehydration that I could hardly make it off
the team bus. After Mr. Woolf checked me into a hotel room,
the rest of the team went on the sight-seeing tour and a doctor was called in to look at me. He told Mr. Woolf that I had a
high temperature and was severely dehydrated and that I
should be woken up at short intervals in order to drink as
many liquids as possible. Around four o'clock in the afternoon, I asked Mr. Woolf if I would be able to play in the game
scheduled for that night and he told me that the doctor had
said that if I could fill a tall glass by game time then I would
be able to play. I must have been feeling a little better by
that time because I started joking around. I said, "I'm glad
it's you, Mr. Woolf, because if Red Auerbach were here, he'd
have brought in a thimble!" Luckily, by that time, I was feeling well enough to visit Bethlehem, as well as the Wailing
Wall in the Old City of Jerusalem so I could take some pictures to bring back to my grandmother.

I was proud to represent the NBA in the Celtics' exhibition
games over in Spain. I am always fascinated with learning
how other people live in other countries. Up until that trip, I
did not realize how knowledgeable and interested people
were in other countries about basketball and particularly
the NBA. It told me what a great job the league is doing to
get out the message. I'll tell you, I'll be the first person to
sign up for any other international trips!

The NBA has grown and prospered so much in the last ten
years that it's really amazing. When I first came into the
league in 1979, I didn't even know who the commissioner

was. Larry O'Brien walked right by me once and I didn't even know who he was. I figured you couldn't even *talk* to him, that it was like getting through to the President of the United States or something.

Then David Stern came in and you could see the changes fairly quickly. You'd meet the executives from his office and they would explain their ideas and you really got excited about your league. And you really did feel it was *your* league. Commissioner Stern also worked well with the NBA Players Association, ably headed by the late Larry Fleisher. You can't say enough about the great job David Stern has done.

While I've never been that comfortable with being a celebrity—by definition anyway—I am grateful that that particular status has allowed me to be in a position where I can support and help to raise money for various charity causes that I support. I've been able to raise money for the Terre Haute Boys' Club, with Max Gibson's help, through an annual golf tournament. I really appreciate the assistance I get from my peers in the NBA, the Celtics, Herb and Mel Simon, the people of Indianapolis, the press and especially the event organizers that I work with to run the Larry Bird All-Star Classic Scholarship basketball game in Indianapolis, which helps to raise money for educational scholarships for kids in Indiana. I have always been a strong believer in education. Many of my endorsement companies, including Converse and Spalding, have assisted me with their support in this project.

It's all been so incredible to experience and I feel very grateful. I think everyone should have the kind of life I've had, going from one extreme to the other. It really makes you appreciate what you have even more. I do know one thing, that whether it's basketball or anything else, I just keep trying to do what Jim Jones always says is the right thing: "Surround yourself with *good* people and good things will happen." Over the years, I do believe I have succeeded in following that advice.

If I had grown up in Terre Haute, where there's eighty thousand people, I think the situation would have been different. It has got to be a real *shock* for the people of French

Lick to have someone come out of there and wind up doing what I'm doing. It's a very small town. Why me? Of all the people in the world, why am *I* playing for the Boston Celtics?

No one can answer that. If the Celtics didn't have both the sixth *and* the eighth picks in the 1978 draft, they probably wouldn't have gambled on me and my whole career would have taken a different course. I'm just happy it worked out the way it did.

When I first came up, all I thought about was establishing myself as a professional, to prove that I *wasn't* too slow and all the other things my critics said I was—or wasn't. Now I've learned there's so much more to being a Celtic than I ever imagined. I'm so glad that I got to know people like Walter Randall and Howie McHugh and Red Auerbach. Red is always talking about Walter Brown, who founded the Celtics in 1946. There's one man I wish I could have met. Red told me how Walter Brown did everything to keep the team and the league together. Red says there wouldn't be a Celtics team or even an NBA without Walter Brown. He paid playoff shares out of his own pocket. Red loved that man, you can tell. Bill Russell and John Havlicek paved the way for me, but who paved the way for them? Walter Brown. I just wish I had known him. If you ever get a chance to meet a man like that, you should take advantage of it.

I love being a Celtic. When I was drafted originally, people said, "What do you think about playing in the Boston Garden?" I said I didn't know anything about it, which was true. When I got there and saw all those championship banners and after you're there awhile and you see John Havlicek and Tom Heinsohn coming around and after you hear people constantly talking about the all-time greats Bill Russell and Bob Cousy, you know there is something *special* about the team. Once you find out a little bit about the history and you hear the stories the old veterans Randy and Howie tell, you really get caught up in it all. Then you realize that the Boston Celtics is the greatest franchise that has ever been put together.

I'll always be a Celtic. If they ever traded me, I'd be shattered. I have no desire to end my career with any other team. At this stage of my career, I'm just thinking about getting healthy again and giving the Celtics some more good years and then getting out. I want to leave while I can still play the game. I've had the operation on my heels and I'm confident that if I get that problem licked I will return at the same level, given the fact that the rest of my body is in great shape and that I still love to play.

People ask me, "Can you get back up there with Magic and Michael?" I believe I can. It's going to be hard, but with my abilities and the way I work at it, I think the only question will be to stay away from injuries. If I can do that, I'm confident I'll get right back up there.

The thing that excites me the most about the rest of my career and the thing that I'll miss the most when I retire isn't basketball, as such. It's the night-in, night-out *competition*. That's what I missed the most when I had to sit out the 1988–89 season. I *want* the challenge of competing against the Magic Johnsons, Michael Jordans, Charles Barkleys, Dominique Wilkinses, Karl Malones, Isiah Thomases and all the great young players coming into the league.

I guess I'll miss basketball when I retire, but I'm not real sure about that. I'll have my two business ventures to take up my time: my hotel in Terre Haute and my Ford dealership in Martinsville, Indiana. And I know I'll be in the stands cheering on the Celtics, but I'm not sure I'll still be involved in any official capacity after I retire.

And when the time does come for me to retire, there will be no big fanfare. Believe me, there will be no Larry Bird Farewell Tour. No ceremonies. I just want to emulate Bill Russell. I respect him and what he stands for. He just walked away. The idea that anyone would compare me to him as a Celtic is all the praise I'll ever need. When the time comes, I just want to be able to walk out on that court one last time and say, "Thank you."